DATE DUE

MAR 1 2 1991		BIRD	1991

Demco, Inc. 38-293

READINGS IN
POWER
IN AMERICA

7.25

Edited by
Robert Bresler

Readings in

POWER in AMERICA

Edited by

ROBERT BRESLER
University of Delaware

McCutchan Publishing Corporation
2526 Grove Street
Berkeley, California 94704

Library of Congress Catalog Card Number: 68-56998

TABLE OF CONTENTS

INTRODUCTION

The selections in this book illuminate a theme basic to the study of politics and construct a debate relevant to its most central concerns. The theme is power. The debate is what theory of power most satisfactory explains the control of influence and resources within the American political system.

We present essentially two conflicting schools of thought. One school can be fairly described as the Pluralists (Parson, Dahl, Knoor, and Bell). Their model of the American system purports: a diffused power structure with no single major influence group (corporations, unions, military) controlling key decisions; a decision making process representing all significant segments of American life and characterized by bargaining and compromise; a solid public consensus on basic political principles and institutional arrangements; stable institutions (economic, political and educational) within which movements for social change can be adequately assimilated and accommodated; a social system offering diversity and choice and moving steadily toward the ideals of equality and opportunitarian democracy.

The Pluralists view mass participation in national or community decision-making as both impractical and undesirable. They accept a system whereby political concerns are articulated by elite controlled interest groups. They assume these interest groups are autonomous and represent the vast majority of Americans. Pluralists generally accept a degree of political apathy as conducive to moderation and stability and a check against political dogmatism and mass movements. They measure the success of the political system by its ability to produce stability and accommodate change. By those standards they view the American political system as unusually successful.

The Elitists, the opposing school, find the pluralist model both misleading and misconstrued. These social critics (here represented by Mills, Baran and Sweezy, Hayden and Pilisuk) see the American system democratic in a formal but not a substantive sense. In their model the power structure is hierarchical and dominated by a corporate-military elite. This elite controls attitudes through the mass media, structures educational policy to service the state, dominates the major political parties and imposes a conservative ideology upon the nation. It has also militarized a major portion of the economy and our foreign policy and has removed from effective public control crucial decisions of our time involving war and peace and the fundamental allocations of our resources.

The Elitists view the American public as a mass society powerless to influence history, alienated from a meaningful political participation and turned inward to a life increasingly private, devoid of many public concerns, and anti-historical. The giant corporation has become in the elitist framework the central political agent dominating the economy, the mass media, the political parties, the federal government and most key decision-making. In their view the major task of American society is not to preserve democracy but to create it.

Which of these perspectives one accepts is crucial to one's viewpoint on the major issues of the day. Does one see creative opportunities for youth in the American economy? Or does the middle-class future seem programmed and sterile? Can the American economic system deal successfully with deep rooted poverty and disintegration of the cities? Does the huge military budget reflect a genuine response to a perceived threat to American security? Or is it a response to pressures from an industrial-military complex with a vested interest in a perpetual arms race? Is American education becoming more sophisticated and relevant to the needs of a technological society? Or is it becoming increasingly impersonal and specialized and unrelated to the inner needs of youth for moral guidance and social relevance?

The choice between these models of American politics and the questions above is in all likelihood not either/or. But an honest facing up to the problems presented here must bring an awareness that we cannot divorce ourselves from history or politics and that the institutions and political system of which we are a part shape our lives, our values, and our view of what we can become.

Robert Bresler

Part 1

AMERICAN DEMOCRACY—THE ELITIST MODEL

THE STRUCTURE OF POWER IN AMERICAN SOCIETY*

C. Wright Mills

I

Power has to do with whatever decisions men make about the arrangements under which they live, and about the events which make up the history of their times. Events that are beyond human decision do happen; social arrangements do change without benefit of explicit decision. But in so far as such decisions are made, the problem of who is involved in making them is the basic problem of power. In so far as they could be made but are not, the problem becomes who fails to make them?

We cannot today merely assume that in the last resort men must always be governed by their own consent. For among the means of power which now prevail is the power to manage and to manipulate the consent of men. That we do not know the limits of such power, and that we hope it does have limits, does not remove the fact that much power today is successfully employed without the sanction of the reason or the conscience of the obedient.

Surely nowadays we need not argue that, in the last resort, coercion is the "final" form of power. But then, we are by no means constantly at the last resort. Authority (power that is justified by the beliefs of the voluntarily obedient) and manipulation (power that is wielded unbeknown to the powerless) —must also be considered, along with coercion. In fact, the three types must be sorted out whenever we think about power.

In the modern world, we must bear in mind, power is often not so authoritative as it seemed to be in the medieval epoch: ideas which justify rulers no longer seem so necessary to their exercise of power. At least for many of the great decisions of our time—especially those of an international sort —mass "persuasion" has not been "necessary;" the fact is simply accomplished. Furthermore, such ideas as are available to the powerful are often neither taken up nor used by them. Such ideologies usually arise as a response to an effective debunking of power; in the United States such op-

position has not been effective enough recently to create the felt need for new ideologies of rule.

There has, in fact, come about a situation in which many who have lost faith in prevailing loyalties have not acquired new ones, and so pay no attention to politics of any kind. They are not radical, not liberal, not conservative, not reactionary. They are inactionary. They are out of it. If we accept the Greek's definition of the idiot as an altogether private man, then we must conclude that many American citizens are now idiots. And I should not be surprised, although I do not know, if there were not some such idiots even in Germany. This—and I use the word with care—this spiritual condition seems to me the key to many modern troubles of political intellectuals, as well as the key to much political bewilderment in modern society. Intellectual "conviction" and moral "belief" are not necessary, in either the rulers or the ruled, for a ruling power to persist and even to flourish. So far as the role of ideologies is concerned, their frequent absences and the prevalence of mass indifference are surely two of the major political facts about the western societies today.

How large a role any explicit decisions do play in the making of history is itself an historical problem. For how large that role may be depends very much upon the means of power that are available at any given time in any given society. In some societies, the innumerable actions of innumerable men modify their milieux, and so gradually modify the structure itself. These modifications—the course of history—go on behind the backs of men. History is drift, although in total "men make it." Thus, innumerable entrepreneurs and innumerable consumers by ten-thousand decisions per minute may shape and re-shape the free-market economy. Perhaps this was the chief kind of limitation Marx had in mind when he wrote, in The 18th Brumaire: that "Men make their own history, but they do not make it just as they please; they do not make it under circumstances chosen by themselves. . . ."

But in other societies—certainly in the United States and in the Soviet Union today—a few men may be so placed within the structure that by their decisions they modify the milieux of many other men, and in fact nowadays the structural conditions under which most men live. Such elites of power

*From Power, Politics and People: The Collected Essays of C. Wright Mills, edited by Irving Louis Horowitz. Copyright (c) 1963 by The Estate of C. Wright Mills. Reprinted by permission of Oxford University Press, Inc.

also make history under circumstances not chosen altogether by themselves, yet compared with other men, and compared with other periods of world history, these circumstances do indeed seem less limiting.

I should contend that "men are free to make history," but that some men are indeed much freer than others. For such freedom requires access to the means of decision and of power by which history can now be made. It has not always been so made; but in the later phases of the modern epoch it is. It is with reference to this epoch that I am contending that if men do not make history, they tend increasingly to become the utensils of history-makers as well as the mere objects of history.

The history of modern society may readily be understood as the story of the enlargement and the centralization of the means of power—in economic, in political, and in military institutions. The rise of industrial society has involved these developments in the means of economic production. The rise of the nation-state has involved similar developments in the means of violence and in those of political administration.

In the western societies, such transformations have generally occurred gradually, and many cultural traditions have restrained and shaped them. In most of the Soviet societies, they are happening very rapidly indeed and without the great discourse of western civilization, without the Renaissance and without the Reformation, which so greatly strengthened and gave political focus to the idea of freedom. In those societies, the enlargement and the co-ordination of all the means of power has occurred more brutally, and from the beginning under tightly centralized authority. But in both types, the means of power have now become international in scope and similar in form. To be sure, each of them has its own ups and downs; neither is as yet absolute; how they are run differs quite sharply.

Yet so great is the reach of the means of violence, and so great the economy required to produce and support them, that we have in the immediate past witnessed the consolidation of these two world centers, either of which dwarfs the power of Ancient Rome. As we pay attention to the awesome means of power now available to quite small groups of men we come to realize that Caesar could do less with Rome than Napoleon with France; Napoleon less with France then Lenin with Russia. But what was Caesar's power at its height compared with the power of the changing inner circles of Soviet Russia and the temporary administrations of the United

States? We come to realize—indeed they continually remind us—how a few men have access to the means by which in a few days continents can be turned into thermonuclear wastelands. That the facilities of power are so enormously enlarged and so decisively centralized surely means that the powers of quite small groups of men, which we may call elites, are now of literally inhuman consequence.

My concern here is not with the international scene but with the United States in the middle of the twentieth century. I must emphasize "in the middle of the twentieth century" because in our attempt to understand any society we come upon images which have been drawn from its past and which often confuse our attempt to confront its present reality. That is one minor reason why history is the shank of any social science: we must study it if only to rid ourselves of it. In the United States, there are indeed many such images and usually they have to do with the first half of the nineteenth century. At that time the economic facilities of the United States were very widely dispersed and subject to little or to no central authority.

The state watched in the night but was without decisive voice in the day.

One man meant one rifle and the militia were without centralized orders.

Any American, as old-fashioned as I, can only agree with R. H. Tawney that "Whatever the future may contain, the past has shown no more excellent social order than that in which the mass of the people were the masters of the holdings which they ploughed and the tools with which they worked, and could boast . . . 'It is a quietness to a man's mind to live upon his own and to know his heir certain.' "

But then we must immediately add: all that is of the past and of little relevance to our understanding of the United States today. Within this society three broad levels of power may now be distinguished. I shall begin at the top and move downward.

II

The power to make decisions of national and international consequence is now so clearly seated in political, military, and economic institutions that other areas of society seem off to the side and, on occasion, readily subordinated to these. The scattered institutions of religion, education and family are increasingly shaped by the big three, in which history-making decisions now regularly occur. Behind this fact there is all the push and drive of a fabulous technology; for these three institutional orders have incorporated this technology and now guide it, even as it shapes and paces their development.

As each has assumed its modern shape, its effects upon the other two have become greater, and the traffic between the three has increased. There is no longer, on the one hand, an economy, and, on the other, a political order, containing a military establishment unimportant to politics and to money-making. There is a political economy numerously linked with military order and decision. This triangle of power is now a structural fact, and it is the key to any understanding of the higher circles in America today. For as each of these domains has coincided with the others, as decisions in each have become broader, the leading men of each—the high military, the corporation executives, the political directorate—have tended to come together to form the power elite of America.

The political order, once composed of several dozen states with a weak federal-center, has become an executive apparatus which has taken up into itself many powers previously scattered, legislative as well as administrative, and which now reaches into all parts of the social structure. The long-time tendency of business and government to become more closely connected has since World War II reached a new point of explicitness. Neither can now be seen clearly as a distinct world. The growth of executive government does not mean merely the "enlargement of government" as some kind of autonomous bureaucracy: under American conditions, it has meant the ascendency of the corporation man into political eminence. Already during the New Deal, such men had joined the political directorate; as of World War II they came to dominate it. Long involved with government, now they have moved into quite full direction of the economy of the war effort and of the post-war era.

The economy, once a great scatter of small productive units in somewhat automatic balance, has become internally dominated by a few hundred corporations, administratively and politically interrelated, which together hold the keys to economic decision. This economy is at once a permanent-war economy and a private-corporation economy. The most important relations of the corporation to the state now rest on the coincidence between military and corporate interests, as defined by the military and the corporate rich, and accepted by politicians and public. Within the elite as a whole, this coincidence of military domain and corporate realm strengthens both of them and further subordinates the merely political man. Not the party politician, but the corporation executive, is now more likely to sit with the military to answer the question: what is to be done?

The military order, once a slim establishment in a context of civilian distrust, has become the largest and most expensive feature of government; behind smiling public relations, it has all the grim and clumsy efficiency of a great and sprawling bureaucracy. The high military have gained decisive political and economic relevance. The seemingly permanent military threat places a premium upon them and virtually all political and economic actions are now judged in terms of military definitions of reality: the higher military have ascended to a firm position within the power elite of our time.

In part at least this is a result of an historical fact, pivotal for the years since 1939: the attention of the elite has shifted from domestic problems—centered in the 'thirties around slump—to international problems—centered in the 'forties and 'fifties around war. By long historical usage, the government of the United States has been shaped by domestic clash and balance; it does not have suitable agencies and traditions for the democratic handling of international affairs. In considerable part, it is in this vacuum that the power elite has grown.

(i) To understand the unity of this power elite, we must pay attention to the psychology of its several members in their respective milieux. In so far as the power elite is composed of men of similar origin and education, of similar career and style of life, their unity may be said to rest upon the fact that they are of similar social type, and to lead to the fact of their easy intermingling. This kind of unity reaches its frothier apex in the sharing of that prestige which is to be had in the world of the celebrity. It achieves a more solid culmination in the fact of the interchangeability of positions between the three dominant institutional orders. It is revealed by considerable traffic of personnel within and between these three, as well as by the rise of specialized go-betweens as in the new style high-level lobbying.

(ii) Behind such psychological and social unity are the structure and the mechanics of those institutional hierarchies over which the political directorate, the corporate rich, and the high military now preside. How each of these hierarchies is shaped and what relations it has with the others determine in large part the relations of their rulers.

Were these hierarchies scattered and disjointed, then their respective elites might tend to be scattered and disjointed; but if they have many interconnections and points of coinciding interest, then their elites tend to form a coherent kind of grouping. The unity of the elite is not a simple reflection of the unity of institutions, but men and institutions are always related; that is why we must understand the elite today in connection with such institutional trends as the development of a permanent-war establishment, alongside a privately incorporated economy, inside a virtual political vacuum. For the men at the top have been selected and formed by such institutional trends.

(iii) Their unity, however, does not rest solely upon psychological similarity and social interminging, nor entirely upon the structural blending of commanding positions and common interests. At times it is the unity of a more explicit co-ordination.

To say that these higher circles are increasingly co-ordinated, that this is one basis of their unity, and that at times—as during open war—such co-ordination is quite wilful, is not to say that the co-ordination is total or continuous, or even that it is very surefooted. Much less is it to say that the power elite has emerged as the realization of a plot. Its rise cannot be adequately explained in any psychological terms.

Yet we must remember that institutional trends may be defined as opportunities by those who occupy the command posts. Once such opportunities are recognized, men may avail themselves of them. Certain types of men from each of these three areas, more far-sighted than others, have actively promoted the liaison even before it took its truly modern shape. Now more have come to see that their several interests can more easily be realized if they work together, in informal as well as in formal ways, and accordingly they have done so.

The idea of the power elite is of course an interpretation. It rests upon and it enables us to make sense of major institutional trends, the social similarities and psychological affinities of the men at the top. But the idea is also based upon what has been happening on the middle and lower levels of power, to which I now turn.

III

There are of course other interpretations of the American system of power. The most usual is that it is a moving balance of many competing interests.

The image of balance, at least in America, is derived from the idea of the economic market: in the nineteenth century, the balance was thought to occur between a great scatter of individuals and enterprises; in the twentieth century, it is thought to occur between great interest blocs. In both views, the politician is the key man of power because he is the broker of many conflicting powers.

I believe that the balance and the compromise in American society—the "countervailing powers" and the "veto groups," of parties and associations, of strata and unions—must now be seen as having mainly to do with the middle levels of power. It is these middle levels that the political journalist and the scholar of politics are most likely to understand and to write about—if only because, being mainly middle class themselves, they are closer to them. Moreover these levels provide the noisy content of most "political" news and gossip; the images of these levels are more or less in accord with the folklore of how democracy works; and, if the master-image of balance is accepted, many intellectuals, especially in their current patrioteering, are readily able to satisfy such political optimism as they wish to feel. Accordingly, liberal interpretations of what is happening in the United States are now virtually the only interpretations that are widely distributed.

But to believe that the power system reflects a balancing society is, I think, to confuse the present era with earlier times, and to confuse its top and bottom with its middle levels.

By the top levels, as distinguished from the middle, I intend to refer, first of all, to the scope of the decisions that are made. At the top today, these decisions have to do with all the issues of war and peace. They have also to do with slump and poverty which are now so very much problems of international scope. I intend also to refer to whether or not the groups that struggle politically have a chance to gain the positions from which such top decisions are made, and indeed whether their members do usually hope for such top national command. Most of the competing interests which make up the clang and clash of American politics are strictly concerned with their slice of the existing pie. Labor unions, for example, certainly have no policies of an international sort other than those which given unions adopt for the strict economic protection of their members. Neither do farm organizations. The actions of such middle-level powers may indeed have consequence for top-level policy; certainly at times they hamper these policies. But they are not truly concerned with them, which means of course that their influence tends to be quite irresponsible.

The facts of the middle levels may in part be understood in terms of the rise of the power elite. The expanded and centralized and interlocked hierarchies over which the power elite preside have encroached upon the old balance and relegated it to the middle level. But there are also independent developments of the middle levels. These, it seems to me, are better understood as an affair of entrenched and provincial demands than as a center of national decision. As such, the middle level often seems much more of a stalemate than a moving balance.

(i) The middle level of politics is not a forum in which there are debated the big decisions of national and international life. Such debate is not carried on by nationally responsible parties representing and clarifying alternative policies. There are no such parties in the United States. More and more, fundamental issues never come to any point or decision before the Congress, much less before the electorate in party campaigns. In the case of Formosa, in the spring of 1955 the Congress abdicated all debate concerning events and decisions which surely bordered on war. The same is largely true of the 1957 crisis in the Middle East. Such decisions now regularly by-pass the Congress, and are never clearly focused issues for public decision.

The American political campaign distracts attention from national and international issues, but that is not to say that there are no issues in these campaigns. In each district and state, issues are set up and watched by organized interests of sovereign local importance. The professional politician is of course a party politician, and the two parties are semifeudal organizations: they trade patronage and other favors for votes and for protection. The differences between them, so far as national issues are concerned, are very narrow and very mixed up. Often each seems to be fifty parties, one to each state; and accordingly, the politician as campaigner and as Congressman is not concerned with national party lines, if any are discernible. Often he is not subject to any effective national party discipline. He speaks for the interests of his own constituency, and he is concerned with national issues only in so far as they affect the interests effectively organized there, and hence his chances of re-election. That is why, when he does speak of national matters, the result is so often such an empty rhetoric. Seated in his sovereign locality, the politician is not at the national summit. He is on and of the middle levels of power.

(ii) Politics is not an arena in which free and independent organizations truly connect the lower and middle levels of society with the top levels of decision. Such organizations are not an effective and major part of American life today. As more people are drawn into the political arena, their associations become mass in scale, and the power of the individual becomes dependent upon them; to the extent that they are effective, they have become larger, and to that extent they have become less accessible to the influence of the individual. This is a central fact about associations in any mass society: it is of most consequence for political parties and for trade unions.

In the 'thirties, it often seemed that labor would become an insurgent power independent of corporation and state. Organized labor was then emerging for the first time on an American scale, and the only political sense of direction it needed was the slogan, "organize the unorganized." Now without the mandate of the slump, labor remains without political direction. Instead of economic and political struggles it has become deeply entangled in administrative routines with both corporation and state. One of its major functions, as a vested interest of the new society, is the regulation of such irregular tendencies as may occur among the rank and file.

There is nothing, it seems to me, in the makeup of the current labor leadership to allow us to expect that it can or that it will lead, rather than merely react. In so far as it fights at all it fights over a share of the goods of a single way of life and not over that way of life itself. The typical labor leader in the U.S.A. today is better understood as an adaptive creature of the main business drift than as an independent actor in a truly national context.

(iii) The idea that this society is a balance of powers requires us to assume that the units in balance are of more or less equal power and that they are truly independent of one another. These assumptions have rested, it seems clear, upon the historical importance of a large and independent middle class. In the latter nineteenth century and during the Progressive Era, such a class of farmers and small businessmen fought politically—and lost—their last struggle for a paramount role in national decision. Even then, their aspirations seemed bound to their own imagined past.

This old, independent middle class has of course declined. On the most generous count, it is now 40 per cent of the total middle class (at most 20 per cent of the total labor force). Moreover, it has become politically as well as economically dependent upon the state, most notably in the case of the subsidized farmer.

The new middle class of white-collar employees is certainly not the political pivot of any balancing society. It is in no way politically unified. Its unions, such as they are, often serve merely to incorporate it as hanger-on of the labor interest. For a considerable period, the old middle class was an independent base of power; the new middle class cannot be. Political freedom and economic security were anchored in small and independent properties; they are not anchored in the worlds of the white-collar job. Scattered property holders were economically united by more or less free markets; the jobs of the new middle class are integrated by corporate authority. Economically, the white-collar classes are in the same condition as wage workers; politically, they are in a worse condition, for they are not organized. They are no vanguard of historic change; they are at best a rear-guard of the welfare state.

The agrarian revolt of the 'nineties, the small-business revolt that has been more or less continuous since the 'eighties, the labor revolt of the 'thirties—each of these has failed as an independent movement which could countervail against the powers that be; they have failed as politically autonomous third parties. But they have succeeded in varying degree, as interests vested in the expanded corporation and state; they have succeeded as parochial interests seated in particular districts, in local divisions of the two parties, and in the Congress. What they would become, in short, are well-established features of the middle levels of balancing power, on which we may now observe all those strata and interests which in the course of American history have been defeated in their bids for top power or which have never made such bids.

Fifty years ago many observers thought of the American state as a mask behind which an invisible government operated. But nowadays, much of what was called the old lobby, visible or invisible, is part of the quite visible government. The "governmentalization of the lobby" has proceeded in both the legislative and the executive domain, as well as between them. The executive bureaucracy becomes not only the center of decision but also the arena within which major conflicts of power are resolved or denied resolution. "Administration" replaces electoral politics; the maneuvering of cliques (which include leading Senators as well as civil servants) replaces the open clash of parties.

The shift of corporation men into the political directorate has accelerated the decline of the politicians in the Congress to the middle levels of power; the formation of the power elite rests in part upon this relegation. It rests also upon the semiorganized stalemate of the interests of sovereign localities, into which the legislative function has so largely fallen; upon the virtually complete absence of a civil service that is a politically neutral but politically relevant, depository of brain-power and executive skill; and it rests upon the increased official secrecy behind which great decisions are made without benefit of public or even of Congressional debate.

IV

There is one last belief upon which liberal observers everywhere base their interpretations and rest their hopes. That is the idea of the public and the associated idea of public opinion. Conservative thinkers, since the French Revolution, have of course Viewed With Alarm the rise of the public, which they have usually called the masses, or something to that effect. "The populace is sovereign," wrote Gustave LeBon, "and the tide of barbarism mounts." But surely those who have supposed the masses to be well on their way to triumph are mistaken. In our time, the influence of publics or of masses within political life is in fact decreasing, and such influence as on occasion they do have tends, to an unknown but increasing degree, to be guided by the means of mass communication.

In a society of publics, discussion is the ascendant means of communication, and the mass media, if they exist, simply enlarge and animate this discussion, linking one face-to-face public with the discussions of another. In a mass society, the dominant type of communication is the formal media and publics become mere markets for these media: the "public" of a radio program consists of all those exposed to it. When we try to look upon the United States today as a society of publics, we realize that it has moved a considerable distance along the road to the mass society.

In official circles, the very term, "the public," has come to have a phantom meaning, which dramatically reveals its eclipse. The deciding elite can identify some of those who clamor publicly as "Labor," others as "Business," still others as "Farmer." But these are not the public. "The public" consists of the unidentified and the nonpartisan in a world of defined and partisan interests.

In this faint echo of the classic notion, the public is composed of these remnants of the old and new middle classes whose interests are not explicitly defined, organized, or clamorous. In a curious adaptation, "the public" often becomes, in administrative fact, "the disengaged expert," who, although never so well informed, has never taken a clear-cut and public stand on controversial issues. He is the "public" member of the board, the commission, the committee. What "the public" stands for, accordingly, is often a vagueness of policy (called "open-mindedness"), a lack of involvement in public affairs (known as "reasonableness"), and a professional disinterest (known as "tolerance").

All this is indeed far removed from the eighteenth-century idea of the public of public opinion. The idea parallels the economic idea of the magical market. Here is the market composed for freely competing entrepreneurs; there is the public composed of circles of people in discussion. As price is the result of anonymous, equally weighted, bargaining individuals, so public opinion is the result of each man's having thought things out for himself and then contributing his voice to the great chorus. To be sure, some may have more influence on the state of opinion than others, but no one group monopolizes the discussion, or by itself determines the opinions that prevail.

In this classic image, the people are presented with problems. They discuss them. They formulate viewpoints. These viewpoints are organized, and they compete. One viewpoint "wins out." Then the people act on this view, or their representatives are instructed to act it out, and this they promptly do.

Such are the images of democracy which are still used as working justifications of power in America. We must now recognize this description as more a fairy tale than a useful approximation. The issues that now shape man's fate are neither raised nor decided by any public at large. The idea of a society that is at bottom composed of a publics is not a matter of fact; it is the proclamation of an ideal, and as well the assertion of a legitimation masquerading as fact.

I cannot here describe the several great forces within American society as well as elsewhere which have been at work in the debilitation of the public. I want only to remind you that publics, like free associations, can be deliberately and suddenly smashed, or they can more slowly wither away. But whether smashed in a week or withered in a generation, the demise of the public must be seen in connection with the rise of centralized organizations, with all their new means of power, including those of the mass media of distraction. These, we now know, often seem to expropriate the rationality and the will of the terrorized or—as the case may be—the voluntarily indifferent society of masses. In the more democratic process of indifference the remnants of such publics as remain may only occasionally be intimidated by fanatics in search of "disloyalty." But regardless of that, they lose their will for decision because they do not possess the instruments for decision; they lose their sense of political belonging because they do not belong; they lose their political will because they see no way to realize it.

The political structure of a modern democratic state requires that such a public as is projected by democratic theorists not only exist but that it be the very forum within which a politics of real issues is enacted.

It requires a civil service that is firmly linked with the world of knowledge and sensibility, and which is composed of skilled men who, in their careers and in their aspirations, are truly independent of any private, which is to say, corporation, interests.

It requires nationally responsible parties which debate openly and clearly the issues which the nation, and indeed the world, now so rigidly confronts.

It requires an intelligentsia, inside as well as outside the universities, who carry on the big discourse of the western world, and whose work is relevant to and influential among parties and movements and publics.

And it certainly requires, as a fact of power, that there be free associations standing between families and smaller communities and publics, on the one hand, and the state, the military, the corporation, on the other. For unless these do exist, there are no vehicles for reasoned opinion, no instruments for the rational exertion of public will.

Such democratic formations are not now ascendant in the power structure of the United States, and accordingly the men of decision are not men selected and formed by careers within such associations and by their performance before such publics. The top of modern American society is increasingly unified, and often seems wilfully co-ordinated: at the top there has emerged an elite whose power probably exceeds that of any small group of men in world history. The middle levels are often a drifting set of stalemated forces: the middle does not link the bottom with the top. The bottom of this society is politically fragmented, and even as a passive fact, increasingly powerless: at the bottom there is emerging a mass society.

These developments, I believe, can be correctly understood neither in terms of the liberal nor the Marxian interpretation of politics and history. Both these ways of thought arose as guidelines to reflection about a type of society which does not now exist in the United States. We confront there a new kind of social structure, which embodies elements and tendencies of all modern society, but in which they have assumed a more naked and flamboyant prominence.

That does not mean that we must give up the ideals of these classic political expectations. I believe that both have been concerned with the problem of rationality and of freedom: liberalism, with freedom and rationality as supreme facts about the individual; Marxism, as supreme facts about man's role in the political making of history. What I have said here, I suppose, may be taken as an attempt to make evident why the ideas of freedom and of rationality now so often seem so ambiguous in the new society of the United States of America.

THE DISTRIBUTION OF POWER IN AMERICAN SOCIETY*

Talcott Parsons

I

It has been remarked that it is relatively rare, in the United States at least, for social scientists to attempt interpretive analyses of major aspects of the total society in which they live. This is particularly true of sociologists,[1] unlike economists, who have made notable attempts in recent years to interpret their societies—for example, Schumpeter's Capitalism, Socialism, and Democracy and Galbraith's American Capitalism. If for this reason alone, the present book of Professor Mills, which must be understood as one of a series as yet far from complete, would be worthy of serious attention.

In the nature of the case, to produce such a study is a very difficult enterprise. However operationally useful precise data may be—and Mr. Mills makes copious and, with some exceptions, relatively good use of them—they cannot suffice for a full empirical grounding of interpretive conclusions, not only because on their own level they are fragmentary and incomplete, but because many of the crucial empirical questions arise on a level at which available operational procedures are not of much or any use. This is not in the least to say that observation is not feasible, but rather that it cannot be precise observation in the usual operational sense.

I am referring to questions of the type which are central to Mr. Mills' argument, as to whether and in what sense a relatively small group of the occupants of "command posts" in the society has acquired a paramount position of power, as to whether the relative power of such a group has greatly increased in the last twenty years, as to how unified such a group is, and the like.

There are technical ways of reducing the ele-

ment of arbitrariness in such judgments and protecting them against at least the grosser sorts of ideological distortion. Checking against all the available precise data is one such method; viewing the problem from the perspective given by wide and deep knowledge, not only of our own society but of others, is another. But I think the most important is exercising control through the use of a relatively well-integrated and technical theoretical scheme. Undertaking as a professional sociologist to review Mr. Mills' book, I am motivated largely by the opportunity to test some of his main conclusions against expectations derived from a type of technical theory that is at best only partially shared by the author of the book. In these terms I wish to take serious issue with Mr. Mills' position on a number of very important points and to outline an alternative interpretation of what I take to be the salient facts of the situation. There are some points at which I differ from Mills on simple questions of fact, but for the most part my criticisms will deal with empirical generalizations and their theoretical background.[2] These generalizations concern not only the facts he chooses to state and emphasize but others he omits or treats as unimportant.

What is the gist of Mills' argument? I am able here to give only a very brief summary. The reader should not depend on this review alone for his information about the contents of the book itself, but should go directly to Mills' own statement of his case.

Mills' central theme is the contention—in contrast to what he refers to as the traditional view of the political pluralism of American society—that there has developed to an unprecedented degree in the last generation or so a concentration of power in the hands of a small, relatively tightly integrated group of people. These are defined as the

---

[1] The main exception here is Robin M. Williams' excellent American Society (New York, 1951), which has received far less general attention than it deserves, perhaps because of its somewhat textbookish orientation.

*From Talcott Parsons, "Distribution of Power in American Society," World Politics, 1957, Vol. X, pp. 123-43. Reprinted by permission.

[2] Mr. Mills is clearly writing only partly for an audience of technical social scientists. Though my own argument will be largely based on considerations of technical theory, I shall not introduce explicit justification of my theoretical judgments into this review, but will try to state my case in relatively non-technical terms.

people occupying the institutional "command posts" of the society, the places where the decisions are made that have the greatest immediate and direct influence on the course of events in the society and on the shaping of its future and that of the rest of the world, so far as that future is dependent on what happens in the United States. Mills argues that the power of this group has grown disproportionately to the growth in size and power of the society as a whole.

The "command posts" in question are centered in large-scale organizations, which are certainly a prominent feature of American society. The power elite are in general those who occupy the decision-making positions in these large organizations. Mills identifies these in only two basic areas, business and government—although for his purposes the field of government is subdivided into the military and the political sectors; indeed, he almost tends to treat the military as independent of the rest of government. He clearly is thinking of the centralized type of organization where a few "top executives" exercise the main immediate decision-making power, in contrast to the democratic association with a somewhat more decentralized structure of authority and influence. It seems to be largely on this ground that he contends that the executive branch of the federal government has gained a pronounced ascendancy over the legislative. He relegates Congress—even the most influential group of Senators—to what he calls the "middle level" of the power structure; such people do not belong to the "power elite."

Mills broadly identifies the power elite with the "upper class." But he does not agree with Lloyd Warner and his group that the primary element of this upper class is a hereditary group of families or lineages; its position clearly depends on occupational status, though there is also emphasis on the importance within it of the "very rich," the majority of whom have inherited their wealth. Contrary to most sociological usage, Mills restricts the term "class" to an economic meaning, so that by "upper class" he means, essentially, the rich. But this still leaves open the question of the substantive relations between inherited and newly acquired wealth, family status relatively independent of at least very large wealth, occupational status within various income ranges, and similar problems.

Generally, Mills is rather vague on the relations between the power elite and other elements which in some sense enjoy rather high prestige. He em-

phasizes the prominence of lawyers among the "political directorate," but there is no clear analysis of the role of professional groups in the occupational structure generally; one presumes that except for a few lawyers who are successful in politics or business, and perhaps some engineers, professional people do not belong to the power elite. Similarly he emphasizes that members of the power elite have more than the average amount of education, and in particular he stresses the proportion who have been to select private schools and to "Ivy League" colleges. In general, he is greatly concerned about the fact that the power elite are not "representative" of the population as a whole in the sense of constituting a random sample by socio-economic origin, by education, by ethnic group, etc. This is a point to which I shall return.

Neither the "higher circles" generally nor the component of the "very rich" (Mills' term) are a leisure class in Veblen's sense; many, if not most of them, "work" in various fields of business and financial management. Furthermore, the processes of recruitment are about what social scientists have come to expect. Mills does not give any exact criteria for what he considers to be "upper class" as a category of social origin, but I have the impression that he puts the line somewhat lower than most sociologists would. But, however that may be, it is clear that there is a considerable element of stability from generation to generation in the higher-status groups in American society. Thus if, to employ a pattern used by Mills, we take a group of prominent persons, the family origin of from two-thirds to three-fourths of them will be the upper third of the American status structure. It is not these essential facts but the interpretation placed upon them which raises questions for us. The only point of fact I would question is whether the recruitment of the very rich has shown a sharper increase through the process of inheritance than through self-earning. It is possible that this is so, but I am inclined to doubt it, and in any case their position does not depend only on the process which Mills calls "cumulative advantage."

Mills radically denies that the group he calls the "very rich" and the "corporate rich" are distinct "classes," in his sense. He explicitly lumps them together and on the whole gives the very rich a greater position of influence than they are usually accorded or than, I think, they actually enjoy. This is in line with his thesis that there is a single, unified power elite. Clearly, it is his contention that the base of the (business) group as a whole lies in command of the very large business enterprises—somewhat erroneously, or at least ambiguously, he puts the primary emphasis on control of property in accounting for this power.

Of the three main subgroups, Mills treats the "political directorate" as by far the weakest. It has, according to him, been greatly infiltrated by the business element, so that it can scarcely be treated as independent. Hence virtually the only element independent of what might be called the business oligarchy is the military—and this, he holds, is coming increasingly to fuse with the business group, or at least to form a close community of interest with it.

The pluralistic components of our older political traditions, Mills feels, are rooted primarily in local groupings—partly, of course, through the constitutional provisions which establish federalism and make Congressional representation dependent on local constituencies. But the operations of the big organizations have become national in scope, and often international. Hence structures rooted in localism have simply been pushed into a secondary position.

But at the same time Mills contends that the structural base of authentic localism has been progressively atrophied through the development of what he calls the "mass society." The most conspicuous phenomena of the mass society are the prevalence and characteristics of the media of mass communication, which tend to serve as instruments of the power elite out of the reach of locally based "publics" and influential elements in them. The theory of the mass society is only very sketchily presented in one chapter near the end of the book, but is clearly meant to provide one of the main components of the total picture of American society which Mills is presenting.

In terms of recent history, one of Mills' main contentions is that the New Deal period did not represent a turning point in social development, but rather a superficial flurry which only momentarily disturbed the process of emergence of the power elite and the dominance of the business contingent within it. Thus Mills speaks of the economic elite as in due course coming "to control and to use for their own purposes the New Deal institutions whose creation they had so bitterly denounced" (pp. 272-73).

Mills repeatedly disavows any intention of presenting a "conspiratorial" interpretation of American social and political development. He stresses the institutional positions occupied by his elite rather than their personalities and conspiratorial activities. Nevertheless he often comes very close to this implication because of his special theory that a peculiar irresponsibility attaches to the elite and their actions. By this he seems to mean the absence or relative ineffectiveness of formal legal restraints or of a system of "checks and balances" of the sort which has traditionally been associated with our political system. His contention thus is that the power elite has been freed from the historic restraints of our society and uses its power in terms of what he calls a "higher immorality"—a conception which is not very clearly explained.

Finally, it should be mentioned that in this, as in some of his previous writings, Mills' general tone toward both men and institutions is sharply caustic. The Power Elite certainly purports to be an exposition and an explanation of what has been happening in American society, but it is equally an indictment. There is no pretense of even trying to maintain a scientific neutrality; the book is a fiery and sarcastic attack on the pretensions of the "higher circles" in America either to competence in exercise of their responsibilities or to moral legitimation of their position. In such a case, the critic must ascertain the moral position from which the indictment is formulated; I shall have something to say about this later. In his combination of often insightful exposition and analysis, empirical one-sidedness and distortion, and moral indictment and sarcasm, Mills reminds one more of Veblen than of any other figure; that he has attained the stature of Veblen I question, but the role he is cutting out for himself is similar.

II

As I have said, the Mills analysis presents what, to me, is a subtle and complex combination of acceptable and unacceptable elements. Let me now attempt, at some of the most important points, to unravel these elements from each other. I want to try this first on the level of empirical generalization and then to raise one or two more strictly theoretical problems. I shall do so more in my own own terms than in those employed by Mills.

In my opinion, two salient sets of processes have been going on in American society during the past half-century, the combination of which encompasses the main facts which are essential to our problem. The first of these is the dynamic of a maturing industrial society, including not only the highly industrialized economy itself but its setting in the society as a whole—notably, its political system and class structure (in a wider sense of the term "class" than Mills')—and the repercussions of the industrial development on the rest of the society. The second concerns the altered position of the United States in world society, which is a consequence in part of our own economic growth, in part of a variety of exogenous changes, including the relative decline of the Western European powers, the rise of Soviet Russia, and the break-up of the "colonial" organization of much of the non-white world. The enormous enhancement of American power and responsibility in the world has taken place in a relatively short time and was bound to have profound repercussions on the characteristics of our own society. Our old political isolation has disappeared and given way to the deepest of involvements.

My first thesis is that these two processes both work in the direction of increasing the relative importance of government in our society and, with it, of political power. But their impact has been all the greater because of the extent to which the United States has been an almost specifically non-political society. This has been evidenced above all in the institutions and tradition of political decentralization already mentioned, one aspect of which is the localism which Mills discusses. A second, however, has been a cultural tradition which has emphasized economic values—an emphasis on enterprise and production in an activist sense, not a merely passive hedonistic valuation of the enjoyment of material well-being. Moreover, the virtually unimpeded process of settlement of a continent in political isolation from the main system of world powers has favored maintenance of this emphasis to a greater extent than would otherwise have readily been possible.

At some points in his discussion, Mills seems to look back to the Jeffersonian picture of a system of economic production consisting mainly of small farmers and artisans, with presumably a small mercantile class mediating between them and consumers. Clearly this is not a situation compatible with high industrial development, in either of two respects. First, the order of decentralization of production where the standard unit is a family-size one is incompatible with either the organization or the technology necessary for high industrialism. Second, the "Jeffersonian" economy is not one in which economic production is differentiated from other social functions in specialized organizations; instead, the typical productive unit is at the same time a kinship unit and a unit of citizenship in the community.[3]

In all salient respects, the modern economy has moved very far from the Jeffersonian ideal. The pace-setting units have become both large and specialized. Their development has been part of a general process of structural differentiation in the society which has led to greater specialization in many fields. An essential aspect of the process of development of the economy as a system in both these senses is greater specialization on at least three levels: first, the specialization of organizations in the functions of economic production as distinguished from other functions; second, the specialization of functions within the economy; and third, the specialization of the roles of classes of individuals within the organization.

Leadership is an essential function in all social systems, which with their increase of scale and their functional differentiation tend to become more specialized. I think we can, within considerable limits, regard the emergence of the large firm with operations on a nation-wide basis as a "normal" outcome of the process of growth and differentiation of the economy. Similarly, the rise to prominence within the firm of specialized executive functions is also a normal outcome of a process of growth in size and in structural differentiation. The question then arises whether the process of concentration of firms, and of executive power within firms, has "gone too far" because it has been greatly influenced by factors extraneous to the process of economic development itself.

Mills makes the assertion that the size of the large firm has exceeded the limits of economic efficiency. He presents no evidence, and I think most competent persons would regard this as an exceedingly difficult question. There is, however, one line of evidence not cited by Mills which has a bearing on it. It is true that the absolute size of firms has steadily increased—General Motors today is larger than any firm of the 1920's. But the relative share of the largest firms in the production of the economy has remained essentially stable for more than a generation, a fact which points to some

---

[3] How far this "Jeffersonianism" thus represents the moral position from which Mills launches his indictment is a question I will discuss at the end of the article. It provides a convenient reference point in terms of contrast both for Mills' characterization of the current society and for my own very different one.

kind of equilibrium condition with respect to the degree of concentration in the system as a whole.

A cognate question is whether the power of the executive or managerial class within industry, and particularly within the large firms, has increased inordinately, which if true would indicate that factors other than the functional needs of the productive process were operating to skew the internal power structure of firms in favor of the executive groups.

Generally speaking, Mills' argument is that the power of the very rich and the corporate rich within the economy is inordinately great and, by virtue of the factor of cumulative advantage, is becoming continually greater. At the very least, I think it can be said that his case is not proved and that there is equally good, if not better, evidence for an alternative view, particularly with reference to the trend.

First, I am not able to accept Mills' close identification of the very rich (i.e., the holders of "great fortunes") with the "corporate rich" (the primary holders of executive power in business organizations) as a single class in any very useful sense. Certainly, in the "heroic age" of American capitalism, from the Civil War to just after the turn of the century, the dominant figures were the entrepreneurs who, mainly as the founders of great enterprises and as the bankers and promoters concerned with mergers and reorganizations and the like, came to control these great organizations. But the dominant sociological fact of the outcome of that era was that these owning groups did not, as a group, succeed in consolidating their position precisely within their own enterprises and in the economy. It is a notorious fact that the very large enterprise still largely under family control through property holdings is much more the exception than the rule. Instead, the control has passed—by no means fully, but for the most part—to professional career executives, who have not reached their positions through the exercise of property rights but through some sort of process of appointment and promotion.

Mills concedes the main facts of this situation but fails, in my opinion, to evaluate them properly. It seems to be clear that the original "captains of industry," the makers of the great fortunes, failed to achieve or to exercise sufficient cumulative advantages to consolidate control of the enterprises in their families and their class ("class" in a sociological, not an economic, sense). This came about essentially because there were factors op-

erating contrary to that of cumulative advantage, which Mills stresses so heavily. The main factor was the pressure to link executive responsibility with competence in such a way that the ascriptive rights of property ownership have tended to give way to the occupational functions of "professionals."

There are, above all, two ways in which Mills' treatment obscures the importance and nature of this shift. First, he continues to speak of power within the economy as based on property. To a considerable degree, of course, this is legally true, since the legal control of enterprise rests with stockholders. But, as Berle and Means first made abundantly clear, very generally it is not substantively true. In the old-style family enterprise, still predominant in the small-business sector of the economy, the functions of management and ownership are fused in the same people. In the larger enterprise they have by and large become differentiated. The fact that executives receive large salaries and bonuses is not to be twisted into an assumption that they control, so far as they do, through their property rights. Paradoxical as it may seem, a relatively backward industrial economy like that of France is far more property-based than is the case with the United States. In general, property holdings have not, of course, been expropriated, except for their diminution through inheritance and income taxes, which are not as negligible as Mills maintains. What has happened is that their relation to the power structure of the economy has been greatly altered. Mills almost entirely passes over this change.

The second problem concerns the process of recruitment in the higher occupational reaches of the economy. It is entirely clear that the process operates in the higher reaches overwhelmingly by appointment, i.e., the decisions of superiors as individuals or in small groups as to who should occupy certain positions. It is also true that the process is relatively unformalized—e.g., there are no competitive examinations and few, if any, formal qualifications of training. But from these facts Mills concludes, and again and again reiterates, that executive competence has very little, if anything, to do with the selection, that it is an overwhelmingly arbitrary process of choosing those who are congenial to the selectors, presumably because they can be counted upon to be "yes men." At the very least this contention is unproved, and I seriously doubt its correctness. There are certainly many difficulties and imperfections in the selection process. But I think it almost certain that higher levels of competence are selected than would on the average be the case through kinship ascription, and that, as such processes go, the levels selected are relatively high.

One final point in this field. It does seem probable that the factor of cumulative advantage has a good deal to do with the high levels of financial remuneration of the higher executive groups and with the discrepancies between their incomes and those of governmental and professional people on comparable levels of competence and responsibility. But this is very far from the great fortune level of the founding entrepreneur type, and the evidence seems to be that the discrepancy has not been cumulatively increasing to an appreciable degree, particularly relative to wages at the labor levels; cases like that of the academic profession are somewhat special.

So far I have been speaking about the nature and power position of the elite within the economy. The general tenor of my argument has been that, given the nature of an industrial society, a relatively well-defined elite or leadership group should be expected to develop in the business world; it is out of the question that power should be diffused equally among an indefinite number of very small units, as the ideal of pure competition and a good deal of the ideology of business itself would have it. But first I question whether the position of power of the business leadership groups is such that a heavy operation of the factor of cumulative advantage must be invoked to account for it. Secondly, I must stress that the business elite is no longer primarily an elite of property-owners, but that its center of gravity has shifted to occupationally professional executives or managers. Differential advantages of family origin, etc., are about the same for admission to this group as to other groups requiring educational and other qualifications. Again the evidence is that the proportion of its members recruited from the upper economic and social groups is and remains relatively high, but it has not, in recent times, been increasing, as the theory of cumulative advantage would lead us to expect.

The problem of an elite within the economy must, however, be clearly distinguished from that of an elite in the society as a whole and the power position occupied by such an elite. There are two main orders of questions bearing on the transition from one to the other. Though a thorough consideration of this transition would lead into very far-reaching questions, for present purposes one can be treated rather briefly. Mills gives us the impression that "eliteness" in any society, including our own, is overwhelmingly a question of the power that an individual or a group can command. By this, he means (I shall further discuss his concept of power presently) influence on the "big" decisions directly affecting what happens in the society in the short run. But there are many elements in the society which are relatively powerless in this sense, but nevertheless of the greatest functional importance. Our society has almost divested kinship units as such of important power in this sense. But this does not mean at all that the family has ceased to be important. Closely linked with this is the question of the feminine role. Women qua women by and large do not have a position of power comparable to that of men; but this is not to say that they are unimportant—otherwise how can we account for the extent of our national preoccupations with questions of sexuality? Finally, there is a distinct difference between the rank-order of occupations—which, relative to other role-types, are closely involved with decision-making in a society like ours—by power and by prestige. The most striking case is the relatively high position of the professions relative to executive roles in business, as revealed by the famous North-Hatt data. Physicians as a group do not exercise great power, but there is no reason to question their very high prestige, which has been demonstrated in study after study.

The second main context, however, directly concerns the question of power. In a complex society the primary locus of power lies in the political system. There are many subtle analytical problems involved in the delineation of this system and its functions in the society which cannot be gone into here; this formula will have to suffice. Two questions are, however, primary for our purposes: the degree of differentiation of the political system from other systems; and its own internal structure. These two problems, it will be noted, parallel those raised with reference to the economy.

For historical reasons it seems clear that the development of the American political system, since the breakdown of the first synthesis associated with the "founders of the Republic," has lagged behind that of the economy. This is a function primarily of the two factors already noted—the economic emphasis inherent in our system of values, and the relative lack of urgency of certain political problems because of our especially protected and favored national position. Relative to the economic structure, which had by that time grown enormously, the political was at its weakest in the period from the Civil War to the end of the century; this situation is sketched by Mills in broadly correct terms. Since then, both internal exigencies and the exigencies of our international position have been stimuli for major changes.

Internally, beyond the more elementary provisions for law and order and essential minimum services—much of this, of course, on a local basis—the main focus of the development of our political system has been control of economic organization and processes, and coping with some of the social consequences of economic growth and industrialization. The process started well before the turn of the century with the Interstate Commerce legislation and the Anti-Trust Act and continued through the New Deal era, not steadily but with waves of new measures and levels of political control.

A major problem in relation to Mills' analysis is whether this is "genuine" control. His view seems to be that at times it has been, but that on balance it is the business power-holders who control government, not vice versa; the above quotation about the outcome of the New Deal puts it succinctly. In my opinion this is a misinterpretation. If genuine and in some sense effective controls had not been imposed, I find it impossible to understand the bitter and continuing opposition on the part of business to the measures which have been taken.[4] Even some of those most completely taken for granted now, like the Federal Reserve system, were bitterly fought at the time. It therefore seems to me to be the sounder interpretation that there has been a genuine growth of autonomous governmental power—apart from the military aspect, which will be discussed presently—and that one major aspect of this has been relatively effective control of the business system. This control and the growth of "big government" have been generally accepted in the society as a whole. The participation of big-business men in governmental processes is by no means to be interpreted as a single index

of their power to dominate government in their own interests, as Mills often seems to maintain.

To me, another indication of Mills' biased view of the governmental situation is his almost complete failure even to mention the political parties, or to analyze their differences. It seems to me broadly true that the Republican party, though a coalition, is more than any other single thing the party of the bigger sector of business. Four years of a Republican administration—two of them without control of Congress—is certainly not enough to indicate that big business through its favorite party organ controls the government on a long-run basis. So Mills is practically forced to the view that the alleged control operates above and beyond the party system. This seems to be connected with his relegation of the legislative branch to the "middle level" of power. I have strong reservations about this, but also it must not be forgotten that the presidency is the biggest prize of all in party politics, and it is its importance which forms the primary integrating focus of our particular type of party system. Surely the presidency is not simply the football of an inner clique which manipulates the executive branch independently of the party.[5]

Mills, of course, recognizes that the aftermath of two world wars, the rise of Communist power, and the relative decline of the older Western Great Powers provide the occasion for the increasing prominence of the military group in our governmental system. Before these changes—and, indeed, to a remarkable extent, as late as the 1930's—the military played a far smaller role in this country than in any other society of comparable scale and organizational and technological development. Part of the change may be interpreted as simply the redressing of a balance. But it seems to me correct to say that for the last ten years there has been a special situation attributable to the extremely unsettled condition of the world at large and to the difficulties entailed for the American system, given its background, in meeting the problem on its own terms. There is thus a sense in which it is true that the higher military officers

---

[4]Cf. F. X. Sutton, et al., The American Business Creed (Cambridge, Mass., 1956), for an excellent analysis of the point of view of business toward its relations to government. The authors make it clear that the present state of affairs is far from being fully accepted in business circles even now.

[5]Somewhat curiously, though tending to suggest that President Eisenhower's elevation to the presidency is symptomatic of the alliance between the "warlords" and the upper business group, Mills does not even mention Adlai Stevenson as a significant figure in the American political scene. To be sure, his book appeared before Stevenson's second nomination. But where does Stevenson fit?

have tended to fill a vacuum in the field of national decision-making. There are two main points to be made about Mills' treatment of the matter. First, more in this field than perhaps any other, Mills' discussion is marred by a hasty tendency to generalize from very recent short-run developments to the long-run prospects of the structure of the society. Even here he fails to mention that in certain crucial questions the recommendations of the military have been overruled by civilian authority, although the President is a former military man. Secondly, the tone of indictment, particularly evidenced by the quite unnecessary and, I think, inappropriate parading of the term "warlord," is stronger in his discussion of this area than in any other, except perhaps the "mass society."

Related to the position of the higher military officers is what Mills calls the "military metaphysic," meaning the definition of international problems in terms of the primacy of military force. That there has been such a tendency, and that it has gone beyond the objective requirements of the situation, seem to be unquestionable. But I very much doubt whether it is as absolute as many of Mills' statements make it appear, and a swing in another direction is discernible already.[6] This seems to be another case of Mills' tendency to make large generalizations about major trends from short-run experience.

Finally, let us say a word about what Mills calls the "political directorate"—that is, the non-military component in the groups most influential in the affairs of government and politics. Again I think there is a certain correctness in his contention that a definite weakness exists here, and that the high participation both of business and of military elements in the exercise of power is related to this. But a difficulty arises in terms of the perspective on American society which I have been emphasizing throughout. Both the non-political stress in American social structure and values generally, and the recency and intensity of the pressures to build up this aspect of our structure, would lead one to predict that it would be a major focus of strain. American society has not developed a well-integrated political-government elite, in the sense that it has developed a relatively well-integrated business-executive group. For this

reason responsibility has been carried—imperfectly, of course—by a very miscellaneous group which includes members of the business and military groups, as would be expected, but also "politicians," in the usual sense of people making an at least partial career out of elective office and the influencing of elections; professional people, particularly lawyers but also economists, political scientists, and even natural scientists (e.g., John von Neumann as Atomic Energy Commissioner); journalists; and, a very important element, upper-class people in more than the purely economic sense that Mills employs, of whom Franklin Roosevelt was one and Adlai Stevenson, though also a lawyer, is another. In my opinion, the structure of the American political leadership group is far from a settled thing. It certainly is not settled in terms of the long-run dominance of a business-military coalition.

Mills holds that the United States has no higher civil service at all, in the European sense, and seems to imply that we should have. There is relative truth in his empirical contention, though I think he tends to underestimate the real influence of "non-political" government officials on longer-run policy.[7] At least it seems highly probable that in the nature of the case the tendency will be toward a strengthening of the element of professional governmental officials who are essentially independent both of short-run "politics" and of elements extraneous to the structure of government and its responsibilities. In fact, the military officer is a special case of this type, and though his role is not stabilized, it presumably must come to be more important than it traditionally has been. However, it is questionable how far the specific models of civil service organization either of Britain or of Continental Europe—particularly, certain of their special connections with the class structure and the educational system—are appropriate to American conditions. Such connections in the American case would accentuate rather than mitigate the prominence of the Ivy League element to which Mills so seriously objects.[8]

---

[6] Whatever may be thought of it in other respects, Mr. Dulles' reluctance to join Britain and France in military measures against Egypt was hardly an expression of the "military metaphysic" now allegedly dominating the government.

[7] Good examples are the Department of Agriculture and the Reclamation Service of the Department of the Interior—and now, increasingly, the Public Health Service. I think that this is even true of the Foreign Service, and that Mills here, as in so many other connections, seriously exaggerates the probable long-run consequences of the McCarthyites' intervention in the affairs of the State Department.

[8] I think it correct to say that five years of Labour government in Britain, far from lessening

Above all, I do not think that Mills has made a convincing case for his contention that the power structure impinging directly on American government is in process of crystallizing into a top business-military coalition with a much weaker political "junior partner" whose main function presumably is, by manipulation of the mass media and the political process in the narrower sense, to keep the great majority of Americans from protesting too loudly or even from awakening to what allegedly is "really" going on. On a number of counts which have been reviewed, there is a case on a short-run basis for part of his interpretation. But I think that the kinds of factors brought out in the previous discussion make it extremely dubious that even the partial correctness of his interpretation of a current situation will prove to be a sound indicator of what is to be expected over such longer periods as a generation or more.

My conviction on this point is strengthened by a variety of other considerations which, for reasons of space, cannot be discussed here, but may be mentioned. First, I am extremely skeptical of Mills' interpretation of what he calls the "mass society," which includes the structural position of the great majority of the American population. In this he ignores both kinship and friendship, and the whole mass of associational activities and relationships. One example is the spread of church membership—which I suppose Mills would dismiss as simply an escape from the boredom of white-collar life, but in my opinion is of considerable positive significance.

Another very important complex which Mills either treats cavalierly or ignores completely involves education at the various levels, and with it the enormous development, over a century, of science and learning and the professions resting upon them. It is true that the people rooted in these areas of the social structure are not prominent in the power elite, and are even subject to some conflicts with it; but they would not be expected to be prominent in this way—their functions in the society are different. Nonetheless, they must be taken very seriously into account in a diagnosis of what has been happening to the society as a whole. One of the most important sets of facts concerns the ways in which the services of technical professional groups have come to penetrate the structures both of business and of government, a circumstance which over a period of time has greatly enhanced the role of the universities as custodians of learning and sources of trained personnel.

Finally, there is one special case of a professional group whose role Mills treats with serious inadequacy—namely, lawyers, First, he dismisses the judicial branch of government as just "trailing along," with the implication that with a slight lag it simply does the bidding of the "real" holders of power. This seems to be a most biased appraisal of the role of the courts. Not to speak of the longer-run record, the initiative taken by the courts in the matter of racial segregation and in the reassertion of civil liberties after the miasma of McCarthyism does not appear to me to be compatible with Mills' views. Similar considerations seem to apply to various aspects of the role of the private legal profession, notably with respect to the control of processes in the business world. Mills tends to assume that the relation between law and business is an overwhelmingly one-way relation; lawyers are there to serve the interests of businessmen and essentially have no independent influence. This, I think, is an illusion stemming largely from Mills' preoccupation with a certain kind of power. His implicit reasoning seems to be that since lawyers have less power than businessmen, they do not really "count."

III

The last problem I wish to raise, therefore, concerns Mills' conception of power and its use as a category of social analysis. Unfortunately, the concept of power is not a settled one in the social sciences, either in political science or in sociology. Mills, however, adopts one main version of the concept without attempting to justify it. This is what may be called the "zero-sum" concept; power, that is to say, is power over others. The power A has in a system is necessarily and by definition at the expense of B. This conception of power then is generalized to the whole conception of the political process when Mills says that "Politics is a struggle for power."

Within limits, every student of social affairs is free to define important concepts the way he prefers; there is no canonically "correct" definition. But choosing one alternative will have consequences which differ from those implied in another, and this is the case with Mills' conception of power. The essential point at present is that, to Mills, power is not a facility for the performance

_____

the prominence of Oxford and Cambridge educations as qualifications for the civil service, in fact increased their relative importance, by increasing the national importance of the civil service itself.

of function in and on behalf of the society as a system, but is interpreted exclusively as a facility for getting what one group, the holders of power, wants by preventing another group, the "outs," from getting what it wants.

What this conception does is to elevate a secondary and derived aspect of a total phenomenon into the central place. A comparison may help to make this clear. There is obviously a distributive aspect of wealth and it is in a sense true that the wealth of one person or group by definition cannot also be possessed by another group. Thus the distribution of wealth is, in the nature of the case, a focus of conflicts of interest in a society. But what of the positive functions of wealth and of the conditions of its production? It has become fully established that the wealth available for distribution can only come about through the processes of production, and that these processes require the "co-operation" or integration of a variety of different agencies—what economists call the "factors of production." Wealth in turn is a generalized class of facilities available to units of the society—individuals and various types and levels of collectivities—for whatever uses may be important to them. But even apart from the question of what share each gets, the fact that there should be wealth to divide, and how much, cannot be taken for granted as given except within a very limited context.

Very similar things can be said about power in a political sense. Power is a generalized facility or resource in the society. It has to be divided or allocated, but it also has to be produced and it has collective as well as distributive functions. It is the capacity to mobilize the resources of the society for the attainment of goals for which a general "public" commitment has been made, or may be made. It is mobilization, above all, of the action of persons and groups, which is binding on them by virtue of their position in the society. Thus within a much larger complex Mills concentrates almost exclusively on the distributive aspect of power. He is interested only in who has power and what sectoral interests he is serving with his power, not in how power comes to be generated or in what communal rather than sectoral interests are served.

The result is a highly selective treatment of the whole complex of the power problem. There is, in the first place, a tendency to exaggerate the empirical importance of power by alleging that it is only power which "really" determines what happens in a society. Against this, I would place the view that power is only one of several cognate factors in the determination of social events. This bias of Mills is particularly evident in his tendency to foreshorten social processes and emphasize overwhelmingly short-run factors. There is, secondly, the tendency to think of power as presumptively illegitimate; if people exercise considerable power, it must be because they have somehow usurped it where they had no right and they intend to use it to the detriment of others. This comes out most conspicuously in Mills' imputation of irresponsibility to his "power elite" and the allegation, vaguely conceived and presented with very little evidence, that they are characterized by a "higher immorality." It is notable that as he approaches the climax indicated by the title of his final chapter the tone of indictment becomes shriller and shriller and the atmosphere of objective analysis recedes.

Back of all this lies, I am sure, an only partly manifest "metaphysical" position which Mills shares with Veblen and a long line of indicters of modern industrial society. I would call it a utopian conception of an ideal society in which power does not play a part at all.

This is a philosophical and ethical background which is common both to utopian liberalism and socialism in our society and to a good deal of "capitalist" ideology. They have in common an underlying "individualism" of a certain type. This is not primarily individualism in the sense that the welfare and rights of the individual constitute fundamental moral values, but rather that both individual and collective rights are alleged to be promoted only by minimizing the positive organization of social groups. Social organization as such is presumptively bad because, on a limited, short-run basis, it always and necessarily limits the freedom of the individual to do exactly what he may happen to want. The question of the deeper and longer-run dependence of the goals and capacities of individuals themselves on social organization is simply shoved into the background. From this point of view, both power in the individual enterprise and power in the larger society are presumptively evil in themselves, because they represent the primary visible focus of the capacity of somebody to see to it that somebody else acts or does not act in certain ways, whether at the moment he wants to or not.

There are, in contemporary society, three main versions of this individualistic utopianism, which may be called "liberal" and "capitalist" and "socialist"—I place all three terms in quotation marks deliberately. The liberal version is mainly "humanistically" oriented to the total welfare of the individual as a person, and in American terms it is very likely to assume a Jeffersonian cast, to hold up the vision of a simpler and hence almost by definition "better" society against the inhumanities and impersonalities of large-scale modern industrialism and all its concomitants.

The capitalist version is, with all the qualifications which such an assertion must occasion, primarily production-oriented. Essentially it says that, whatever the cost to individuals—including even businessmen themselves, or especially so—production must be achieved, carried on, and so far as possible increased. This is the focus of what has been called the "business creed."[9] Understandably it has been highly sensitive to "interferences" on both fronts, from liberal sources which would sacrifice productivity to humanistic values, and from governmentalist sources which would "interfere" with the businessman's primary responsibility for production. Social organization beyond the level of the firm is thus presumptively a limitation of its freedom.

The socialist version has been a secondary theme in American ideology largely because of the apolitical character of American society, which, as I have noted, has been prominent historically. The opposition to capitalism has centered on two fronts, the control of the economy in the interests of preventing abuses of power and the steering of the benefits of productivity in the humanistic direction of "welfare." But the socialist questions whether control of the abuses of private enterprise is possible at all; to him, for the state to take over production directly is the only way. From this perspective, furthermore, the "Jeffersonian" version of romantic utopianism seems particularly unrealistic and unacceptable.

From one point of view, the socialist romanticizes the state and the political process. Whereas he distrusts private interests almost totally and feels that they cannot be entrusted with any responsibility, he romantically believes that if public authority alone is entrusted with all responsibilities, all will be well—because some mystical "popular will" or "public interest" controls it—forgetting that public authority, like other forms of social organization, is administered by human beings.

And that he does not fundamentally trust even public authority is evidenced by his ultimate ideal that the state should "wither away" and the spontaneous co-operation of institutionally unorganized human beings should take over. The socialist has been put in a particularly difficult position in the contemporary world by the development of communism which, while still paying lip service to the eventual withering-away of the state, carries the enforcement of its predominance over all private interests, including the liberties of its citizens, to the totalitarian extreme.

Mills does not make his own position explicit in this book. As noted, at times he speaks like a nostalgic Jeffersonian liberal. I understand, however, that he professes to be a socialist—non-Communist, of course. But a basic strain of his thinking is consistent with both wings of the liberal-socialist dilemma on the basically individualistic premises that I have outlined: either that social organization beyond the level of the family and the local community is a bad thing in toto, or that it is instrumentally justified only to get society over a particular hump, the threat of the capitalist evil.

Mills seems to be suggesting that the development of the power elite is bringing that capitalist evil to a climax, to a situation which is intolerable to liberals and socialists alike. I suggest an alternative view: that, though of course accompanied by a whole range of "abuses," the main lines of social development in America are essentially acceptable to a humanistic ethic which in my case is closer to the liberal than to either of the other two outlined here. But it differs in not being in the older sense an individualistic liberalism. If the individualistic assumptions are modified in favor of a set which not only admit the necessity but assert the desirability of positive social organization, much of the ideological conflict between the three positions as total "systems" evaporates. Above all, it can be positively asserted that power, while of course subject to abuses and in need of many controls, is an essential and desirable component of a highly organized society. This position, in asserting and justifying the increased importance of government, thus grants that there is a grain of truth in the "socialist" theme. There is, however, also some justification for the existence of "capitalism," if by that is meant the institutionalization of responsibility for the larger part of economic production in the hands of a variety of private, non-governmental agencies. To my mind, there is no more reason why all important economic production

9 Cf. Sutton, et al., op. cit.

should be controlled by government than why all
scientific research should be.

Hence, in my opinion, many of the difficulties
of Mills' analysis of a crucial problem in American society arise from his failure to transcend the
dilemmas inherent in much of the individualistic
tradition in American and, more broadly, in Western thought. It seems to me that he is clearly
and, in the degree to which he pushes this position,
unjustifiably anti-capitalist. He is partly pro-lib-
eral and probably even more pro-socialist. But in
the American scene a choice between these old alternatives of ideological orientation is no longer
enough. It is necessary not only to criticize existing conditions from the older philosophical or ideological points of view, but to take serious stock of
the ideological assumptions underlying the bulk of
American political discussion of such problems as
power.

Part 2

AMERICAN DEMOCRACY—THE PLURALIST MODEL

ON THE SPECIES HOMO POLITICUS*

Robert Dahl

We have described the long-run changes from oligarchy to pluralism; we have analyzed the distribution and patterns of influence; we have traced the short-run changes from spheres of influence to an executive-centered order. We know now how the system works. Can we explain why?

Let us start with man himself: with his opportunities and resources for gaining influence and the way he exploits—or more often neglects to exploit—his political potentialities.

Homo Civicus

Civic man is, at heart, simply man; man is the child grown up; the child is the human species after millions of years of evolution. In spite of ideas and ideals, the human organism still relentlessly insists on its primordial quest for gratifications and release from pain. The child and the youth learn various forms of gratifying experience; they learn of love, and food, of play, work, and rest, of the pursuit of curiosity, the perception of order and pattern, sex, friendship, self-esteem, social esteem. Throughout man's life, experiences like these channel his efforts, his energies, his attention. They represent his hungers, his needs, his wants.

The child, the budding civic man, learns all too soon that he cannot indulge himself without stint. Constraints are imposed on his liberty to gratify himself, both by nature herself in the form of physiological, mechanical, and psychological limitations and also by other individuals—his family, to begin with, then playmates, teachers, and later a host of others. The child struggles, resists, and is caught, more or less firmly, in a net woven by himself and his society.

He learns how to delay his gratifying experiences; because of the various barriers imposed on him, the routes he now chooses to his goals are frequently complex and time-consuming, sometimes boring, occassionally painful, at times dangerous.

He discovers that just as others constrain him in his efforts to achieve his primary goals, he too has resources that he can use to influence others to gain his own ends. At first these resources are closely attached to his own person and consist of simple, direct actions and reactions like affection, friendliness, anger , hostility, crying, destructiveness. But the world, as he gradually learns, contains many resources that can be used more indirectly. In our own culture, for example, he soon finds that money has a magical power to induce the compliance of many different people for many different purposes.

Thus homo civicus begins to develop strategies, ways of using his resources to achieve his goals. Even in choosing strategies, he discovers, he does not enjoy complete freedom. Some strategies are banned, some are permissible, others are encouraged, many are all but unavoidable. Schooling and a job are presented to him as compulsory strategies; it is made clear that any attempt to depart from these paths will be visited not only by a great loss in his capacity to attain his goals but possibly even by outright punishment. Schooling is considered instrumental in gaining knowledge, and knowledge is a resource of widespread applicability; a job is instrumental in acquiring income and social standing, resources that are important for a variety of ends.

Young homo civicus learns that his choices are constrained by laws enforced by the police, by courts, and by many other officials. He learns of clusters of institutions and men called governments, toward some of which he develops sentiments of loyalty or cynicism. He may accept the constraints on his choices flowing from the actions of these governments, or he may try to evade them, but in either case he gradually learns that the range of permissible strategies in dealing with governments is a good deal wider and includes many subtler alternatives than he had first assumed. Among his resources for influencing officials, homo civicus discovers the ballot. Although the prevailing public doctrine of American society places a high value on this resource, and homo civicus may himself give lip service to that doctrine, in fact he may doubt its value and rarely if ever employ it, or he may vote merely out of habit and sense of duty. Or

*From Robert Dahl, Who Governs?, Yale University Press, 1961. Copyright (c) 1961 by Yale University. Reprinted by permission.

26

he may see the ballot as a useful device for influencing politicians.

Homo civicus has other resources, too. For example, he can forego a movie or two in order to make a contribution to a political campaign; he can forego an evening of television in order to distribute propaganda for a candidate. But the chances are very great that political activity will always seem rather remote from the main focus of his life. Typically, as a source of direct gratifications political activity will appear to homo civicus as less attractive than a host of other activities; and, as a strategy to achieve his gratifications indirectly, political action will seem considerably less efficient than working at his job, earning more money, taking out insurance, joining a club, planning a vacation, moving to another neighborhood or city, or coping with an uncertain future in manifold other ways.

Sometimes, however, the actions or inactions of governments may threaten the primary goals of homo civicus. Then homo civicus may set out deliberately to use the resources at his disposal in order to influence the actions of governments. But when the danger passes, homo civicus may usually be counted on to revert to his normal preoccupation with nonpolitical strategies for attaining his primary goals.

Homo civicus is not, by nature, a political animal.

Homo Politicus

Despite several thousand years of richly insightful speculation, not much can be said with confidence about the factors that shape homo politicus out of the apolitical clay of homo civicus. Presumably, in the course of development some individuals find that political action is a powerful source of gratifications, both direct and indirect. If and when the primary goals that animate homo civicus become durably attached to political action, a new member of the genus homo politicus is born. Political man, unlike civic man, deliberately allocates a very sizable share of his resources to the process of gaining and maintaining control over the policies of government. Control over policies usually requires control over officials. And where, as in the United States, key officials are elected by voters, political man usually allocates an important share of his resources to the process of gaining and maintaining influence over voters. Because the acquiescence of homo civicus is always a necessary

condition for rulership, and to gain his consent is often economical, in all political systems homo politicus deliberately employs some resources to influence the choices of homo civicus. Political man invariably seeks to influence civic man directly, but even in democratic systems civic man only occasionally seeks to influence political man directly.

Like civic man, political man develops strategies that govern the ways in which he uses the resources at his disposal. Like civic man, political man chooses his strategies from a narrowly limited set. In some political systems, the limits imposed on homo politicus are broad; in others the limits are relatively narrow. In pluralistic, democratic political systems with wide political consensus the range of acceptable strategies is narrowed by beliefs and habits rooted in traditions of legality, constitutionality, and legitimacy that are constantly reinforced by a great variety of social processes for generating agreement on and adherence to political norms. Whoever departs from these acceptable strategies incurs a high risk of defeat, for the resources that will be mounted against the political deviant are almost certain to be vastly greater than the resources the political deviant can himself muster. Even homo civicus (under the prodding of rival political leaders) can be counted on to rise briefly out of his preoccupation with apolitical goals and employ some of his resources to smite down the political man who begins to deviate noticeably in his choice of strategies from the norms prescribed in the political culture.

Resources

The resources available to political man for influencing others are limited, though not permanently fixed. For our purposes in this book, a resource is anything that can be used to sway the specific choices or the strategies of another individual. Or, to use different language, whatever may be used as an inducement is a resource.

How one classifies resources is to some extent arbitrary. It would be possible to list resources in great detail, distinguishing one from the other with the utmost subtlety or to deal in very broad categories. One could search for a comprehensive and logically exhaustive classification or simply list resources according to the dictates of common sense. One could employ elaborate psychological categories derived from theories of modern psychology, or one could use more commonplace terms to classify resources. It will do, I think, to use categories dictated by common sense; to do more at this stage of our knowledge would be pseudoscientific window dressing.

Some resources can be used more or less directly as inducements. Or, put another way, the kinds of effective and cognitive experiences mentioned a moment ago as peculiarly fundamental and universal depend rather directly on some kinds of resources and more indirectly on others.

A list of resources in the American political system might include an individual's own time; access to money, credit, and wealth; control over jobs; control over information; esteem or social standing; the possession of charisma, popularity, legitimacy, legality; and the rights pertaining to public office. The list might also include solidarity: the capacity of a member of one segment of society to evoke support from others who identify him as like themselves because of similarities in occupation, social standing, religion, ethnic origin, or racial stock. The list would include the right to vote, intelligence, education, and perhaps even one's energy level.

One could easily think of refinements and additions to this list; it is not intended as an exhaustive list so much as an illustration of the richness and variety of political resources. All too often, attempts to explain the distribution and patterns of influence in political systems begin with an <u>a priori</u> assumption that everything can be explained by reference to only one kind of resource. On the contrary, the various manifestations of influence described earlier can be explained, as we shall see, only by taking into account a number of different political resources.

Although the kinds and amounts of resources available to political man are always limited and at any given moment fixed, they are not, as was pointed out a moment ago, permanently fixed as to either kind or amount. Political man can use his resources to gain influence, and he can then use his influence to gain more resources. Political resources can be pyramided in much the same way that a man who starts out in business sometimes pyramids a small investment into a large corporate empire. To the political entrepreneur who has skill and drive, the political system offers unusual opportunities for pyramiding a small amount of initial resources into a sizable political holding. This possibility will prove to be highly important, as we shall see, in accounting for changes in influence.

Hypotheses

In Book I, we saw how the monopoly over public life enjoyed by the Congregational patrician families of New Haven was destroyed, how the entrepreneurs without inherited social position and education acquired the prerogatives of office, and how these men were in their turn displaced by ex-plebes who lacked the most salient resources of influence possessed by their predecessors: hereditary social status, wealth, business prominence, professional attainments, and frequently even formal education beyond high school. The change in the New Haven political system from the election of Elizur Goodrich in 1803 to John W. Murphy in 1931—the first a descendant of a sixteenth-century Anglican Bishop, a Yale graduate, a Congregationalist, a lawyer, a judge, congressman, Federalist; the second a descendant of Irish immigrants, a Catholic, a Democrat, and a union official in Samuel Gompers' old Cigar Makers International Union—represented nothing less than an extended and peaceful revolution that transformed the social, economic, and political institutions of New Haven.

This change in New Haven is fully consistent with three of the key hypotheses in this study. First, a number of old American cities, of which New Haven is one, have passed through a roughly similar transformation from a system in which resources of influence were highly concentrated to a system in which they are highly dispersed. Second, the present dispersion is a consequence of certain fundamental aspects of the social, economic, and political structures of New Haven. Third, the present dispersion does not represent equality of resources but fragmentation. The revolution in New Haven might be said to constitute a change from a system of <u>cumulative inequalities</u> in political resources to a system of noncumulative or <u>dispersed inequalities</u> in political resources.

This system of dispersed inequalities is, I believe, marked by the following six characteristics.

1. Many different kinds of resources for influencing officials are available to different citizens.

2. With few exceptions, these resources are unequally distributed.

3. Individuals best off in their access to one kind of resource are often badly off with respect to many other resources.

4. No one influence resource dominates all the others in all or even in most key decisions.

5. With some exceptions, an influence resource

is effective in some issue-areas or in some specific decisions but not in all.

6. Virtually no one, and certainly no group of
more than a few individuals, is entirely lacking in
some influence resources.

A CRITIQUE OF THE ELITIST THEORY OF DEMOCRACY*

Jack L. Walker

During the last thirty years, there have been numerous attempts to revise or reconstitute the "classical" theory of democracy: the familiar doctrine of popular rule, patterned after the New England town meeting, which asserts that public policy should result from extensive, informed discussion and debate.[1] By extending general participation in decision-making the classical theorists hoped to increase the citizen's awareness of his moral and social responsibilities, reduce the danger of tyranny, and improve the quality of government. Public officials, acting as agents of the public at large, would then carry out the broad policies decided upon by majority vote in popular assemblies.

Although it is seldom made clear just which of the classical democratic theorists is being referred to, contemporary criticism has focused primarily on the descriptive elements of the theory, on its basic conceptions of citizenship, representation and decision making.[2] The concept of an active, informed, democratic citizenry, the most distinctive feature of the traditional theory, is the principal object of attack. On empirical grounds it is argued that very few such people can be found in Western societies. Public policy is not the expression of the common good as conceived of by the citizenry after widespread discussion and compromise. This description of policy making is held to be dangerously naive because it overlooks the role of demagogic leadership, mass psychology, group coercion, and the influence of those who control concentrated economic power. In short, classical democratic theory is held to be unrealistic; first because it employs conceptions of the nature of man and the operation of society which are utopian, and second because it does not provide adequate, operational definitions of its key concepts.

Since contemporary scholars have found the classical theory of democracy inadequate, a "revisionist" movement has developed, much as it has among contemporary Marxists, seeking to reconstitute the theory and bring it into closer correspondence with the latest findings of empirical research. One major restatement, called the "elitist theory of democracy" by Seymour Martin Lipset,[3] is now employed in many contemporary books and articles on American politics and political behavior and is fast becoming part of the conventional wisdom of political science.

The adequacy of the elitist theory of democracy, both as a set of political norms and as a guide to empirical research, is open to serious question. It has two major shortcomings: first, in their quest for realism, the revisionists have fundamentally changed the normative significance of democracy,

---

[1] For discussions of the meaning of the classical theory of democracy see: George Sabine, "The Two Democratic Traditions," The Philosophical Review, 61 (1952), 451-474; and his A History of Political Theory (New York, 1958), especially chs. 31 and 32. Also see J. Roland Pennock, Liberal Democracy: Its Merits and Prospects (New York, 1950); and Sheldon Wolin, Politics and Vision (Boston, 1960), especially chs. 9 and 10.

[2] Criticism of the descriptive accuracy of the classical theory has been widespread in recent years. The best statement of the basic objections usually made is Joseph Schumpeter, Capitalism, Socialism and Democracy (New York, 1942), Part IV. See also Bernard Berelson et al., Voting (Chicago, 1954), chapter 14; articles by Louis Hartz and Samuel Beer in W. N. Chambers and R. H. Salisbury (eds.), Democracy in the Mid-20th Century (St. Louis, 1960); Seymour Martin Lipset, Political Man (New York, 1960); Robert Dahl, A Preface to Democratic Theory (Chicago, 1956), and Who Governs? (New Haven, 1961), especially

pp. 223-325; V. O. Key, Public Opinion and American Democracy (New York, 1961), especially Part VI; Lester W. Milbrath, Political Participation (Chicago, 1965), especially Chapter VI; and for a general summary of the position: Henry Mayo, An Introduction to Democratic Theory (New York, 1960).

[3] Introduction by Lipset to the Collier Books paperback edition of Robert Michel's, Political Parties (New York, 1962, p. 33.

*From Jack Walker, "A Critique of the Elitiest Theory of Democracy," American Political Science Review, 1966, Vol. LX, pp. 283-305. Reprinted by permission of the American Political Science Association and the author.

rendering it a more conservative doctrine in the process; second, the general acceptance of the elitist theory by contemporary political scientists has led them to neglect almost completely some profoundly important developments in American society.

I. Normative Implications of the Elitist Theory

At the heart of the elitist theory is a clear presumption of the average citizen's inadequacies. As a consequence, democratic systems must rely on the wisdom, loyalty and skill of their political leaders, not on the population at large. The political system is divided into two groups: the elite, or the "political entrepreneurs,"[4] who possess ideological commitments and manipulative skills; and the citizens at large, the masses, or the "apolitical clay"[5] of the system, a much larger class of passive, inert followers who have little knowledge of public affairs and even less interest. The factor that distinguishes democratic and authoritarian systems, according to this view, is the provision for limited, peaceful competition among members of the elite for the formal positions of leadership within the system. As Joseph Schumpeter summarized the theory: "the democratic method is that institutional arrangement for arriving at political decisions in which individuals acquire the power to decide by means of a competitive struggle for the people's vote."[6]

Democracy is thus conceived primarily in procedural terms; it is seen as a method of making decisions which insures efficiency in administration and policy making and yet requires some measure of responsiveness to popular opinion on the part of the ruling elites. The average citizen still has some measure of effective political power under this system, even though he does not initiate policy, because of his right to vote (if he chooses) in regularly scheduled elections. The political leaders, in an effort to gain support at the polls, will shape public policy to fit the citizens' desires. By anticipating public reaction the elite grants the citizenry a form of indirect access to public policy making, without the creation of any kind of formal institutions and even in the absence of any direct communication. "A few citizens who are nonvoters, and who for some reason have no influen-

tial contact with voters, have no indirect influence. Most citizens, however, possess a moderate degree of indirect influence, for elected officials keep the real or imagined preferences of constituents constantly in mind in deciding what policies to adopt or reject."[7] An ambiguity is created here because obviously leaders sometimes create opinions as well as respond to them, but since the leaders are constantly being challenged by rivals seeking to gain the allegiance of the masses it is assumed that the individual citizen will receive information from several conflicting sources, making it extremely difficult for any one group to "engineer consent" by manipulating public opinion. As Lipset puts it: "Representation is neither simply a means of political adjustment to social pressures nor an instrument of manipulation. It involves both functions, since the purpose of representation is to locate the combinations of relationships between parties and social bases which make possible the operation of efficient government."[8]

There has been extensive research and speculation about the prerequisites for a democratic system of this kind. There is general agreement that a well developed social pluralism and an extensive system of voluntary groups or associations is needed, along with a prevailing sense of psychological security, widespread education and limited disparities of wealth. There must be no arbitrary barriers to political participation, and "enough people must participate in the governmental process so that political leaders compete for the support of a large and more or less representative cross section of the population."[9]

Elitist theory departs markedly from the classical tradition at this point. Traditionally it was assumed that the most important prerequisite for a stable democracy was general agreement among the politically active (those who vote) on certain fundamental policies and basic values, and widespread acceptance of democratic procedures and restraints on political activity. Political leaders would not violate the basic consensus, or "democratic mold," if they wished to be successful in gaining their objectives, because once these fundamental restraints were broken the

---

[4] The phrase is Dahl's in Who Governs? p. 227.

[5] Ibid., p. 225.

[6] Schumpeter, op. cit., p. 269.

[7] Dahl, Who Governs?, p. 164.

[8] Lipset, Introduction to Michels, op. cit., p. 34.

[9] Robert Dahl and Charles Lindblom, Politics, Economics and Welfare (New York, 1953), p. 309.

otherwise passive public would become aroused
and would organize against the offending leaders.
Elitist theorists argue instead that agreement on
democratic values among the "intervening structure of elites," the very elements which had been
seen earlier as potential threats to democracy, is
the main bulwark against a breakdown in consti-
tutionalism. Writing in 1959 David Truman dis-
cards his notion of "potential groups," a variation
of the traditional doctrine of consensus, and calls
instead for a "consensus of elites," a determination on the part of the leaders of political parties,
labor unions, trade associations and other voluntary associations to defend the fundamental procedures of democracy in order to protect their
own positions and the basic structure of society
itself from the threat of an irresponsible demagogue. [10] V. O. Key, in his Public Opinion and the
American Democracy, concludes that "the critical element for the health of a democratic order
consists in the beliefs, standards, and competence of those who constitute the influentials, the
opinion-leaders, the political activists in the order."[11] Similarly, Robert Dahl concludes in his
study of New Haven that the skillful, active political leaders in the system are the true democratic
"legitimists."[12] Since democratic procedures
regulate their conflicts and protect their privileged
positions in the system the leaders can be counted
on to defend the democratic creed even if a majority of the voters might prefer some other set of
procedures. [13]

It has also been suggested by several elitist
theorists that democracies have good reason to
fear increased political participation. They argue
that a successful (that is, stable) democratic system depends on widespread apathy and general political incompetence. [14] The ideal of democratic
participation is thus transformed into a "noble lie"
designed chiefly to insure a sense of responsibility
among political leaders. As Lester Milbrath puts
it:

> . . . it is important to continue moral ad-
> monishment for citizens to become active
> in politics, not because we want or expect
> great masses of them to become active,
> but rather because the admonishment helps
> keep the system open and sustains a belief
> in the right of all to participate, which is
> an important norm governing the behavior
> of political elites. [15]

---

[10]David Truman, "The American System in
Crisis," Political Science Quarterly, (December,
1959), pp. 481-497. See also a perceptive critique
of Truman's change of attitude in Peter Bachrach,
"Elite Consensus and Democracy," The Journal
of Politics, 24 (1962), 439-452.

[11]Key, op. cit., p. 558. See also Key's "Public Opinion and the Decay of Democracy," The
Virginia Quarterly Review, 37 (1961), 481-494.

[12] Dahl's position on this issue seems to have
undergone a transformation somewhat similar to
Truman's. Compare Dahl and Lindblom, op. cit.,
Chapter 11 with Dahl, Who Governs?, Books IV,
V, VI.

[13]Dahl, Who Governs?, pp. 311-325. It is important to note that these conclusions about the
crucial function of an elite consensus in democracy were based on little empirical evidence. Truman, Key and Dahl seem to rely most heavily on
Samuel Stouffer, Communism, Conformity, and

Civil Liberties (New York, 1955), a study based
on national opinion surveys which was concerned
with only one issue (McCarthyism) and did not investigate the relationship between the expressed
opinions of its subjects and their behavior under
stress; and James Prothro and Charles Grigg,
"Fundamental Principles of Democracy: Bases
of Agreement and Disagreement," Journal of Politics, 22 (1960), 276-294, a study of attitudes in
two small cities. More recently, however, Herbert McClosky has produced more convincing data
in his "Consensus and Ideology in American Politics," this REVIEW, 58 (1964), 361-382. On page
377 McClosky concludes that widespread agreement on procedural norms is not a prerequisite to
the success of a democratic system: "Consensus
may strengthen democratic viability, but its absence in an otherwise stable society need not be
fatal, or even particularly damaging." McClosky's
conclusions are called into question by data presented by Samuel Eldersveld, Political Parties:
A Behavioral Analysis (Chicago, 1964), pp. 183-
219; and Edmond Constantini, "Intra-party Attitude
Conflict: Democratic Party Leadership in California," Western Political Quarterly, 16 (1963),
956-972.

[14] See Bernard Berelson, et al., op. cit., Chap-
ter 14; Lipset, op. cit., pp. 14-16; W. H. Morris-
Jones, "In Defense of Apathy," Political Studies,
II (1954), 25-37.

[15] Milbrath, op. cit., p. 152.

If the uninformed masses participate in large numbers, democratic self-restraint will break down and peaceful competition among the elites, the central element in the elitist theory, will become impossible.

The principal aim of the critics whose views we are examining has been to make the theory of democracy more realistic, to bring it into closer correspondence with empirical reality. They are convinced that the classical theory does not account for "much of the real machinery"[16] by which the system operates, and they have expressed concern about the possible spread among Americans of either unwarranted anxiety or cynical disillusionment over the condition of democracy. But it is difficult to transform a utopian theory into a realistic account of political behavior without changing the theory's normative foundations. By revising the theory to bring it into closer correspondence with reality, the elitist theorists have transformed democracy from a radical into a conservative political doctrine, stripping away its distinctive emphasis on popular political activity so that it no longer serves as a set of ideals toward which society ought to be striving. [17]

_____

[16] Louis Hartz, "Democracy: Image and Reality," in Chambers and Salisbury (eds.), op. cit., p. 26.

[17] Several articles have recently appeared which attack the elitist theory on normative grounds. The best and most insightful is Lane Davis, "The Cost of Realism: Contemporary Restatements of Democracy," Western Political Quarterly, 17 (1964), 37-46. Also see: Graeme Duncan and Steven Lukes, "The New Democracy," Political Studies, 11 (1963), 156-177; Steven W. Rousseas and James Farganis, "American Politics and the End of Ideology," British Journal of Sociology, 14 (1963) 347-360; and Christian Bay, "Politics and Pseudopolitics," this REVIEW, 59 (1965), 39-51. The subject is also treated in: Henry Kariel, The Decline of American Pluralism (Stanford, 1961), Chapters 9 and 11; T. B. Bottomore, Elites and Society (London, 1964), 108-110; Robert Presthus, Men at the Top (New York, 1964), 3-47; and Robert Agger, Daniel Goldrich and Bert Swanson, The Rulers and the Ruled (New York) (1964), 93-99, 524-532. For an insightful critique of the work of Dahl and Mills, conceived of as opposing ideological positions see: William E. Connolly, Responsible Political Ideology: Implications of the Sociology of Knowledge for Political Inquiry, (unpub-

The most distinctive feature, and the principal orienting value, of classical democratic theory was its emphasis on individual participation in the development of public policy. By taking part in the affairs of his society the citizen would gain in knowledge and understanding, develop a deeper sense of social responsibility, and broaden his perspective beyond the narrow confines of his private life. Although the classical theorists accepted the basic framework of Lockean democracy, with its emphasis on limited government, they were not primarily concerned with the policies which might be produced in a democracy; above all else they were concerned with human development, the opportunities which existed in political activity to realize the untapped potentials of men and to create the foundations of a genuine human community. In the words of John Stuart Mill:

> . . . the most important point of excellence which any form of government can possess is to promote the virtue and intelligence of the people themselves. The first question in respect to any political institutions is how far they tend to foster in the members of the community the various desirable qualities, . . . moral, intellectual, and active. [18]

In the elitist version of the theory, however, emphasis has shifted to the needs and functions of the system as a whole; there is no longer a direct concern with human development. The central question is not how to design a political system which stimulates greater individual participation and enhances the moral development of its citizens, but how "to combine a substantial degree of popular participation with a system of power capable of governing effectively and coherently?"[19]

The elitist theory allows the citizen only a passive role as an object of political activity; he exerts influence on policy making only by rendering

_____

lished doctoral dissertation, University of Michigan, 1965), pp. 18-39. This section of this article depends heavily on Lane Davis' analysis.

[18] John Stuart Mill, Considerations on Representative Government (New York, 1862), pp. 39-40.

[19] Samuel Beer, "New Structures of Democracy: Britain and America," in Chambers and Salisbury (eds.), op. cit., p. 46.

judgements after the fact in national elections. The safety of contemporary democracy lies in the high-minded sense of responsibility of its leaders, the only elements of society who are actively striving to discover and implement the common good. The citizens are left to "judge a world they never made, and thus to become a genteel counter-part of the mobs which sporadically unseated aristocratic governments in eighteenth- and nineteenth-century Europe."[20]

The contemporary version of democratic theory has, it seems, lost much of the vital force, the radical thrust of the classical theory. The elitist theorists, in trying to develop a theory which takes account of the way the political system actually operates, have changed the principal orienting values of democracy. The heart of the classical theory was its justification of broad participation in the public affairs of the community; the aim was the production of citizens who were capable enough and responsible enough to play this role. The classical theory was not meant to describe any existing system of government; it was an outline, a set of prescriptions for the ideal polity which men should strive to create. The elitist theorists, in their quest for realism, have changed this distinctive prescriptive element in democratic theory; they have substituted stability and efficiency as the prime goals of democracy. If these revisions are accepted, the danger arises that in striving to develop more reliable explanations of political behavior, political scientists will also become sophisticated apologists for the existing political order. Robert Lane, in concluding his study of the political ideologies of fifteen "common men" in an Eastern city, observes that they lack a utopian vision, a well-defined sense of social justice that would allow them to stand in judgement on their society and its institutions.[21] To some degree, the "men of Eastport" share this disability with much of the American academic elite.

II. The Elitist Theory as a Guide for Research

The shortcomings of the elitist theory are not confined to its normative implications. Serious questions also arise concerning its descriptive accuracy and its utility as a guide to empirical research. The most satisfactory element in the theory is its concept of the passive, apolitical, common man who pays allegiance to his governors and to the sideshow of politics while remaining primarily concerned with his private life, evenings of television with his family, or the demands of his job. Occassionally, when the average citizen finds his primary goals threatened by the actions or inactions of government, he may strive vigorously to influence the course of public policy, but "Homo Civicus" as Dahl calls him, "is not, by nature, a political animal."[22]

It was the acceptance of this concept that led the elitist theorists to reject the traditional notion of consensus. It became implausible to argue that the citizenry is watchful and jealous of the great democratic values while at the same time suggesting that they are uninvolved, uninformed and apathetic. Widespread apathy also is said to contribute to democratic stability by insuring that the disagreements that arise during campaigns and elections will not involve large numbers of people or plunge the society into violent disorders or civil war.

No one can deny that there is widespread political apathy among many sectors of the American public. But it is important to ask why this is so and not simply to explain how this phenomenon contributes to the smooth functioning of the system. Of course, the citizens' passivity might stem from their satisfaction with the operation of the political system, and thus they would naturally become aroused only if they perceived a threat to the system. Dahl, for one, argues that the political system operates largely through "inertia," tradition or habitual responses. It remains stable because only a few "key" issues are the objects of controversy at any one time, the rest of public policy having been settled and established in past controversies which are now all but forgotten. Similarly, Nelson Polsby argues that it is fallacious to assume that the quiescent citizens in a community, especially those in the lower income groups, have grievances unless they actually express them. To do so is to arbitrarily assign "upper-

[20]Davis, Op. Cit., p. 45.

[21] Robert Lane, Political Ideology (New York, 1962), p. 475. See also Donald Stokes' comments on the same topic in "Popular Evaluations of Government: An Empirical Assessment," in Harlan Cleveland and Harold Lasswell (eds.), Ethics and Bigness (Published by the Conference on Science, Philosophy and Religion in their relation to the Democratic Way of Life, 1962), p. 72.

[22] Dahl, Who Governs?, pp. 225.

and middle-class values to all actors in the community."[23]

But it is hard to believe, in these days of protest demonstrations, of Black Muslims and the Deacons of Defense and Justice, that the mood of cynical apathy toward politics which affects so many American Negroes is an indication of their satisfaction with the political system, and with the weak, essentially meaningless alternatives it usually presents to them. To assume that apathy is a sign of satisfaction in this case is to overlook the tragic history of the Negroes in America and the system of violent repression long used to deny them any entrance into the regular channels of democratic decision-making.

Students of race relations have concluded that hostile attitudes toward a racial group do not necessarily lead to hostile actions, and amicable feelings do not ensure amicable actions. Instead, "it is the social demands of the situation, particularly when supported by accepted authority figures, which are the effective determinants of individual action. . . ."[24] This insight might apply to other areas besides race relations. It suggests that a society's political culture, the general perceptions about the nature of authority and the prevailing expectations of significant reference groups, might be a major influence on the political behavior of the average citizen regardless of his own feelings of satisfaction or hostility. There have been sizable shifts in rates of political participation throughout American history which suggests that these rates are not rigidly determined. A recent analysis indicates that rates of voter participation are now lower than they were in the Nineteenth Century even though the population is now much better educated and the facilities for communication much better developed.[25]

Other studies indicate that there are marked differences in the political milieu of towns and cities which lead citizens of one area to exhibit much more cynicism and distrust of the political system than others.[26] Although the studies showed no corresponding changes in feelings of political competence, cynical attitudes might inhibit many forms of participation and thus induce apathy.

Political apathy obviously has many sources. It may stem from feelings of personal inadequacy, from a fear of endangering important personal relationships, or from a lack of interest in the issues; but it may also have its roots in the society's institutional structure, in the weakness or absence of group stimulation or support, in the positive opposition of elements within the political system to wider participation; in the absence, in other words, of appropriate spurs to action, or the presence of tangible deterrents.[27] Before the causes of apathy can be established with confidence much more attention must be directed to the role of the mass media. How are the perceptions of individual citizens affected by the version of reality they receive, either directly or indirectly, from television, the national wire services, and the public schools[28] —and how do these perceptions affect their motivations? Political scientists have also largely neglected to study the use of both legitimate and illegitimate sanctions and private intimidation to gain political ends. How do the activities of the police,[29] social workers, or elements of organized

[23] Nelson Polsby, Community Power and Political Theory (New Haven, 1963), p. 117.

[24] Herbert Blumer, "Recent research [on race relations in the] United States of America," International Social Science Bulletin (UNESCO), 10 (1958), p. 432. Similar arguments concerning the relationship of beliefs and action can be found in J. D. Lohman and D. C. Reitzes, "Deliberately Organized Groups and Racial Behavior," American Sociological Review, 19 (1954), 342-344; and in Earl Raab (ed.), American Race Relations Today (Garden City, 1962).

[25] Walter Dean Burnham, "The Changing Shape of the American Political Universe," this REVIEW, 59 (1965), 7-28.

[26] Robert Agger, Marshall Goldstein and Stanley Pearl, "Political Cynicism: Measurement and Meaning," The Journal of Politics 23 (1961), 477-506; and Edgar Litt, "Political Cynicism and Political Futility," The Journal of Politics, 25 (1963), 312-323.

[27] For a brief survey of findings on this subject, see Milbrath, op. cit.; and for a clear, brief summary, see: Morris Rosenburg, "Some Determinants of Political Apathy," Public Opinion Quarterly, 18 (1954-55), 349-366. Also see David Apter (ed.), Ideology and Discontent (New York, 1964), especially chapters by Converse and Wolfinger, et al.

[28] A major study of the influence of secondary schools on political attitudes is underway at the University of Michigan under the direction of M. Kent Jennings.

[29] An extensive investigation of the role of the police and the courts in city politics is being conducted at Harvard University by James Q. Wilson.

crime affect the desires and the opportunities available for individual political participation?

Certainly the apparent calm of American politics is not matched by our general social life, which is marked by high crime rates, numerous fads and crazes, and much inter-group tension. [30] One recent study showed that during the civil rights protests in Atlanta, Georgia, and Cambridge, Maryland, crime rates in the Negro communities dropped substantially. [31] A finding of this kind suggests that there is some connection between these two realms of social conflict and that both may serve as outlets for individual distress and frustration. High crime (or suicide) rates and low rates of voting may very well be related; the former may represent "leakage" from the political system. [32]

Once we admit that the society is not based on a widespread consensus, we must look at our loosely organized, decentralized political parties in a different light. It may be that the parties have developed in this way precisely because no broad consensus exists. In a fragmented society which contains numerous geographic, religious and racial conflicts, the successful politican has been the man adept at negotiation and bargaining, the man best able to play these numerous animosities off against each other, and thereby build ad hoc coalitions of support for specific programs. Success at this delicate business of coalition building depends on achieving some basis for communication among the leaders of otherwise antagonistic groups and finding a formula for compromise. To create these circumstances sharp conflicts must be avoided;

highly controversial, potentially explosive issues shunned. Controversy is shifted to other issues or the public authorities simply refuse to deal with the question, claiming that they have no legitimate jurisdiction in the case or burying it quietly in some committee room or bureaucratic pigeonhole. [33]

In other words, one of the chief characteristics of our political system has been its success in suppressing and controlling internal conflict. But the avoidance of conflict, the suppression of strife, is not necessarily the creation of satisfaction or consensus. The citizens may remain quiescent, the political system might retain its stability, but significant differences of opinion remain, numerous conflicts are unresolved and many desires go unfulfilled. The frustrations resulting from such deprivations can create conflict in other, non-political realms. Fads, religious revivals, or wild, anomic riots such as those which occurred in the Negro ghettos of several large American cities during the summers of 1964 and 1965, phenomena not directly related to the achievement of any clearly conceived political goals, may be touched off by unresolved tensions left untended by the society's political leaders.

The American political system is highly complex, with conflicting jurisdictions and numerous checks and balances. A large commitment in time and energy must be made, even by a well-educated citizen, to keep informed of the issues and personalities in all levels of government. Most citizens are not able or willing to pay this kind of cost to gain the information necessary for effective political participation. This may be especially true in a political system in which weak or unclear alternatives are usually presented to the electorate. For most citizens the world of politics

---

[30] It is very difficult to compare crime rates or other indications of social disorganization in the United States with those in other countries. For a discussion of some of the difficulties see: UNESCO 1963 Report on the World Social Situation (New York, 1963).

[31] Fredric Solomon, Walter L. Walker, Garrett O'Connor and Jacob Fishman, "Civil Rights Activity and Reduction of Crime Among Negroes," Archives of General Psychiatry, 12 (March, 1965), 227-236.

[32] For an excellent study of the Black Muslims which portrays the movement as a non-political outlet for the frustration and bitterness felt by many American Negroes see the study by an African scholar: E. V. Essien-Udom, Black Nationalism: A Study for an Identity in America (Chicago, 1962).

---

[33] Herbert Agar makes a similar analysis and argues for the retention of the system in The Price of Union (Boston, 1950). On page 689 he states:

The lesson which Americans learned [from the Civil War] was useful: in a large federal nation, when a problem is passionately felt, and is discussed in terms of morals, each party may divide within itself, against itself. And if the parties divide, the nation may divide; for the parties, with their enjoyable pursuit of power, are a unifying influence. Wise men, therefore, may seek to dodge such problems as long as possible. And the easiest way to dodge them is for both parties to take both sides.

is remote, bewildering, and meaningless, having no direct relation to daily concerns about jobs or family life. Many citizens have desires or frustrations with which public agencies might be expected to deal, but they usually remain unaware of possible solutions to their problems in the public sphere. This group within our political system are citizens only from the legal point of view. If a high degree of social solidarity and sense of community are necessary for true democratic participation, then these marginal men are not really citizens of the state. The polity has not been extended to include them. [34]

For the elitist theorist widespread apathy is merely a fact of political life, something to be anticipated, a prerequisite for democratic stability. But for the classical democrat political apathy is an object of intense concern because the overriding moral purpose of the classical theory is to expand the boundaries of the political community and build the foundations for human understanding through participation by the citizens in the affairs of their government.

III. Leaders and Followers

While most elitist theorists are agreed in conceiving of the average citizen as politically passive and uncreative, there seems to be a difference of opinion (or at least of emphasis) over the likelihood of some irrational, anti-democratic outburst from the society's commom men. Dahl does not dwell on this possibility. He seemingly conceives of homo civicus, the average citizen, as a man who consciously chooses to avoid politics and to devote himself to the pleasures and problems of his job and family:

> Typically, as a source of direct gratifications political activity will appear to homo civicus as less attractive than a host of other activities; and, as a strategy to achieve his gratifications indirectly political action will seem considerably less efficient than working at his job, earning more money, taking out insurance, joining a club, planning a vacation, moving to another neigh-

borhood or city, or coping with an uncertain future in manifold other ways. [35]

Lipset, on the other hand, seems much more concerned with the danger that the common man might suddenly enter the political system, smashing democratic institutions in the process, as part of an irrational, authoritarian political force. He sees "profoundly anti-democratic tendencies in lower class groups," [36] and he has been frequently concerned in his work with Hitler, McCarthy and other demagogic leaders who have led anti-democratic mass movements.

Although there are obviously some important differences of opinion and emphasis concerning the political capacities of average citizens and the relative security of democratic institutions, the elitist theorists agree on the crucial importance of leadership in insuring both the safety and viability of representative government. This set of basic assumptions serves as a foundation for their explanation of change and innovation in American politics, a process in which they feel creative leadership plays the central role.

Running throughout the work of these writers is a vision of the "professional" politician as hero, much as he is pictured in Max Weber's essay, "Politics as a Vocation." Dahl's Mayor Lee, Edward Banfield's Mayor Daley, Richard Neustadt's ideal occupant of the White House all possess great skill and drive, and are engaged in the delicate art of persuasion and coalition building. They are actively moving the society forward toward their own goals, according to their own special vision. All of them possess the pre-eminent qualities of Weber's ideal-type politician: "passion, a feeling of responsibility, and a sense of proportion." [37] As in Schumpeter's analysis of capitalism, the primary source of change and innovation in the political system is the "political entrepreneur"; only such a leader can break through the inherent conservatism of organizations and shake the masses from their habitual passivity.

It is obvious that political leaders (especially chief executives) have played a very important role in American politics, but it is also clear that the American system's large degree of internal

---

[34] For a study of several important factors affecting the degree of participation in American politics see: E. E. Shattschneider, The Semi-Sovereign People (New York, 1960), especially chs. 5 and 6.

[35] Dahl, Who Governs?, p. 224.

[36] Lipset, op. cit., p. 121.

[37] Hans Gerth and C. Wright Mills (eds.), From Max Weber: Essays in Sociology (New York, 1946), p. 115.

bargaining, the lack of many strong hierarchical controls and its numerous checks and balances, both constitutional and political, place powerful constraints on the behavior of political executives. American presidents, governors and mayors usually find themselves caught in a web of cross pressures which prevent them from making bold departures in policy or firmly attaching themselves to either side of a controversy. The agenda of controversy, the list of questions which are recognized by the active participants in politics as legitimate subjects of attention and concern, is very hard to change.

Just as it can be argued that the common citizens have a form of indirect influence, so it can also be argued that the top leaders of other institutions in the society, such as the business community, possess indirect influence as well. As Banfield suggests in his study of Chicago, the top business leaders have great potential power: "if the twenty or thirty wealthiest men in Chicago acted as one and put all their wealth into the fight, they could easily destroy or capture the machine."[38] The skillful politician, following Carl Friedrich's "rule of anticipated reactions,"[39] is unlikely to make proposals which would unite the business community against him. The aspiring politician learns early in his career, by absorbing the folklore which circulates among the politically active, which issues can and cannot be exploited successfully. It is this constellation of influences and anticipated reactions, "the peculiar mobilization of bias" in the community, fortified by a general consensus of elites, that determines the agenda of controversy.[40] The American political system, above all others, seems to be especially designed to frustrate the creative leader.

But as rigid and inflexible as it is, the political system does produce new policies; new programs and schemes are approved; even basic

procedural changes are made from time to time. Of course, each major shift in public policy has a great many causes. The elitist theory of democracy looks for the principal source of innovation in the competition among rival leaders and the cleaver maneuvering of political entrepreneurs, which is, in its view, the most distinctive aspect of a democratic system. Because so many political scientists have worn the theoretical blinders of the elitist theory, however, we have overlooked the importance of broadly based social movements, arising from the public at large, as powerful agents of innovation and change.

The primary concerns of the elitist theorists have been the maintenance of democratic stability, the preservation of democratic procedures, and the creation of machinery which would produce efficient administration and coherent public policies. With these goals in mind, social movements (if they have been studied at all) have usually been pictured as threats to democracy, as manifestations of "political extremism." Lipset asserts that such movements typically appeal to the "disgruntled and the psychologically homeless, to the personal failures, the socially isolated, the economically insecure, the uneducated, unsophisticated, and authoritarian persons at every level of the society."[41] Movements of this kind throw the political system out of gear and disrupt the mechanisms designed to maintain due process; if the elites were overwhelmed by such forces, democracy would be destroyed. This narrow, antagonistic view of social movements stems from the elitist theorists' suspicion of the political capacities of the common citizens,[42] their fear of instability

---

[38] Edward Banfield, Political Influence (New York, 1961), p. 290.

[39] Carl Friedrich, Constitutional Government and Politics (New York, 1939), pp. 17-18.

[40] This point is made persuasively by Peter Bachrach and Morton Baratz, "The Two Faces of Power," this REVIEW, 56 (1962), 947-952. Also see their "Decisions and Nondecisions: An Analytical Framework," this REVIEW, 57 (1963), 632-642; and Thomas J. Anton, "Power, Pluralism and Local Politics," Administrative Quarterly, 7, (1963), 425-457.

[41] Lipset, op. cit., p. 178.

[42] Ruth Searles and J. Allen Williams, in a study of Negro students who took part in the sit-in demonstrations, found no evidence that they were authoritarian or posed threats to democracy. "Far from being alienated, the students appear to be committed to the society and its middle class leaders": "Negro College Students' Participation in Sit-ins," Social Forces, 40 (1962), p. 219. For other studies of this particular social movement see: Robert Coles, "Social Struggle and Weariness," Psychiatry, 27 (1964), 305-315; and three articles by Fredric Solomon and Jacob Fishman; "Perspectives on Student Sit-in Movement," American Journal of Ortho-psychiatry, 33 (1963), 872-882; "Action and Identity Formation in First Student Sit-in Demonstration," Journal of Social

and their failure to recognize the elements of rigidity and constraint existing in the political system. But if one holds that view and at the same time recognizes the tendency of the prevailing political system to frustrate strong leaders, it becomes difficult to explain how significant innovations in public policy, such as the social security system, the Wagner Act, the Subversive Activities Control Act of 1950, or the Civil Rights Bill of 1964, ever came about.

During the last century American society has spawned numerous social movements, some of which have made extensive demands on the political system, while others have been highly esoteric, mystical, and apolitical. These movements arise because some form of social dislocation or widespread sense of frustration exists within the society. But dissatisfaction alone is not a sufficient cause; it must be coupled with the necessary resources and the existence of potential leadership which can motivate a group to take action designed to change the offending circumstances.[43] Often such movements erupt along the margins of the political system, and they sometimes serve

the purpose of encouraging political and social mobilization, of widening the boundaries of the polity.[44] Through movements such as the Negroes' drive for civil rights, or the Midwestern farmers' crusade for fair prices in the 1890's, the Ku Klux Klan, or the "radical right" movements of the 1960's, "pre-political people who have not yet found, or only begun to find, a specific language in which to express their aspirations about the world"[45] are given new orientation, confidence, knowledge, sources of information and leadership.

Social movements also serve, in Rudolf Heberle's words, as the "creators and carriers of public opinion."[46] By confronting the political authorities, or by locking themselves in peaceful—or violent[47] —conflict with some other element of the society, social movements provoke trials of strength between contending forces or ideas. Those trials of economic, political or moral strength take place in the court of public opinion and sometimes place enormous strain on democratic institutions and even the social fabric itself. But through such trials, as tumultuous as they may sometimes be, the agenda of controversy, the list of acceptable, "key" issues may be changed. In

Issues, 20 (1964), 36-45; and "Psychosocial Meaning of Nonviolence in Student Civil Rights Activities," Psychiatry, 27 (1964), 91-99. Also see the October, 1964 issue of The Journal of Social Issues, entitled "Youth and Social Action," edited by Fredric Solomon and Jacob Fishman; and Jack L. Walker, "Protest and Negotiation: A Case Study of Negro Leaders in Atlanta, Georgia," Midwest Journal of Political Science, 7 (1963), 99-124.

[43] Sociologists usually study social movements under the rubric of collective behavior. For general treatments see: Herbert Blumer, "Collective Behavior" in J. B. Gittler (ed.), Review of Sociology (New York, 1957); Rudolph Heberle, Social Movements, (New York, 1951); Lewis Killian, "Social Movements" in Robert Faris (ed.), Handbook of Modern Sociology (Chicago, 1964); Charles King, Social Movements in the United States (New York, 1956); Karl Lang and Gladys Lang, Collective Dynamics (New York, 1961); Neil Smelser, Theory of Collective Behavior (New York, 1963); Ralph Turner and Lewis Killian, Collective Behavior (Englewood Cliffs, N. J., 1957). For a brief historical sketch of some American social movements see: Thomas Greer, American Social Reform Movements: Their Pattern Since 1865 (Englewood Cliffs, N.J., 1946).

[44] For a book which investigates social movements which have served this function among Italian peasants see: E. J. Hobsbawn, Primitive Rebels (Manchester, 1959). See also: Vittorio Lanternari, The Religions of the Oppressed (New York, 1963) for a study of the relationship of Messianic Cults and revolutionary movements on five continents; and George Rude, The Crowd in History (New York, 1964) for a study of popular uprisings in England and France from 1730-1848.

[45] Hobsbawn, op. cit., p. 2.

[46] Heberle, op. cit., pp. 417-418.

[47] American political scientists have not been sufficiently concerned with the role of violence in the governmental process. Among all the articles published in The American Political Science Review between 1906 and 1963, there was only one whose title contained the word "violence," only one with the word "coercive" (it concerned India), and none with the word "force." During the same period there were forty-nine articles on governmental reorganization and twenty-four on civil service reform. See Kenneth Janda (ed.), Cumulative Index to The American Political Science Review (Evanston, 1964). Efforts to retrieve this situation have begun in: Harry Eckstein (ed.), Internal War (New York, 1964).

an effort to conciliate and mediate, the political leaders fashion new legislation, create unique regulatory bodies and strive to establish channels of communication and accommodation among the combatants.

Of course, members of the political elite may respond to the movement by resisting it, driving it underground or destroying it; they may try to co-opt the movement's leaders by granting them privileges or by accepting parts of its program, or even by making the leaders part of the established elite; they may surrender to the movement, losing control of their offices in the political system in the process. The nature of the political leader's response is probably a prime determinant of the tactics the movement will adopt, the kind of leadership that arises within it, and the ideological appeals it develops. Other factors might determine the response of the leadership, such as the existence of competing social movements with conflicting demands, the resources available to the political leaders to satisfy the demands of the movement, the social status of the participants in the movement, the presence of competing sets of leaders claiming to represent the same movement, and many other elements peculiar to each particular situation. In this process social movements may be highly disruptive and some institutions may be completely destroyed; the story does not always have a happy ending. But one major consequence (function, if you will) of social movements is to break society's log jams, to prevent ossification in the political system, to prompt and justify major innovations in social policy and economic organization.[48]

This relationship of challenge and response between the established political system and social movements has gone without much systematic study by political scientists. Sociologists have been concerned with social movements, but they have directed most of their attention to the causes of the movements, their "natural history," and the relationship between leaders and followers within them.[49] Historians have produced many

case studies of social movements but little in the way of systematic explanation.[50] This would seem to be a fruitful area for investigation by political scientists. But this research is not likely to appear unless we revise our concept of the masses as politically inert, apathetic and bound by habitual responses. We must also shift our emphasis from theories which conceive of the "social structure in terms of a functionally integrated system held in equilibrium by certain patterned and recurrent processes," to theories which place greater emphasis on the role of coercion and constraint in the political system and which concentrate on the influences within society which produce "the forces that maintain it in an unending process of change."[51] The greatest contribution of Marx to the understanding of society was his realization that internal conflict is a major source of change and innovation. One need not accept his metaphysical assumptions to appreciate this important insight.

IV. Conclusion

In a society undergoing massive social change, fresh theoretical persepctives are essential. Political theorists are charged with the responsibility of constantly reformulating the dogmas of the past so that democratic theory remains relevant to the stormy realities of Twentieth Century American society with its sprawling urban centers, its innumerable social conflicts, and its enormous bureaucratic hierarchies.

In restating the classical theory, however, contemporary political scientists have stripped democracy of much of its radical élan and have diluted its utopian vision, thus rendering it inadequate as

---

[48] Lewis Coser has discussed the role of conflict in provoking social change in his The Functions of Social Conflict (Glencoe: 1956); and in his "Social Conflict and the Theory of Social Change" British Journal of Sociology, 9 (1957), 197-207. See also Irving Louis Horowitz, "Consensus, Conflict and Cooperation: A Sociological Inventory," Social Forces, 41 (1962), 177-188.

[49] For an insightful and stimulating example,

see Joseph Gusfield, Symbolic Crusade (Urbana, 1963), which makes an excellent analysis of the causes of the Temperance movement and changes in its leadership but makes only brief mention of the movement's impact on the government and the responses of political leaders to its efforts.

[50] John Higham is somewhat of an exception of this generalization. See his Strangers in the Land: Patterns of American Nativism 1860-1925 (New York, 1963). Also see his: "Another Look at Nativism," Catholic Historical Review, 44 (1958), 147-158; and his "The Cult of the 'American Consensus': Homogenizing Our History," Commentary (February, 1959), p. 159.

[51] Ralf Dahrendorf, Class and Class Conflict in Industrial Society (Stanford, 1959), p. 159.

a guide to the future. The elitist theorists generally accept the prevailing distribution of status in the society (with exceptions usually made for the American Negro), and find it "not only compatible with political freedom but even . . . a condition of it."[52] They place great emphasis on limitations of the average citizen and are suspicious of schemes which might encourage greater participation in public affairs. Accordingly, they put their trust in the wisdom and energy of an active, responsible elite.

Besides these normative shortcomings the elitist theory has served as an inadequate guide to empirical research, providing an unconvincing explanation of widespread political apathy in American society and leading political scientists to ignore manifestations of discontent not directly related to the political system. Few studies have been conducted of the use of force, or informal, illegitimate coercion in the American political system, and little attention has been directed to the great social movements which have marked American society in the last one hundred years.

If political science is to be relevant to society's pressing needs and urgent problems, professional students of politics must broaden their perspectives and become aware of new problems which are in need of scientific investigation. They must examine the norms that guide their efforts and guard against the danger of uncritically accepting the values of the going system in the name of scientific objectivity. Political scientists must strive for heightened awareness and self-knowledge; they must avoid rigid presumptions which diminish their vision, destroy their capacities for criticism, and blind them to some of the most significant social and political developments of our time.

---

[52] Sabine, "The Two Democratic Traditions," op. cit., p. 459.

Part 3

CORPORATE POWER

CORPORATIONS*

David Bazelon

The very existence of America's massive and
bountiful corporations was for many years neglected, if not denied, by conventional thinking. The
revolutionary issue they represent was lost somewhere between Adam Smith's ideal irrelevancies
and what was most often referred to as "the monopoly problem" or, even more delicately, as "the
question of imperfect competition." That the most
obvious fact of economic life in this country, the
central position of major corporations, could have
been thus obscured is a testament both to the right-
thinking energies of our official mentors and the
credulity of our educated citizenry. When one reflects that Adam Smith was opposed to corporations
and did not welcome them into his eighteenth-
century world, this obscurantism becomes even
more impressive. It is occasionally even funny
that the self-exploitation of the small proprietor
still lingers in our minds as a model of American
enterprise, while the major corporations which
supply most of our needs remain theoretical ano-
malies. All of this is now beginning to change,
however, and a deeply significant discussion has
commenced which assumes: 1) that ours is a
corporate economy with each industrial or business area typically dominated by a few large organizations, which dominate no less effectively
because they are not technical monopolies; and
2) that this rather obvious fact has a welter of
far-reaching implications and is going to take
an awful lot of explaining.

A vice president and general counsel of the
Ford Motor Company has stated out loud: "It is
not inaccurate to say that we live in a corporate
society." This assertion is still somewhat in-
delicate, but we can now take it as certain that
it is no longer inaccurate.

It may not be saying too much to assert also
that the new thinking about collective enterprise,
or managerialism, is about to be recognized as
constituting a great theological crisis, on the order of the one that accompanied the introduction
of Darwin's work, or even the social and political

pillars of the ideology which has dominated Western
thought for several hundred years. A "new man"
has entered onto the historical stage, and the required new explanation of him is in the making.
Comprehending the corporate economy, his milieu,
is central to this effort. It is, in our terms, the
institutional bedrock of the Paper Economy.

"Corporation" has become one of the more important words in the language, and the people who
run them, called "managers," properly count
themselves among the more powerful groups to be
found on this power-ridden planet. Well, what
is a corporation? Technically, it is a legal entity—what is called a creature of the law—which
remark, I am sure, does nothing for anyone.
Reinhold Niebuhr has referred to them suggestively
as "these dubious sovereignties," which I like very
much but is probably too poetic for present purposes. Roger Blough's speechwriters see the
big American corporation as a voluntary association of free men, which dovetails nicely with the
familiar "just folks" metaphysics of our commercial culture. Writing early in this century, Veblen
defined the corporation as "a conspiracy in re-
straint of production"; this contains an essential
insight but cannot qualify as a well-rounded Aris-
totelian definition. To be official, the main thing
about a major corporation is that it organizes and
directs large masses of men and material in a
more or less limited technological area. So I
suggest that a corporation is a form of industrial
or technological or financial government.

The two basic points about corporations were
made decades ago, by Veblen and by Berle and
Means. Around the turn of the century, Veblen
demonstrated that large business organizations,
especially financial institutions, dominated and
distorted the new technological forces, and that
these control-organizations used paper—that is,
capitalization—primarily to make money out of
making and not making goods. To his mind, profit and production were substantially opposed to
each other, especially the profit derived from the
issuance of paper, which is the chief kind. The
second basic point about corporations was made
thirty years ago by Berle and Means, who suggested that large publicly held corporations were

an anomaly in the supposed system of private property. That pronouncement in The Modern Corporation and Private Property, published in 1932, will probably turn out to be one of the more resounding understatements in the history of social thought. Because in fact the big American corporation is engaged in a pleasant, leisurely, and continuingly decisive destruction of the previously existing system of private property. In a very neat, one-line summary, Berle and Means put it this way: "The corporate system has done to capital what the factory system did to labor."

John P. Davis, the chief American historian of corporations, wrote in 1905: "The growth of corporations in Western Europe and the United States signifies nothing less than a social revolution." That statement is more obviously true today than when it was made.

The history of corporations contains a few choice points for our purposes. The modern part of the story begins with the Dutch East India Company, which was chartered in 1602—the first stock corporation. (There were "bodies corporate"— that's a redundant phrase—before the modern period, such as churches, guilds, some various types in Rome, etc.) As an economic form, the stock corporation grew out of certain risk-sharing procedures in the early ship trade. The corporate form was useful, of course, where no investment was forthcoming without a guarantee of limited personal liability for the investor, and where large sums of money were required in high speculative but potentially very profitable schemes. The early English corporations were established by royal charter for trading and colonizing, and were in effect grants of substantial monopoly power. In some instances, the power granted covered immense geographical areas, as for example, India New York, the Massachusetts Bay Colony, Canada more or less, Virginia, and so on.[1]

_____
[1] We may note as an historical footnote that the magical paper-creating power of corporations was discovered—and violently reacted to—a bare century after the first stock corporation was set up. The occasion was the famous bursting of the famous South Sea Bubble in 1720. So many people had been hurt by their own greed and ignorance of corporate paper that prohibitive legislation was passed which, according to A. A. Berle Jr., "practically blanked out [corporations] for a little over a hundred years in English life. The

The most important historical point about corporations is that until recently they had always been considered public agencies—in effect, specific governments. Not nation-states, even when they ruled what we would consider whole countries; but nevertheless, governments. This was nicely put by Henry C. Adams, in his presidential address to the American Economics Association in 1896:

Corporations originally were regarded as agencies of the State. They were created for the purpose of enabling the public to realize some social or national end without involving the necessity for direct governmental administration. They were in reality arms of the State, and in order to secure efficient management, a local or private interest was created as a privelege or property of the corporation. A corporation, therefore, may be defined in the light of history as a body created by law for the purpose of obtaining public ends through an appeal to private interests.

America was founded by colonizing corporations which subsequently became state governments. A political scientist from Amherst, Earl Latham, asserts that "the basic form of the public government in America derived from the provenance of a commercial corporation," an ordinance of The Virginia Company in 1621. This entrancing historical circumstance might be characterized, in legal corporate language, as follows: the kings of England, in their corporate majesty, formed subsidiaries which then became greater than the parent; some time later these subsidiaries—now independent governments—formed other subsidiary corporations which have since become, again, greater than their parents. Moreover, if America was founded by English corporations, it seems that it was also lost to the Empire as the result of an effort to "control the market" for the benefit of one of them. The purpose of the English Tea Act which in high school led to the Boston Tea Party which in turn led to the American Revolution, was to bail out the East India Company—the same which, in

_____
theory was that they were too dangerous." That was a fascinating early episode in the forming of the modern paper system—the emotional essence of capitalism gone wild.

someone's beautiful phrase, is said to have acquired India for the British Empire "in a moment
of inadvertence." Apparently the Company lost
us in a moment of ineptitude.

Royal charters were succeeded by charters
granted by state legislatures. A special act of
the legislature was the only way to create a corporation until the first corporate statute was enacted by New York in 1811. It remained the usual
way during most of the first half of the century;
but finally the statutory procedure became common
among the states. They have since become a common joke, the states having competed strenuously
in making their laws attractive by abandoning serious supervision of their legal creatures: Delaware
gives the biggest premiums, and has an inordinate
number of customers. In 1800 there were only a
few score corporations in all the thirteen states.
Today there are 150,000 to 200,000 new ones
created each year: it costs only about $100 to
start one. (It is an interesting historical side-
light that The Federalist Papers do not mention
corporations at all; but this basic document, which
contains our initial theory of government, does not
mention political parties either.)

So in the beginning there was no difference between a charter for a corporation and a franchise
for a public utility. Today, the right to incorporate for any purpose at all has become generally
available; incorporation is now as common as contract. Corporations began as public bodies with
responsibilities to the public. It was only after
decades of struggle, the courts with technical
problems (the Supreme Court decided in 1886 that
the word "person" in the Fourteenth Amendment
included corporations) and society with this great
new source of private power, that they were established before the law as legal persons—with no
more legal responsibility than any other person.
The public relations aspect of the legal fiction
established them in the pantheon of legal-econo-
mic ideology as hard-working persons with individual initiative and other business emotions that
could be damaged as a person's feelings can be
hurt. To a very substantial extent, General Motors today—with its better than 10-billion-dollar
cash flow annually— stands before the government
and the law as a person just as you and I do. Now
isn't that silly! A cash flow of that size is equal
to about a tenth of the Federal government's—the
Federal government which shares with major central banks the national power to create the cash
that flows. Besides, the value of General Motors

stock increases rather steadily, while that of
Federal Reserve Notes does not: the market value
of GM's paper doubled between 1953 and 1958,
while Federal currency was declining in value.
But this doesn't make GM a person—it simply
makes GM a more effective institution than the
Federal government. Which will come as news
to no one.

The briefest possible history of the beginning of
corporate power in the United States would be this:
Toward the middle of the nineteenth century the
Federal government and the states turned over
substantial amounts of their power and property
to increasingly sizable corporate enterprizes.
Starting with the first grant to the Illinois Central
in 1850, the Federal government conveyed about
130 million acres of America to the railroad companies. State and local authorities added perhaps
another 25 million acres. Just to indicate what
was involved here, railroad companies were literally given one-quarter of the states of Washington
and Minnesota. Understand that this was not
merely land for track, but was a means of financing
the construction of the roads. The land was sold
to homesteaders, and only after considerable ac-
reage had been given away to the railroad corporations was the Homestead Act passed in 1862.
Also, this land giveaway was supplemented by
tax forgiveness on the part of the governmental
authorities.

The railroads were the beginning of big cor-
porate-financial enterprise in the United States.
Although railroad-building required a mass community effort, the community shared in the benefit only by having a railroad running through the
area: the profits went to the companies. Most
of this came from selling railroad securities,
rather than from building and operating the roads
themselves. Moreover, the middle and late nineteenth-century railroad-paper provided the airy
basis for a world of later paper, and greatly expanded paper-trading as a national pastime. As
a result of all the feverish activity that accompanied
the building of the railroads, we have not only the
roads and the paper but also a very deep tradition
of corruption in local politics, since so many leg-
islators were bought on so many occasions.

Now it is a little easier to understand what the
"free" in free enterprise stands for. It is the word
"private" in private enterprise that remains obscure. All the taking was done in public, of the
public wealth, so I don't see where it was private
at all.

This governmental giveaway to "private" profit-seeking enterprise has characterized American economic history from the building of the railroads to the development of atomic energy and communication by means of space satellites. In fact, it is our economic history. Literally and historically, governments distribute their plenary power to business corporations in order to accomplish a particular function, whether or not such government could have accomplished the purpose on its own, or by some other means, or at a lesser cost. That is our characteristic way of getting things done. That is what corporations mean.

The early corporations were all acknowledged monopolies—clear grants of governmental power—established and tolerated for acknowledged public purposes. It is both historically recent and somewhat quaintly American that such power is claimed to exist without an accompanying public responsibility. Before the railroad land-grab got underway in the nineteenth century, the prior canal system had been built by means of state enterprise. The canals worked all right, and Erie Canal bonds were one of the earliest pieces of good paper in America—but then came the railroads, by which I mean a new and superior form of travel and free-wheeling, land-grabbing enterprise and reams of railroad paper.

The kind of corporate paper system we now live under is not only not provided for in the Constitution, it was not even a necessary outgrowth of our early history. Somewhere along the way a choice was made: the leading people in society decided to unleash the impulse to get rich quick by stealing—and they also decided to join in the fun. So they stole the continent, with the cooperation of most governments. (Except for the very early days, we Americans have frequently been embarrassed by the quality of our ruling classes.)

The suggestion was made earlier that our large corporations are properly defined as industrial or technological governments. Consequently, understanding the corporation is as much an exercise in political as in economic theory. As a political form, the modern corporation has assumed its present leading role for the simplest and most compelling reason: it was necessary—to administer men and things in large aggregates. In the nature of the case, the technological revolution could not proceed unorganized and unplanned. The major corporations, as stewards of the technological upheaval, have come into being in response to the imperatives of such organization and planning. Their work is political work, in any reasonable meaning of the term. This governing function—of the most important areas of activity in American life—was taken on by unofficial corporate bodies rather than by the pre-existing, legally constituted government because: 1) the corporate order grew out of the previous system of private property administered by dominant financial interests, which was itself not a duly constituted government; and 2) the alternative, to entrust this overridingly important work to the government in Washington, would have contradicted our entire political history since that weak authority had never been entrusted with anything more important than partial participation in raising and operating armies.

The corporate order is a system of private government. This privacy, however, is not to be comprehended in terms of private property or the private discretion of individuals. The corporate order is largely private from—from public accountability, whether indirectly through that other national government or directly to any of its various constituencies. The rulers of the corporate system are not elected by anybody, and they are not answerable for the exercise of their more important powers to any elected officials. The privacy of this private government serves mainly to ensure its authoritarian nature—it has nothing to do with the free action of individuals, which is what most of us usually think of when the word "private" is used. Professor Edward S. Mason, one of our leading authorities on the corporate system, has suggested that the corporation was inevitable because of the enlarged "entrepreneurial discretion" the form allows—meaning the capacity to command large groups of men and materials toward a particular purpose, much the same as in an army. And like an army, the individual corporation is (except in very rare instances) a one-party state. In other areas of government, we have no difficulty in recognizing this as a feature of dictatorship; it is only the studied absence of clear thinking that keeps us from recognizing the political fact in this area. The significance of these authoritarian centers for our otherwise somewhat democratic order is sharpened when we note, for instance, that Peter Drucker has called the few hundred business enterprises dominating the American economy "the only meaningful units of local government."

Further attesting to their essential authoritarianism, the really important activities of private corporate governments are not governed by any constitution. Originally, the charter was intended to serve this purpose: not until the charter was cheapened to the level of contract was it seriously asserted that the lack of a constitution was a positive virtue. Without the fundamental law of a constitution, the corporation is—to put the matter succinctly—a lawless institution. A particular one may very well be a benevolent dictatorship; its benevolence may make it tolerable, or even popular—it can never make it legal. Because of the legal fiction that a corporation is a "person," the Supreme Court of the United States is unable to apply the protections of that other Constitition we all revere for the benefit of the millions of individuals making up the communities of our corporate order. Even more important, it is intellectually embarrassed in dealing with the corporation in its own terms. One perceptive theorizer (Professor Arthur S. Miller) has put the matter this way:

> Under orthodox constitutional theory, only two entities are recognized: the State and the individual person. Nothing intermediate is envisaged. The rise of groups, a development which in its present extensive form is unprecedented, has brought the need for new constitutional theories and patterns of doctrine.

This problem is of course bigger than that of the corporation alone, having to do with the relation between the individual and all of the large organizations which are in fact the characteristic power centers of our society.

A constitution or rule of law for the corporation (or any big organization) would deal with policy and procedure governing both individuals and groups. The latter refers to the constituencies making up the corporate community—labor (including white-collar workers and middle-management), suppliers, dealers, stockholders, and even ultimate consumers. These should be organized for their own protection (thus mirroring the actual political forms in American life)—and it is perhaps a happy harbinger that the only group currently well organized, labor, has accomplished a great deal in "constitutionalizing" the place of its members in the industrial community. Indeed, from one source or another, the unions have been impelled to more progress in the internal rule of law than other typical large organizations. Walter Reu-

ther's U. A. W. Public Review Board is an imaginative and apparently sincere departure—not copied by any major corporation or, in fact, many other unions. Another constituency, dealers, were moved a few years ago to a little political self-help. GM for a number of years had a private judiciary in which hearings were heard on complaint of an automobile franchise-holder, although (or perhaps because) these franchise contracts are not clearly enforceable in a true court of law. It was partly the poor quality of the justice dispensed in these private proceedings that led to the passage of the Automobile Franchise Dealers Act of 1956, which was lobbied through Congress by the dealers.

Reinhold Niebuhr remarks relevantly: "You must allow quasi-sovereignties, whether they are corporations, church, or educational institutions. The more quasi-sovereignties you have, the better protection you have against totalitarianism." But the gain against totalitarianism is certainly lost if the quasi-sovereignty is more authoritarian in nature than the alternative plenary national power. There is more law today running in favor of individual rights in the armed services than there is in any of our major corporate communities. I see no reason why the industrial army should not be at least as democratic as the other one. In fact, there is no good reason in the world why The People should not participate generally in the processes of our private governments. And there is every good reason to believe that our so-called democracy has a limited longevity unless it begins soon to address itself with more energy to the relevant governments in our society. Otherwise our highly organized future will overwhelm us.

The framers of the Constitution did their work too well in checking and balancing power, with the effect that, when an individualistic agricultural society was replaced by a collective industrial one, too much concentrated, illegal, and unchecked and unbalanced power grew up elsewhere than in Washington. After all, if you believe in democracy and accept the premise that a democracy need not by definition be weak, then the basic power in the society should have been centered in Washington. It was excessive rationalism at the beginning which has created our biggest continuing historical problem.

If the corporation is private property, nobody but the stockholder-owners are legitimately concerned with its government; and if the stockholder's vote ensures the property-owners control by democratic means, the managers who run the corporation are property-servants operating under a legitimate mandate. But if these related propositions are not true, then our major corporations are authoritarian private baronies legitimated by nothing more than their existence. In fact, the propositions are not true—they are simply loudly and continuously endorsed by the people who control the properties of which they are not true.

Large publicly held corporations are not private property and they are not controlled by their shareholders. Where did anybody get the idea that they were? It comes from the fact that the corporate order "grew out of" the previously existing system of private property was facilitated by convenient, justifactory misrepresentations of that system, and finally buttressed by an overwhelming barrage of public relations nonsense, which by an act of rhetorical will has succeeded in assimilating the new corporate system to readily available fantasies concerning the democratic significance of voting. It is, for me at least, strangly disturbing that this conception of the magic of the vote has so much in common with the concept in Communist states, where one also votes not to make a choice, but as a ritualistic submission to unassailable power.

While shareholders are considered a continual annoyance and an occasional threat by corporate managements, it is just not true that anybody on the inside believes for one moment that they own or control anything—certainly not the corporation, and certainly not by means of the stock vote. But General Electric, pushing that low-grade Madison Avenue concoction called "People's Capitalism," is perfectly willing—to the tune of expensive full-page advertisements—to say in public that "The 376,000 owners with savings invested in General Electric are typical of America, where nearly every citizen is a capitalist." (Emphasis supplied.) First of all, there are that large number of GE stockholders exactly to ensure that the GE management shall not be inconvenienced by their ownership; secondly, only about one out of ten families own any stock at all; thirdly and most importantly, it is an unfortunate illustration of the dangers of such free and illegimate corporate power that it can be used to peddle such degrading junk. The statement is a shameful lie, and whoever wrote it and whoever hired him to write it, knew it was a lie when it was written. This kind of national lying spree—which smells up the whole cultural atmosphere in the country—is one of the conse-

quences of the irresponsible managerial power which, along with its periodic productiveness, is the main feature of our corporate system.

It is very difficult for the layman to grasp the fact that no one owns a big corporation like General Motors. The ordinary way of thinking about property and things produces a certain horror at the idea of anything so big and so valuable striding the earth unowned. The difficulty dissolves easily enough, however, when we realize that we have been assuming ownership means control. It is very hard to conceive of something like General Motors as not being controlled, and I will not ask anyone to strain himself to do so. But I must insist on the effort to see it as unowned.[2]

Paper mechanics and other managers and manipulators of modern property forms understand quite well that ownership is frequently irrelevant—the main thing is control. And control is often achieved exactly because ownership is abandoned. For example, management control of a big corporation is ensured by distribution of the irrelevant ownership paper, stock certificates, among as large a public as possible: in numbers there is weakness. (Corporate managers typically follow the changes in the stock list on a careful daily basis, looking for warning signs of an accumulation of a bloc which might revive the threat of ownership-control.)

The simple fact of the matter is that the major economic institutions are too big to be owned. Too big, that is, to be owned by any individual: Standard Oil of New Jersey is today too much for a Rockefeller—even for a group of Rockefellers, unless that group is organized on the same principles as the institution being owned. In other words, big institutions can only be owned by other big institutions, which in turn are not effectively owned. Stop and think for a moment: How could an industrial government like AT&T be "owned"? By means of stock certificates? That's like trying to attach some significance to the notion that I own a piece of Central Park because I live in New York City. The assets of AT&T, well over $20 billion worth, are owned by the corporation itself. There are more than two million shareholders in the company. Over half of these have investments of less than $2,000. Now what is $2,000 worth of $20 billion? It is .0000001 per

---

[2] The sense of ownership is so profound in us that its negation literally feels like infinity—the wonder-state of what is "outside" of outside.

The unlegitimated power of corporate managements without basis in ownership has not gone unnoticed. It was most specifically noticed by Berle and Means in 1932, and by the early New Deal and its securities legislation. Ever since then, the moral reform of corporations has been most noticeably in the hands of what must be one of the strangest reform movements in American history. I refer to the "corporate democracy" caper—better recognized popularly by the name of its leading field captains, the Gilbert brothers.

There are a lot of entertaining anecdotes and other charming details about the Gilberts, John Campbell Heinz, and Wilma Soss, chairman of the lady's auxiliary—anybody who has had to sit through the unspeakable farce of a stockholders' meeting can add to the lore. I will never forget the look of demonic fury on Lewis Gilbert's face when, in the midst of one of those rarely significant meetings in which control of a big corporation actually was being decided, he experienced a little difficulty in being recognized by the chair to make his usual thundering demand for a bigger and better post-meeting report. He started to charge down the aisle in order to complete his fit closer to the official steno-typist, lacking only a battle-torn tricolor in his hands to complete the picture of Democracy Outraged.

But the serious point about this weird movement is that it couldn't be more effectively misdirected if it were entirely an espionage arm of the corporate powers it presumes to attack and reform. The professional stockholder's suit was actually an effective agency for reform, so it was mostly done away with and, to be polite about the matter, partly "taken over." The corporate democracy movement has not been fought—it was first tolerated with irritation and finally welcomed.

I have come across no single detail that better characterizes the studied irrelevance of "corporate democracy" than this: it would hardly exist at all apart from the efforts of a handful of individuals. This is nicely demonstrated by the fact that out of 2,000 proxy statements filed with the SEC in 1956, only 3 per cent contained shareholder proposals—which were supposed to be one of the vital elements in the schemata of the movement. The total number of proposals was 102, and 78 of these were sponsored by the two Gilbert brothers and John Campbell Heinz. Other items in the "corporate democrats" pastiche are: stockholders meetings in accessible cities rather than out-of-the-way places of incorporation, cumulative

voting, public directors, post-meeting reports, independent auditors, token ownership of stock by management, and so on. None of it makes any real difference. Professor Bayless Manning[4] of Yale has shrewdly noted:

> The nostrums of Corporate Democracy have a vaguely familiar quality, for the prescription is largely taken from the municipal reformers of the turn of the century. . . . Nearly all of the planks in the platform of Corporate Democracy find their analogues in the reform agitations of 1900 for the long ballot, initiative and referendum, the direct primary, proportionate representation and women's suffrage.

The stock-vote of scattered, impotent stockholders cannot be relied upon to make corporate managements responsible, even to the owners. Moreover, the idea "is misconceived because the shareholders are not the governed of the corporation whose consent must be sought," as Professor Abram Chayes has correctly pointed out: the governed are all of the constituencies previously mentioned. "The forms and mechanisms of shareholder democracy divert attention from the real problems of holding business management to a desirable standard of responsibility," says Manning. Indeed, if we abandon the fiction that the stockholder "owns" the corporation and "controls" his property by means of the vote, we more easily notice the very rickety structure of enforcing even property-responsibility, much less institutional or public accountability, upon managements. With the facade of the vote working in their favor, managements have succeeded in escaping even the common law rigors of the personal responsibility of trustees. Livingston, in the book Manning reviewed, is rather indignant about the special deal that was made between the Ford family and the New York Stock Exchange, to overcome the Exchange's rule about not listing non-voting common stock: under the terms of the stock issue, the Fords could retain

_____
[4] Manning is the author of an essay-review of J. A. Livingston's The American Stockholder which appeared in Volume 67, page 1477, of The Yale Law Journal in 1958, and quickly became a minor classic; it sets forth a completely devastating case against the illusion of corporate democracy, and is unreservedly recommended to anyone who needs further convincing.

cent—a technical piece of Central Park. (Even when you consider the biggest institution investors, no stockholder in AT&T holds more than a fraction of 1 per cent of the outstanding stock.)

Now how can anyone call something like this private property or private enterprise? It is owned by a disorganized impotent public, and controlled by a private self-perpetuating managerial clique. The control is important, the ownership is not. Ownership of this kind is just a very limited charge on production and, paradoxically, the means of maintaining managerial control of the corporate enterprise.

The notion that GM (or any one of the great majority of public corporations) is "owned" proceeds from the time-honored assumption that to own stock is to own the corporation. If we examine this old-fashioned "self-evident" truth empirically, we note that what the public stockholder actually has is three double-edged rights: 1) he can sell his stock at a profit or at a loss; 2) he can receive or fail to receive a variable dividend; and 3) he can vote Yes or No on certain issues affecting control of the corporation and the disposition of its properties. The first two items indicate that he owns a negotiable instrument of a certain character—consisting of an "iffy" return on capital and a lottery ticket on market appreciation. Let's look more closely at the third item, the only one of the three that even looks like ownership of the corporation itself. What does the stockholder's vote mean? To skip over several stages of a dull argument, it means that the vote can effect changes of control over "his" property, the corporation, or it means approximately nothing. Can he do this? The answer is no, not unless an ambitious, well-heeled syndicate mounts a campaign to do so, and thus gives <u>him</u> the opportunity to support <u>them</u>. This does not happen at all often.[3]

_____
[3] A control bloc of stock, usually put at between 20 per cent and 51 per cent, affords a means of translating ownership into control; but this is a feature of the aggregate, not of individual shares—and the courts are now seeing it this way. There is a considerable body of law a-building to the effect that sale of a control bloc at a premium over the market value of individual shares is actionable on the part of other shareholders. This clearly means that the control feature is a separate element; and conversely, there is no real control quality in a single share of stock. In other words, the point is so obvious that even the courts are beginning to recognize it.

A mite of ownership, indeed. Especially when one considers that the essential difference between the incumbent and contending control groups is apt to be that the one has been at that particular trough for a period of time and the other has not. Moreover, in the absence of blatant mismanagement or special business reverses, it is next to impossible to unseat an in-group that is on the alert and well advised by experts. (Leopold Silberstein, who has accomplished a certain amount of unseating, has said: "It's very tough to buy control in the market if the management controls ten to twenty percent.") Unlike a campaign for political office, the "ins" have at their disposal not only the corporate patronage but also the corporate treasury; and the voting apathy of the citizen is a form of frenzied activity compared to that of the lottery-ticket holder. Not only are most corporate "elections" carried out with only one yes-or-no slate of directors available to the electorate, but there is also no real public opinion concerning the nominees. Only in a heavily financed fight does such an opinion develop, and it is then even paler and more foolish than the usual "fantasy of issues" in our more familiar political elections. This also indicates the strained quality of democracy in our autocratic private governments.

As Bayless Manning so felicitously put it, "The modern proxy contest is at best a device for tempering autocracy by invasion." An invasion is called a "raid"—and only "bad guys" undertake them. Dean Rostow of the Yale Law School has pointed out: "Raiding is regarded as something more than uncouth; increasingly, it is treated as almost illegal." Which again reveals how far corporate authoritarianism has progressed, since a raid is the only practical means of changing a management, the professional stockholder's suit, was held in such fearful disdain by the "ins" that they passed a seemingly democratic law against it: and now the great "giant-killers" of earlier decades are no more.) Following the New York Central and Montgomery Ward fights, in theory the SEC put the final kibosh on the matter by promulgating proxy-fight regulations which ensure that only nice people fighting a good clean fight may now do battle in the arena of what is charmingly called "corporate democracy."

The fundamental meaning of private property is private control over the property one owns, and all the stock-holders own is a share of stock. The corporation is not private property—only the share of stock is.

40 per cent of the voting rights in the 3-billion-dollar company with only 5.1 per cent of the equity. Two points: 1) the public didn't care, if it noticed at all—300,000 shareholders are perfectly content if the stock goes up, and are not mollified by the vote if it does not; and 2) no one can demonstrate any actual difference at all between, say, General Motors and Ford in the quality of managerial responsibility—certainly not in favor of the "fairly" elected officials of GM.

What is the real nature of the established corporate power? Simply, that the strength and purpose of the nation are in the hands of the few thousand men who control the few hundred bureaucracies which dominate the economy. These organizations and men are the stewards of the permanent technological revolution which is the economy, and which it is not too dramatic to call the hope and the despair of mankind.

There are many ways of stating or characterizing the institutional concentration of economic power which, being the heart of American power and not subject to public control, is far and away the overriding political fact of our social order. The usual way is to state the number of corporations which own what per cent of productive assets. For example: a study by the Federal Trade Commission in 1947-1949 disclosed that 113 corporations with assets of over $100 million held 46 per cent of the total assets of manufacturing firms. Or the figures which Professor Berle frequently repeats: ". . . about two-thirds of the economically productive assets of the United States, excluding agriculture, are owned by a group of not more than 500 corporations." But I think that we should not rest with this quick characterization of so important an aspect of our environment: to make certain that the dominating significance of size is conveyed we might run through the following miscellany.

Corporation income-tax returns, in a recent compilation, "showed 525,000 active nonfinancial corporations reporting a total of $413 billion of assets. The 202 corporations . . . each with assets of $250 million or more—owned 40% of this total."

The minimum amount of assets required for inclusion in the 100 largest nonfinancial corporations in 1950 was $329 million; in 1960 it was $698 million. Over this same period the number of "billion-dollar" corporations better than doubled—increasing from 22 to 54.

You get down to number 405 on Fortune's list of industrial corporations before you find one that had sales in 1961 of less than $100 million; up front, you get to number 42 before you find a little item called Eastman Kodak which had sales in that year of less than a billion dollars.

If you rank big corporations and governments according to revenue, you have eight corporations after the Federal government before you get to the first state, California; then another five before arriving at New York State and New York City; and ten more before Pennsylvania. Out of fifty-five organizations with a billion or more annual revenue (1958), only nine are official governmental units.

When we say that America is a corporate economy and that the concentration of corporate power is extreme, we must still put this fact in a proper context—that is, place it in the general business population. At the beginning of 1960 there were about 4.6 million operating business concerns in the United States. The number has been increasing slowly throughout the postwar period, with net gains of about 60,000 firms a year. (These figures do not include agriculture and professional services; but the firms so defined account for 85 per cent of income originating to the private economy.) The Survey of Current Business makes the following precise statement on the matter: "Small firms comprise the bulk of the business population—two-fifths have no employees at all—and only one firm in 20 employs 20 or more." In other words, a substantial amount of self-exploitation: a great number of marginal retail establishments, many examples of a carpenter or two appearing in the statistics under "Contract Construction," a lot of filling stations, a bunch of "candy-stores."

There are over 4 1/2 million "firms"; but to see the proper context we have been thinking of, compare all of them to, say, just one firm, the Metropolitan Life Insurance Company, with $17 billion in assets. This company has as many health and accident policyholders as there are firms in the country. But here is a figure to conjure with in the course of thinking about bigness: the Metropolitan Life Insurance Company has 38 million life insurance policyholders.

Another approach is to look at employment. The Survey for November 1959 informs us:

About 30 million full-time equivalent workers are employed by corporations, or somewhat under one-half of the total number of persons engaged in production. Proprietorships and partnerships provided work for another 21 million persons, who are about equally divided between employees and self-employed (businessmen, farmers, or professional persons). An additional 10 million workers are employees of governments—Federal, State, and local—and the other 4 million persons engaged in production are working in households, or nonprofit institutions.

And further: "In 1956 as in 1951, slightly less than one per cent of all firms had 100 or more employees; however, these larger firms accounted for nearly three-fifths of all paid employment."

All of these smaller firms still manage to survive in retail and service trades because it remains "economic" for one or two individuals to exploit themselves mercilessly. Selling television sets, once a strong trade in this area, was profitable enough to be concentrated in discount and shopping-center operations. But there is no TV repair chain: there, it is still "economic" for one technician to exploit himself—and of course part of the exploitation is the price he pays for parts.

We talk about "big" corporations and "big" business so much that the words turn flat and tend to slip by too easily. How big is big?

We try to conceive of size by referring to so many millions of this and so many billions of that, and if you make the imaginative effort, this can do the job for you. But it would be most worthwhile to freshen up our perception of industrial, economic and financial size, because size is essential to our story. It is because of size that private property is irrelevant; that major corporations can be understood only as forms of government; and it is also and finally because of size that our system has been transformed, has become the very new thing it is.

The question is important: the bigger the institution, the smaller the individual who lives in its shadow. This small individual must at least try to understand the source of the shadow.

But really, how big is big? General Motors is supposed to be the biggest industrial corporation in the world. We can begin to take its measurements by noting that the American public has decided that it is worth $12-13 billion—but that's just dollar value, and in my opinion GM is worth a lot more than that to all of us. As a matter of

fact, I don't think we could get along without it at any price. If, God help us, it refused to get into the ballgame, 600,000 people around the world would have to scrape together $3.5 billion of income from some other source, and I wonder where they would find it. Some 750,000 stockholders would have to find some other paper to play with; upwards of 27,000 suppliers would lose one sweetheart of a customer; 20,000 wholesalers and 200,000 retailers would also experience great sorrow in adjusting to a GM-less world.

GM was not always so important to so many people. As a matter of fact, it celebrated its fiftieth birthday as recently as 1958, at which time it was noticed that about 68 million cars and trucks had been produced by it since the beginning. But any large corporation produces paper as well as products, so it should also be noticed that a $100 share of General Motors common purchased in 1908 was worth or had brought in more than $150,000 over the same time-span. Whether looked at from the point of view of cars or paper, that is still one hell of a lot of internal combustion.

Let's go back to those 27,000 suppliers for a minute. GM dispenses about $5 billion a year to them for materials and services. The publicity gentlemen at the Company make a rather large point of the fact that these suppliers are Small Business, and in this connection they inform us that 70 per cent of them employ fewer than 100 people: U.S. Steel, du Pont, etc., I suppose, are in the other 30 per cent. There is a great deal of power in spending that kind of money and, unlike UAW production workers, these small businesses are not organized to protect themselves. (For the time being I leave you with the thought.)

One of the things GM is supplied with is advertising, about $200 million a year. It is in fact the nation's largest advertiser—the greatest single prop for this wonderful mass culture of ours. The corporation advertises a great many things, including itself in the pure state. About thirteen advertising agencies are needed to handle the Company's business. (GM has twenty-seven publications for its employees alone.)

So there we have some aspects of big GM. I might also mention that this organization does not live by cars alone, but fabricates numerous other fabrications, and I wouldn't be surprised if it could make almost anything it wanted to make. Mostly it wants to make money, and consequently does very well at that.

General motors is not the biggest corporation in

the country—the biggest one is AT&T. But AT&T is a utility rather than a free-wheeling industrial outfit; and it is so big as to be almost indescribable. [5]

It has gross assets of over 30 billion dollars, and these include the Bell Telephone Laboratories, The Western Electric Company, and most of the telephones in the country. But then there are a lot of big corporations in America. Bigness at du Pont, for example, means among other things 12,000 managerial promotions each year—about one every ten minutes of working time. There has been some new bigness, too: through both merger and regular growth, Olin Mathieson Chemical Corporation grew from a six-plant, $67 million-a-year producer of metals and guns in 1946 to nearly $550 million in 1958. Just as the rich get richer, the big get bigger. (Incidentally, we have no inheritance laws to keep the major corporations from growing as big as the sky.)

Standard Oil of New Jersey, which always follows General Motors as No. 2 on the Fortune list, had sales of nearly $8 billion. That's a lot of gasoline, but then General Motors with its sales of $11 billion-plus produced a lot of cars, so it all figures. Standard of New Jersey is a very careful corporation: it has built a little sixty-acre "remote-control center" in New Jersey so that if in the event of a thermonuclear attack New York City should be lost, at least Standard of Jersey would be able to carry on. These apocalyptic facilities afford living and working accomodations for sixty-five executives—sort of a skeleton force. It would appear that Standard of New Jersey takes quite seriously the provision in its charter that it shall exist in perpetuity.

All this concentration of assets and general institutional size means a good deal more than it seems to mean. A big corporation is much bigger than its balance sheet, and much bigger than the percentage of industry assets that it may own. Corporate governments do not rule by ownership alone. Berle puts it this way: "The ability of the large corporation to make decisions and direct operations overflows the area of its ownership. Its power travels farther than its title. . . ." This factor can stand some elaboration.

---

[5] Berle: "American Telephone and Telegraph . . . based on combined population and wealth, would be somewhere around the 13th state of the Union in terms of budget, and certainly larger than many of the countries of South America."

Notice first that those business areas with the greatest number of firms—wholesale and retail trade, contract construction and the service industries—are all middlemen, that is, they are customers of heavy industry and salesmen to the public. They are therefore "controlled" insofar as heavy industry dominates the markets in which they buy. The institutional concentration of power is much more effective than any simple statistics will indicate: a small, highly disciplined military unit can always control a larger population. This has been accomplished too many times throughout history to be any longer disputable. The argument here is that the same historical factor applies in finance and industry. The fact that the operator of a small TV repair shop owns his tools, fixtures, etc., is merely a matter of convenience to General Electric, RCA, etc. As if GE were to force its workers to supply their own hand tools. This is another, if somewhat more obscure, virtue of non-ownership in the modern American property system.

The point is that big corporations not only dominate their own industries, but are also centers of power around which are clustered thousands upon thousands of satellite enterprises which are wholly or substantially dependent on the center. The satellites may be suppliers or dealers or customers. The dependence is not altered by the role: a manufacturer, 80 per cent of whose volume consists of supplying door handles to Ford, is as dependent on the corporation as any Ford dealer or repair agency. Logically enough, the dominating corporation as buyer may look for suppliers who are both small and tied to the one big purchaser for distribution of a substantial portion of output. (This is announced policy of Sears, Roebuck and Company.) In these circumstances, whether the satellite is an owned division or an independent contractor is a matter of indifference. To try to assimilate this situation to the image of free, competitive market dealings is about as helpful as denominating widespread stock ownership as People's Capitalism and assuming this means democratic control of corporations. The markets in which giants and satellites trade are completely structured and dominated by the giants; it is somewhat gratuitous to call them markets at all, and considerably less than candid to call these dubious markets "free." (What we have here is the primary illusion in the assumption of justice in free contract: there never was a free and just contract between non-equals because the contract must always reflect the inequality.) Professor Arthur S. Miller:

"It can validly be concluded that a widespread system of satellite coercion characterizes business operations. Whether the satellite is a supplier or a dealer, he exists in a position of vastly inferior economic power." His relation to the large corporation has more of status than of contract in it.

The traditional economist sees a market as a Grand Image of All-Justifying Freedom, to be submitted to with adoration by all right-thinking people. A practicing businessman sees it as something to be organized before its dangerous potential is realized. The historical purpose of big corporations is to organize markets. In a sense that is all they are—organized markets. Or: the center of power around which and by means of which markets are organized. (At one time financial power alone was sufficient for this purpose; then it was discovered that combining industrial and financial power in one organization had much to recommend it. Corporations today are as much financial as industrial centers of power; they are the newest form of banking, resulting from the fact that productive capacity, or captured technology, has replaced gold as the backing for all the paper.) Professor Mason says: "As a firm grows, transactions that could conceivably be organized through the market price mechanism are transferred to the administrative organization of the firm." In other words, with big corporations markets are "ingested" or internalized. Thus, by "owning" part of the market, much more of it can be dominated and organized.[6]

Once a market area is organized, the centralized power of the dominating corporation may indeed become superfluous. But it will persist—as a distorting effect of the Paper Economy. For example, the size of our major corporations today is probably based more on considerations of finance than of production. It is safer to be big and diversified—safer in terms of survival. This is recognized by the corporations, obliquely, in their present accelerated movement toward decentralization,

---

[6]Mason makes a helpful distinction between monopoly and concentration. He says that "the degree of general concentration depends fundamentally upon the extent of industrialization." On the other hand, a monopoly can be small—as, for example and for obvious reasons, local brick companies. If industrialism equals concentration, then the classic pattern is that of Standard Oil wherein competition—real and brutal competition—occurs in the early expanding stage of an industry,

plant autonomy, divisional responsibility, etc. Markets must be organized, and basic producing units protected, to ensure the rational and continuing flow of goods—to ensure that productive capacity shall not, unknowingly, become a highly stylized form of hara-kiri. This technological rationalization is one thing; finance, in the Paper Economy, is another. GM needs profit instead of production only as a form of self-protection—and of course there is never enough of that. This requires maintenance of the price level, especially by curtailing production. Veblen called this "sabotage" (after a very precise definition). We can call it Scarcity Regained.

This is not the only size-distortion resulting from the Paper Economy: To the extent that the early liberal reformers were successful in thwarting the accumulation of great fortunes over generations, by means of the estate tax laws, they merely accelerated the growth of big and bigger corporations, the only true and lasting form of perpetuity. Decisive bigness changed its form but did not disappear.

As centers of industrial and financial power, market-organizers, and general governing bodies, big corporations are necessarily planning agencies. Planning is nothing but looking ahead—and using your head in the process. It is intelligence and knowledge applied in the administration of our complex social technology: planning and technology go together, they are common imperatives. You can, then, easily see that: 1) planning is indispensable; 2) it is in glaring contradiction to our free enterprise ideology; 3) it is something that takes both superior intelligence and training, which signifies the heightened importance of intellectual experts; and finally 4) the problem of power in the modern setting cannot be dissociated from it. Since it is so close to the real issues of power in our day, and since it involves a very significant upgrading of intellectual classes, and since to be accomplished effectively it must be carried out over large industrial areas which requires the use of national, i.e., Federal, power—therefore, the existing private power centers necessarily oppose it when carried on by any other groups than themselves, and always obscure it no matter who does it, or why.

---

and one of the essential jobs in building productive capacity is to do away with this unwelcome and expensive phenomenon.

Big business borrows Federal power when necessary in furtherance of its planning activities—as with the Federal Reserve System: this is a fundamental pattern in the working out of dual government in American history. There are numerous examples: the planned introduction of color television and FM radio—planned by the business groups concerned, using the FCC as a medium of control; the Federal super-highway plan—something of a necessity for the oil and automotive industries; and so on. But business also plans all on its own: "There is no such thing as an unplanned corporation. . . ." Diversification programs typically involve judgments based on five and ten year perspectives. Capital investment programs, plant location, the institutionalizing of technical discovery, executive training programs, all involve present allocation of resource in response to long-range perspectives. "Du Pont often publicizes its Chart Room, where decisions are made about the rate at which the company's technological innovations are to be permitted to flow into the market." (Du Pont spent $27 million from 1928 to 1940 on nylon before it sold its first commercial unit.) All this is planning.

It is unfortunately necessary to point out that one can plan ahead without being omnipotent. That is, not all plans are perfectly relevant, not all of them are completely prescient, all must be continually modified, and every once in a while one has to be abandoned altogether. But that has always been true of thinking; and there are no new reasons to believe that thinking is useless simply because it is less than perfectly omnipotent. But if you get into a discussion about national planning with most businessmen, the first argument would in fact be an attack on your suggestion of omnipotence in The Plan. The most devastating argument against any form of national planning is that no goddamn bureaucrat can know everything, therefore no one should plan anything, and anybody who even thinks about it is a Communist. But behind the facade of these childish arguments, competent corporate executives are planning everything they can—strenuously, and with great effect.

An article in the Harvard Business Review of July-August 1956 contains a review of the limited writing by business professionals on this subject of long-range planning. The rundown reads like an elementary course in how to think effectively. For example, it is discovered that "long-range planning puts possibly a greater premium on con-

ceptual skills of the manager (as opposed to technical and human relations skills) than does any other phase of top management." It is also pointed out that long-range plans should be revised frequently. (I have no objection: I revise my own long-range plans frequently. Doesn't everybody?) The writers of a book entitled Principles of Management suggest three types of planning—where the What being planned is not in the control of the planning enterprise, where It is partially controlled, and lastly where It is characteristically controlled. To which one can only murmur bemused assent. It seems that where the individual firm is concerned, businessmen can be cozied into thinking beyond the carpe diem of the next big production order.

Unfortunately, corporations plan only for themselves—which is terribly selfish. It is difficult to understand why the executives who plan for their own firms are not more insistent about integrating these plans with over-all industry plans and even inter-industry, nationwide plans in pursuance of agreed-upon national purposes. Their individual plans are necessarily puny and failing of full effect, even for individual purposes, because not so integrated.

Also unfortunately, one of the things corporations have taken to planning is the early obsolescence of their products. Not all of them, of course: I am sure that U.S. Steel would not stand for built-in obsolescence in the new oxidizing furnaces it is buying. Nor would an electric power company go along with very much stylish product weakness when it buys big generators. At that level, technological obsolescence is about all a purchaser is willing to live with—he won't take any cleverly devised decay. But in many consumer areas of the economy, the big producers have already instituted as the law of the land what Aldous Huxley in Brave New World suggested would have to be the law of the future: thou shalt consume—endlessly. So industry helps the administration of this law along by making stuff that falls apart on schedule.

Superficial product obsolescence which is planned by business to stimulate sales (at a paper-creating price level: to make money rather than things) is such a widely understood and uncomfortable part of our economy that even two out of three businessmen consider it "not in the long-run interest of the United States." A few years back, the Harvard Business Review surveyed business opinion on this guilt-laden issue. The editors were quite surprised by the heavily emotional responses they received. It seems that businessmen had already been doing a lot of thinking about the matter, none of it comforting. The two out of three who thought that there was already too much artificial obsolescence were admitting to themselves a feeling which was in clear contradiction, in many cases, to the policies of their companies. [7]

We are talking about product obsolescence which is intended by the producer, but not merely as a rational response to advances in technology (what used to be called progress, until it became such a problem). We are talking about artificial obsolescence, which is effected in two basic ways: 1) you can build the thing itself so that it just won't last—inferior materials, poor inspection, etc.; and 2) you can attack the psychological utility of the item in the hands of the consumer. Madison Avenue is the moving force in this last form of uselessness. For example, you don't sell refrigerators, you sell a new design of a refrigerator. And often enough we get a rich mixture of aspects of uselessness, as where a manufacturer builds up an inventory of minor technological improvements and doles them out to the public as part of otherwise scheduled model changes. Anyway, these are details, and the main question is, Is this the ballgame we all came out here to watch? Because something else could be done with the time and effort and industrial capacity devoted to these practices. It is hardly news, but it should be mentioned again that we might instead build schools, new cities, commuter railroads, improve diet and health facilities, and so forth. As a result of which we could all live longer and better.

A corporation is known by its balance sheet; and the top corporate executive is first and foremost a balance-sheet tender—an impressario of the profit-and-loss statement.

Financial statements are a fundamental piece of paper in the Paper Economy. They are prepared for all public corporations periodically by accountants, lawyers, and public relations men,

_____
[7] Only 18 per cent of the respondents reported that their companies changed models less than once a year; but 25 per cent stated that there were five or more model changes in the course of a year; while the minority who defended the practice were tensely shrill in doing so—one of them in textiles went deep into history for his justification and found that "planned obsolescence . . . really started with Adam and Eve." He just blamed it on female foolishness.

on the basis of internally supplied data—with the active "cooperation" of the managers who are to be judged by what the statements reveal. As previously suggested, the main thing about a corporation is its capacity to earn a profit, and just about everything outsiders know about this magical capacity is derived from the corporation's financial statements. So you can see how important they are.

But according to Leonard Spacek, one of the leading accountants in the country, writing in the Harvard Business Review in 1958, our corporate financial statements too often show "misleading results," too often are neither fair nor accurate reports on financial operations, and generally speaking are substantially below the level of which the accounting profession has proven itself capable. How does this happen? By the use of inconsistent principles of accounting, with the choice between contrasting principles being made by the management itself for its own purposes. The key phrase in the traditional certificate of a public auditor states that the results shown in the financial statements are fairly presented "in accordance with generally accepted accounting principles." Mr. Spacek's simple point is that there are none, and that to suggest that there are is pertinently misleading.

Mr. Spacek makes the main point very nicely when he notes that "the need for proper accounting mounts as more people become interested in an enterprise or institution." Then he ties this down by saying: "Different groups may argue as to how the profits may be distributed, but what the profits are should not be subject to confusion and controversy." I think we have to say that the balance sheet and operating statement, which are basic instruments of business policy, have been to a large extent assimilated to the system of distortion engineered by public relations men and other top management counsel by means of which American business presents its fuzzy public image.

If you are devoted to producing profit instead of goods, you simply cannot afford to be candid about the accounting facts of your operation—any more than if the shoe were on the other foot, a manufacturer would be apt to say: "These are lousy washing machines, but we already made 'em, so you buy 'em. OK?" Financial statements are a very delicate area in the Paper Economy because, like inventory and price-setting, they exist in a nexus where the reality and the paper meet. I repeat: if you want to understand the Paper Economy, either for esthetic reasons or in order to make it work, you must look for those areas where paper and thing meet—and avoid the magical incantations of the high priests of paper.

Prepared in this fashion, the balance sheet determines the price of the corporation's paper; the price of goods determines the balance sheet. Again, we are back to this ubiquitous question of price.

There are approximately two ideas current today about how prices are set. One view has it that neither individuals nor institutions exercise discretion, unless they have sinned deeply and are "monopolies," but that prices are set and reset every hour on the half-hour by a Great Force better than any candy-store operator, including General Motors, and this Great Force is called the Free Market. The other idea, which is both obvious and not quite decent as yet, is that where markets are dominated they are not "free," and the dominating economic institutions have, among their other powers, the power to set prices with a certain independent attitude. The latter have come to be called "administered prices." The process of price administration presumes price administrators who engage in thought prior to decreeing their prices, who do not respond automatically to impersonal forces. This is simply the view that "somebody" sets prices. The alternative view is that "nobody" sets prices, and this is why all prices are exactly correct, and need not be discussed further. When "nobody" sets prices they are not only "right," but also "free" and even "competitive." From the point of view of peace of mind, you can't beat 'em.

The main thing to be understood about administered prices is that they are not to be understood at all apart from long-range business planning. That is, a particular price is based on the idea that you are going to sell a particular quantity with given fixed costs and given unit costs. In order to figure that way you have to plan to produce and sell x quantity of the thing. Once you decide this, the "right" price follows. So the main thing price does, in the mind of the price administrator, is to determine how much shall be sold in the first place. For example, it is reported that General Motors uses a "standard volume" system for setting prices. It wants 20 per cent profit after taxes, and figures its price in order to earn this on an "estimated average rate of planned operation." This latter has been calculated on the basis of about 55 per cent of capacity. Sales were higher than the standard volume

in seven of the eight years after 1950, so GM made much more profit than it had figured itself entitled to. Which has boosted its net worth $3 billion in the decade 1947-57.

Even if the administrators of a big corporation tried their hardest to live up to the principles of automatic competitive pricing which they learned in college economics courses, it would be beyond their best capacity. International Harvester, for instance, establishes prices for 250,000 parts. It takes a large staff of people just to know <u>where</u> a price is, much less <u>what</u> it is, or whether it's "right": how could an organization of such magnitude possibly be market-sensitive concerning every price? No, big corporations know what they are even if classical theorists don't. They set prices and production quantities in tandem according to over-all and long-range objectives. Anything else would be much too dangerous for a major institution. They have the power to protect themselves, and they use it.

Perhaps, from their own point of view, the major achievement of our best industrial organizations is their low break-even points—the per cent of unused capacity they can tolerate before losing money. U. S. Steel, which must set some 50,000 prices, now has a break-even point of 32 per cent of capacity; the Company could cut its prices 10 per cent and still break even at 50 per cent of capacity, which is the national average. But I doubt if they will. Even if they moved more steel at the lower prices, the whole maneuver would be too risky; they might end up needing customers as much as the customers needed them: the terrible dangers of inventory—"real" wealth—could be realized. U. S. Steel might then find itself in a genuine "competition" between its own productive potential and the capacity of the rest of the country to consume steel.

But while the big producing units play it safe on the down-side—to not cut prices and risk the dangers of inventory—they also exercise care on the up-side, and do not charge every last dollar they could get away with. The corporation is primarily a government: its function is to rule various constituencies while satisfying certain needs, and like a government, its ultimate concern is to preserve the organization.

Our big corporations administer not only prices in our society, but also progress. By progress I mean, naturally, this great potential pool of technique for achieving everything the human race has dreamed and nightmared about for centuries—scientific technology.

Even so, private industry does not create all the technology, or even pay for most of it; but it does regularly end up controlling its development and application, generally speaking. Universities had established research laboratories before General Electric set up the first one in industry in 1900; the Navy hired inventors in 1789, and sponsored research has been substantially dependent on the military since then. In 1959, private industry spent $9.6 billion on research and development—$4 billion of their own and $5.6 billion of government money. An additional $3 billion of R&D was performed by universities and other nonprofit institutions—and, again, the Federal government. Whoever pays for it, and whatever the direction given by the military, there is not much question about the technological stewardship of our business organizations.

At the level of productive capacity we have reached in the United States, and considering the current runaway force of technology, the price-and-profit system is an increasingly distorting factor in the plans of isolated (read: unarticulated) institutions. One expert says: "Intentional duplication of effort is an inevitable result of the patent system and industrial secrecy." Everybody in-business-for-himself is here quite wasteful—of exactly those energies and capacities which are most valuable: we are forced to spend an inordinate amount of time discovering what is already known. This process is much facilitated by the practice among the bigger organizations of not bothering to patent their discoveries, which requires disclosure, but of exploiting them at leisure as industrial secrets. But that is a bit understandable since the patent system is not much to be relied on—60 per cent of the patents litigated in the last two decades have been declared invalid by Federal appellate courts. It is also rather patriotic not to patent since the Russians can buy a copy of any American patent for pennies and use it throughout the appropriate industrial sector in Russia—a privilege not accorded to American companies.

Now could there be a sweeter, more poignant illustration of the inevitable imperatives of technology-wide industrial articulation? I mean, what can the most sincere belief in private property contribute toward the solution of this perfectly technical problem?

Let me state the articulation (planning) problem, for the moment, this way: Why tolerate a monstrosity like General Motors at all if you are not going to take the full tour and rationalize the whole automotive industry on the same principles which justify GM's existence in the first place? You may say that we are not politically prepared for this quantity of rational articulation. True enough. About as little prepared for that as we were for the whole technological revolution, the completion of which demands exactly the aforementioned articulation.

The big 500 corporations which dominate two-thirds of the industry of the United States are also in charge of the accumulation of approximately 60 per cent of the capital which is applied to industrial use. So the most important thing the corporations administer is the better part of our future.

We can think of this as "administered financing," and it is hardly second in significance to the great power involved in administering prices. Between 1946 and 1953, $150 billion of capital expenditures were made in the United States by non-financial corporations and other businesses. Sixty-four per cent of this money came from internal sources—retained earnings and depreciation. Eighteen per cent came from current borrowing from banks, twelve per cent by the issue of bonds (mostly privately placed), and only six per cent or $9 billion by the issue of stock. Berle discribes this neatly as follows: "The capital is there; and so is capitalism. The waning factor is the capitalist." So economic initiative has been taken over by massive organizations and is no longer a function of individuals. One by one, it would seem, the classical attributes of capitalist enterprise have been institutionalized in the form of the major industrial corporation, or the major financial intermediary. These organizations, run as political units, each involve and affect the lives of tens upon tens of thousands of human beings. They are, there is no question, governments. A new society has been born.

This point about internal financing, and the consequent money-autonomy of the bigger corporations, received special emphasis from Adolf Berle in his most recent book, Power Without Property. For a good reason: this is one more market-force from which the corporations are freeing themselves—in this case, the capital market. They have become their own bankers. The source of these "banking" funds is not limited to profit and depreciation—in addition there is tax-accrual money and current obligations or trade accounts. The latter is "pure" corporate money, since it serves as such only between and among the corporations themselves: it has been estimated to amount to nearly $50 billion, one-tenth of the book value of all corporate assets.

Even an important critic of Berle's position such as John Lintner of the Harvard Business School grants that there has been "a marked decline in the relative importance of security issues" in manufacturing (as is well known, not in utilities which are regulated industries with very heavy capital requirements). But of course there remains some external financing, even in manufacturing and other unregulated industries—some bank-borrowing and security issues, both debt and equity. Professor Lintner assumes that this external financing means "dependence" on external sources, and a consequent lessening of corporate power. I wonder. I think it is inaccurate to say that General Motors is dependent on the Chase Manhattan Bank because it borrows a few hundred million dollars from it. Dependence would be a proper term if GM were borrowing up to the hilt—then, indeed, it might have to beg for a few hundred million more. But as it is, it is an honor to do business with them, and instead of being dependent on the Chase Manhattan, GM is actually doing the latter a favor when it borrows from it.

Rather than the non-financial corporations being dependent on capital markets, probably the opposite is true: the one fundamental fact underlying the whole structure of paper values is the earning capacity of the major corporations which, sustained by government purchase, credit, and other policy, sustains all else in the economy. For example, this is true not only of the $400 billion or so in stock exchange value but, more subtly, mortgages and bank financing of retail stores may be entirely dependent on the plant of a particular corporation located in the area. Real estate values in New York, since it has become the corporate headquarters of the nation, are clearly dependent on that event—and they amount to billions, with values shared between the equity of individual owners and the debt priority of large financial institutions.

As for being dependent on stockholders, we have already looked into that matter. It is also noticeable that the big corporations such as U.S. Steel prefer to get necessary expansion funds from the public by raising prices instead of selling stock. That way "dividends" are more purely discretion-

ary, being "paid" only in reduced prices—and there haven't been any lately.

Lintner points out, properly enough, that in such industrial financing as there is, the typical situation involves trained corporate managers on one side of the table bargaining in a sophisticated fashion with trained financial managers on the other side of the table. Again, I see no compelling reason to assume that one side is more "dependent" than the other. This is financing administered in a decidedly managerial setting. When the representatives of big organizations deal with each other, I am sure that considerable dust can be raised in well-appointed board-rooms. If you call this action "competition," I don't see what has been added to the analysis. And much has been subtracted from from it if that loaded term is taken to revive the image of a really dusty produce-market.

Let us at last be reasonable about things and note the substantial difference between market and institutional competition. The latter is much closer to statesmanlike collusion.

On the intellectual question of the American corporate system and the ideological issues presented by its robust existence, the thought of Adolf Berle is a great deal of the whole show. There are few intellectual areas in which the name of one man becomes and remains quite so pervasively meaningful. It all began with the publication in 1932 of The Modern Corporation and Private Property, which certainly marked a turning point in American social thought. The very title implies that something about the corporation calls into question some-something about the system of private property. This book, written with the economist Gardiner C. Means, has become the kind of unassailable historical event which it is no longer wise to discuss freshly. I am a very careful—and very indebted—reader of Berle; I find that it is not so much this book as the brilliant suggestiveness of his later (and scattered) thought that has made his current contribution to the subject so important. Berle would be the first to say that the purpose of his 1932 thesis was to stimulate speculation, and he himself has been speculating on its implications for more than a quarter-century. We would all do well to begin our own speculation by tracing his.

Berle can be placed in a general way by seeing him as a specifically American off-to-the-side variant of the capitalism/socialism argument. Bypassing this great oppositional debate is almost an American intellectual tradition—Veblen did it,

too. There is an historical validity in this maneuver, which of course has been buttressed by the
general population's startling lack of interest in
the socialist alternative. A great deal of the force
behind the socialist movement in Europe derived
from egalitarian sentiments which expressed themselves in the demand for the kind of democratic
forms and official rhetoric which had early become
an accepted part of the American landscape. An
even larger part of the force behind the movement
was garden-variety class-conflict, which simply
fought for a bigger cut of the produce—again, less
of a problem here because our system was the
first to become modern-productive, in which people as consumers are recognized as a business
necessity. And lastly, everything happened so
quickly here on this tabula rasa of a continent,
with an unprecedented amount of physical and social shifting, that socialism never had a chance
to become a class tradition—a very important
quality of the movement in European countries.
On the other hand, we never lacked for anti-capitalist sentiments; but they were always crudely
expressed and seldom achieved a sophisticated
pattern (compare Veblen as to high quality and
low influence, to Bryan and the muckrakers—or
even, to be brutal about the matter, to Teddy
Roosevelt). Let's face it, we have had a very
strange political history, which has followed none
of the traditional markers with any real faithful-
ness: where else, for example, could this national
liberal effluvia of ours be tolerated culturally,
much less taken as a political point of view?

Following Veblen, Berle largely bypassed the
egalitarian issue (as also Thurman Arnold and,
more recently, J. K. Galbraith) and emphasized
the analytical side of the matter. He has asserted
that the world revolution following World War I
was "technical far more than it was social," add-
ing, "The philosophical and scientific discoveries
of the 19th century were put to work in the 20th,
and whole civilizations changed as a result." The
corporation was the chosen vehicle of this technical
revolution. As a new form of social organization
in the modern setting, the corporation is a major
revolutionary force. And not least revolutionary
in contradicting all of the traditional capitalist assumptions—the privacy of property, the freedom
of markets, the economic importance of individualism, and the role of the government.

The last is especially significant since, as we
have noted, the corporation is itself a form of
government. This is the basic dramatic confront-

ation out of which Berle's thought and insight flows,
with one added factor: observing the process of
the corporation as the dominant form of economic
government in development, it is immediately
noticeable that the separate corporate governments
are only primitively articulated. A more sophisticated articulation—beyond the present much too
loose confederation—is the major work of the corporate system yet to be accomplished. The problem in this country is that this requires a much
larger borrowing of Federal power, or more substantial amalgamation with it. Which in turn would
necessarily call upon the corporations either to
legalize themselves, or turn the national government itself into an illegal instrumentality. (Some
years ago the latter possibility was called "fascism," and is still quite unpopular when identified
by that name.) This is the context in which the discussion of planning becomes predominant: it is to
this subject that Berle's thought most recently and
most strongly tends.

That—and the overriding political, legal, and
even spiritual problem of legitimacy.

Before we get to this final issue in our discussion of the corporation, let me point out one of
the grand ironics of history—the accidental con-
junction of capitalism and the scientific revolution.
The revival of learning and later free intellectual
inquiry was a bourgeois phenomenon as much as the
trading society which accompanied it; and we tend
to think of nineteenth-century industrialism, with
its mechanical and chemical inventions, as capitalism proper. But there seems to have been a
geometric progression in technology, not equal
to the growth of capitalism nor directly caused by
it. In science we have experienced, in this century at least, the most permanent of permanent
revolutions. Capitalism, the price-and-paper
system, has demonstrably done as much to har-
ness as to unleash the force of science (this would
be much more noticeable in the absence of the progressive effect of the military). The system of
business enterprise happened to be there when
science, so to speak, took off. The new dynamic
factor which kept the contradictions between the
two from tearing society apart more than has actually occurred was—the modern corporation, an
equivocally capitalist if not non-capitalist institution. This had to be accomplished by the corporation (along with the military) in such short order
that it may be excused its early illegitimacy: there
wasn't time for a proper birth certificate. But
the excuse is wearing thin; and modern dynamic

technology cannot be contained, certainly not furthered at its own pace, without rationalizing the corporate system: <u>without national planning</u>.

The only nationally planned, fully articulated application of technology we now have, of any scale, is that of the military. Indeed, I think that may be one of the main reasons that we still have a big military—which has become exactly as much of a danger to its own domestic population as it is to the enemy population. The military provides an excuse to do what has to be done, without taking that terrible leap into the future—admitting what we're doing while we're doing it. Such admission is the very beginning of a legal order. And a legal order would not have to rely so exclusively on the on the military direction of the economy.

So the dominance of the corporate system finally raises two questions: 1) is it technically adequate? and 2) is the power it represents "legitimate" within the assumptions of the whole society?

The answer to both questions is No. And the answers are related.

Let us be quite clear at the outset that the legitimacy of a power system, or the lack of it, is an important issue for any society. No law governing the exercise of power ever equals perfect justice, which is like saying that law is just law. But having experienced the totalitarianisms of this century, we should not doubt that law that is just law is invaluable to us poor mortals who are just mortals. Law can never get very far in contradicting a power system (although it can express the contradictions existing in one); but in its presumptive rationality, it <u>regularizes</u> the exercise of power and it <u>justifies</u> that exercise. Law justifies power—"gives it legitimacy"—by relating its exercise to more basic assumptions of the social order. Such justification can be, and often is, quite thin—which puts you smack in the middle of politics (the solvent and source of law), arguing for more substantial justification, or referring to some more basic or some other basic assumptions. And all the while, in law and in politics, people typically become so enthusiastic in justifying that they just naturally falsify in unconscionable quantities. But the commonly accepted need to justify gives a point to the lies. Without this need, why lie? It is in the nature of power not to rely on crude force. I am serious when I say that the discovery and wide use of fraud and deception marked a considerable advance in human history: it is so much easier and more effective to con people into doing what you

want them to do, than hit all of them over the head to convince them—and you cover more social ground. Of course we have in our current century managed to carry this to a seemingly ultimate point of sophistication; but that is another matter. (Machiavelli thought so of his century, too, I would imagine.)

When we raise the question of the legitimacy of the corporate order, we are asking what basic assumptions of the society justify its power—and then asking whether they are really basic. The difficulty is immediately apparent: there are none—or they aren't.

The first defense of the system, still relied on by many ill-informed persons, is that it doesn't exist. In the course of this defense it is imagined that corporations are private property, operate in free markets, etc. In other words, <u>capitalism</u> is justified and this is thought to carry us forward with the problem of understanding and justifying the corporate order. It doesn't really, and since this is a regular subject of most other sections of this book, I will not dwell on it here.

Frequently, the next defense is, What difference does it make? It "works." This is obviously contemptible, and beneath discussion. (See below for discussion.)

Berle has been greatly concerned with this question of legitimacy. And he has come up with something like an answer. I say "something like" because I am not sure whether he is prognosticating—describing a process whereby the corporate order <u>may become</u> legitimated—or identifying a current legitimation. In any event, his view is that corporations are developing a "conscience" because they exist in an environment of opinion that states what they ought and ought not to do. He calls this "the consensus," which consists not only of the opinion-pressures of the corporate constituencies, but (apparently even more significantly) of general intellectual opinion—university professors, independent journalists, and so on, which he calls "the forum of accountability." At times he refers to the core of the consensus as the Lord's Spiritual, as opposed to the corporate executives, the Lord's Temporal, on a medieval analogy. He has suggested that what we are looking for is a moral substitution for the Medieval Church and the nineteenth-century Free Market, now that neither is any longer adequate. He defines the corporate conscience as "a lively apprehension by the present senior instruments of production that they had better try to anticipate what is wanted and conform to it rather than wait until there is conflict." (But he later says: "The corporate conscience is merely a lively apprehension of possible state intervention of some kind.")

Berle's conscience-consensus theory is the best known and best accepted justification of the corporate order for those who recognize that there is anything to be justified in the first place. Before criticizing this idea, I should note that he will also make statements like this: "A consensus that economy-by-accident is not good enough for our complicated domestic and international society is beginning to form." And: "The corporation having won its place in the economic system must fill it." With Professor Berle available to identify consensus and specify conscience, the perspective is rhetorically useful and, as usual with him, quite interesting. In the hands of the speech-writers of leading executives, however. . .

I don't doubt that a consensus concerning proper corporate behavior exists, and that the corporate managers worry about it somewhat. I can even see that some professors have helped to create it. But one of the things that is wrong with this notion is that it can be taken to justify almost anything that both exists, and is tolerated by intelligent people. Another thing wrong with it is that the consensus which is to judge the corporations is largely created by them, as well as for their benefit. To the extent that it is not a creation of Madison Avenue's mass culture, it is as well described as the better conversation about corporations. As conversation, it is just as reasonable to say that the consensus accompanies the illegitimacy of corporate power in the United States as it is to say that it legitimates it.

I think that the consensus really is part of the quality of the power wielded by corporate managers. The organizations which give them their power are integral with the community, and so they must concern themselves with community views; but these institutions dominate the community economically, and no amount of conversation is apt to change the fact. The consensus indicates how to use the great concentrated power of our major corporations: it is not a functioning factor dealing with the why and the wherefore of this power. It can be seen in its more serious aspects as the capitalization of a possible political future; it cannot be seen as a substitute for politics, present or future. In the end, the idea of the consensus is not much more than a Happy Thought. It comes from a very idealistic view of things: "We have yet to see the time in

America when ideas do not eventually establish themselves to the extent merited by their validity," Berle says. If so, then only because in our short history we have not had enough "eventually" as yet.

The consensus is inadequate as a source of legitimacy and as a control technique because the present powers in the country guided by the consensus they choose to be guided by have not achieved the basic existing potentiality of the people, namely, full production. Full production is not a "fancy" requirement: it is what the people want in the crudest and most direct way. To have devoted ourselves to industrialism with such single-minded fervor and then, possessing this magnificent industrial plant, not to use it to produce all the goods it is designed to produce is not only illegitimate but criminal. I would just have to include myself out of any consensus that didn't account for this point.

Very simply, the reason there is so much difficulty in legitimating the corporation is that it is an illegitimate institution. It is an authoritarian form of industrial government in a purportedly democratic society. All the talk about constitutionalizing the corporation, giving it a finer conscience by making it responsibly subject to elite opinion, and in other ways spiritually domesticating it, are all attempts to answer the unanswerable. The problem simply will not be confronted head-on by any of these conversational means. The corporation is an illegitimate form of baronial government. The fact must be stated and understood. And we should not be in a hurry to scour up some legitimation for a developing and unfinished illegitimate system. The easiest way to make the corporate order "consistent" with the basic assumptions of our society would be to ignore or downgrade the latter, especially in their democratic orientation.

The system was born in illegality: I notice nothing outstandingly legal about the way in which Vanderbilt, Gould, Morgan, et al went about creating it. Of course it is better behaved now: it has achieved the power for which it struggled. I should imagine that all new societies are born with the essential assistance of alien, illegitimate midwives. The new is not legal—it is just imperative, or irresistible, or terribly important.

The reason that the corporation, this dominant form of government in the United States, has assumed its crucial role in our world is that we wanted done what only the corporation in the first instance could do, but we were not ready enough to admit that we wanted it done and to make the doing of it legal. The corporation is a primary American illegal instrumentality, just as the political party is, and syndicate crime is. Indeed, I think a very good case could be made out that the real history of the United States is a history of illegal instrumentalities, or legal instrumentalities operated by illegal means.

And beyond the bruited issue of legitimacy, there is the further question of responsibility.

The power of the corporation is unavoidable, but it should exist for a particular purpose, not for its own sake. If the purpose is generally accepted, the power is in fact legitimate; if it is actually used for that purpose, it is responsible. The great power of the corporate system is both illegitimate and irresponsible because in form it has not been made coherent with other purposes in the society, and in fact it is not devoted to fulfilling the purpose for which it was created and is tolerated—production.

There is not just the question of regularizing and justifying the actions of a new power system—there is also the question of the rights of individuals who exist under it, and the duty of the power-wielders to them. Whether and to what extent individuals can experience freedom and liberty in relation to these great structures does not really depend on whether or not an acceptable theory accounting for their existence has been formulated. Note that it took some centuries to achieve what individual rights we have vis-a-vis the state; now we are faced with a similar struggle with regard to non-state organizations. Who can doubt that this is a long-term affair? And who can believe that this struggle is mainly a theoretical one? Besides, the historically immediate point is that the structure of the corporate system itself is incomplete, because modern technology requires a higher level of integration between the separate corporate empires than now exists. The individuals "involved under" these private governments can, must, should assert themselves wherever possible against the dominant and domineering bureaucratic structures. But already we, as individuals, have made great sacrifices in order to create these private industrial governments which produce the goods we so much desire, and these sacrifices will go for nothing if the industrial system is not made coherent enough to fulfill its practical purpose of the maximum production of goods. Once the system is complete, particularly with effective automation and other institutionalized science, we can

then concentrate solely on individual self-assertion. As things stand now, however, our devotion to the monster is unconsummated.

To the question, Should and will the corporation be subject to the guarantys of the Fourteenth Amendment which protects individuals against governing bodies? Berle replies with an historical affirmative. If corporations are private governments, then the citizen's rights under the Fourteenth Amendment are made shallow if that constitutional provision does not govern the exercise of corporate power in relation to them. In other words, to allow the system of corporate power to exist outside of constitutional guarantys is to negate constitutional due process.

The growth of corporate power in the United States has, pari passu, repealed the Constitution. Veneration of the repealed document has become a perverse means of embracing the primary illegality of our social order.

THE GIANT CORPORATION*

Paul Baran and Paul Sweezy

I

Scientific understanding proceeds by way of constructing and analyzing "models" of the segments
or aspects of reality under study. The purpose of
these models is not to give a mirror image of reality, not to include all its elements in their exact
sizes and proportions, but rather to single out and
make available for intensive investigation those
elements which are decisive. We abstract from
nonessentials, we blot out the unimportant to get
an unobstructed view of the important, we magnify
in order to improve the range and accuracy of our
observation. A model is, and must be, unrealistic in the sense in which the word is most commonly used. Nevertheless, and in a sense paradoxically, if it is a good model it provides the key
to understanding reality.

There are no rules for model-building, and, as
the literature of economics attests, it is much
easier to build a bad one than a good one—a bad
model being one which abstracts from essentials
and therefore leads to neither insight nor understanding.[1] Nor are there any simple a priori
tests by which a model can be judged. The proof
of the pudding is in the eating. We can only start
with certain hypotheses and ideas; we can use them
to separate the unimportant from the important;
out of the residue of the important we can shape
what look like the parts and elements of a system;
we can assemble the parts and elements, refining
and polishing as we proceed. When we finally get
our model, there is one test to which we must subject it: does it help to make sense of the real
world? Or, to put the matter in another way, does
it help us to see connections to which we were pre-

---

[1]As Duesenberry rightly says: "Knowing how
to simplify one's description of reality without neglecting anything essential is the most important
part of the economist's art." James S. Duesenberry, Business Cycles and Economic Growth,
New York, 1958, pp. 14-15.

*From Paul A. Baran and Paul M. Sweezy,
"The Giant Corporation", Monopoly Capital.
Copyright (c) 1966 by Paul M. Sweezy, reprinted
by permission of Monthly Review Press.

viously blind, to relate effects to causes, to replace
the arbitrary and the accidental by the regular and
the necessary? In a word, does it help us to understand the world and act in it intelligently and effectively?

These are the general ideas and aims by which
we have been guided in constructing a model of the
monopoly capitalist economy. It is intended to
put at the center of the stage and play the spotlight
on those features which, despite all diversity and
underneath whatever overlay of detail, make the
system what it is. And in order to accomplish
this, we start, for reasons which have been indicated in the preceding chapter, with an analysis
of the typical unit of Big Business, the modern
giant corporation.

Once again: we are not interested in realism
of a photographic kind. There undoubtedly are corporations which correspond closely to the "ideal
type"—to use Max Weber's expression—with which
we shall be concerned, but the analysis would lose
none of its relevance even if there were not. The
point is that the decisive units of the economy are
unmistakably moving toward a definite, recogniz-
able pattern, and this pattern itself is much more
important than any of the concrete approximations
to it. A model of which the major component parts
are corporations of the ideal type will display with
sharpness and clarity what may appear in everyday
economic life in a disguised form, difficult to recognize and easy to misinterpret.

II

The corporate paradigm on which we wish to
focus attention has a number of characteristic features, of which we may single out the following:

(1) Control rests in the hands of management,
that is to say, the board of directors plus the chief
executive officers. Outside interests are often
(but not always) represented on the board to facili-
tate the harmonization of the interests and policies
of the corporation with those of customers, suppliers, bankers, etc.; but real power is held by
the insiders, those who devote full time to the corporation and whose interests and careers are tied
to its fortunes.

(2) Management is a self-perpetuating group.
Responsibility to the body of stockholders is for

all practical purposes a dead letter. Each generation of managers recruits its own successors and trains, grooms, and promotes them according to its own standards and values. The corporate career recognizes two characteristic forms of advance: rising from lower to higher positions within a given company, and moving from a smaller company to a larger one. The acme of success is the presidency or board chairmanship of one of the biggest corporations.

(3) Each corporation aims at and normally achieves financial independence through the internal generation of funds which remain at the disposal of management. The corporation may still, as a matter of policy, borrow from or through financial institutions, but it is not normally forced to do so and hence is able to avoid the kind of subjection to financial control which was so common in the world of Big Business fifty years ago.

Before we investigate the behavior of giant corporations of this type, a few words of explanation and clarification may be useful.

In the first place, there is no implication in our description of the corporate paradigm that great wealth, or family connections, or large personal or family stockholdings are unimportant in the recruiting and promotion of management personnel —that, for example, the chances of a David Rockefeller's getting a job at the Chase Manhattan Bank and rising to the top position are the same as those of anyone else with similar personal and intellectual attributes. On the contrary, wealth and connections are of the utmost importance, and it may indeed be taken for granted that they are normally decisive. What we are implying is something quite different: that stock ownership, wealth, connections, etc., do not as a rule enable a man to control or exercise great influence on a giant corporation from the outside. They are rather tickets of admission to the inside, where real corporate power is wielded. Mills put the essential point in a nutshell:

Not great fortunes, but great corporations are the important units of wealth, to which individuals of property are variously attached. The corporation is the source of, and the basis of the continued power and privilege of wealth. All the men and the families of great wealth are now identified with large corporations in which their property is seated. [2]

What needs to be emphasized is that the location of power inside rather than outside the typical giant corporation renders obsolete the conception of the "interest group" as a fundamental unit in the structure of capitalist society. In traditional usage, an interest group is a number of corporations under common control, the locus of power being normally an investment or commercial bank or a great family fortune. [3] Thus a Morgan company was one under the control of the investment banking firm of J. P. Morgan & Company, a Rockefeller company one under the control of the Rockefeller family, and so on. The members of an interest group would naturally coordinate their policies; and in the case of conflicts, the interests of the controlling power (or of the whole group as interpreted by the controlling power) would prevail.

A whole series of developments have loosened or broken the ties that formerly bound the great interest groups together. The power of the investment banker was based on the urgent need of the early corporate giants, at the time of foundation and in the first stages of growth, for outside financing. Later this need declined in importance or disappeared altogether as the giants, reaping a rich harvest of monopoly profits, found themselves increasingly able to take care of their financial needs from internally generated funds. At the same time, the domineering founders of family fortunes were dying off, leaving their stockholdings to numerous heirs, foundations, charities, trust funds, and the like, so that the ownership unit which once exercised absolute control over many enterprises became increasingly amorphous and leaderless. Thus the larger corporations gradually won more and more independence from both bankers and dominant stockholders, and their policies accordingly were geared to an ever greater extent each to its own interests rather than being subordinated to the interests of a group.

We are not of course maintaining that interest groups have disappeared or are no longer of any importance in the United States economy. We do hold that they are of rapidly diminishing importance and that an appropriate model of the economy no longer needs to take account of them. It is not the

[2] C. Wright Mills, The Power Elite, New York, 1956, p. 116.

[3] An analysis of interest groups in the American economy as of the mid-1930's will be found in Appendix 13 to Part 1 of the National Resources Committee's well-known report, The Structure of the American Economy, Washington, 1939 (reprinted in Paul M. Sweezy, The Present as History, New York, 1953, Chapter 12).

purpose of the present work to support this view
with empirical evidence, despite its ready availability. But since belief in the crucial importance
of interest groups is a deeply rooted tenet of left-
wing thought, it seems wise to cite one specific
example of the dissolution process as it has affected what would once have been generally admitted
to be one of the two most powerful interest groups,
the Rockefeller group.

The core of the Rockefeller interest group was
the original Standard Oil Company which, after
its break-up in 1911 under the Sherman Antitrust
Law, became a number of separate companies operating in different regions of the country. There
is ample evidence that these companies remained
in one interest group under firm Rockefeller control through the 1920's. They respected each other's marketing areas and generally worked together
against the rapidly rising independents. An attempt
by the President of Standard of Indiana in 1929 to
wrest control of his company from the Rockefeller
family via a proxy contest for stockholder support
was decisively defeated and the would-be rebel
was unceremoniously fired.

In the years after 1929, great changes came to
the oil industry: the international cartel was
formed; the rich Middle Eastern fields were opened
up; domestically, the depression-born prorationing
system brought what amounted to government enforcement of monopoly prices; the tripling of the
number of motor vehicles in three decades and the
widespread substitution of fuel oil for coal sent
demand and production skyrocketing. How did
Rockefeller companies react to these developments? Did they continue to act as a team, all
doing their best to promote the interests of the
group as a whole, as the interest-group theory
would lead us to expect? Or did each seek to exploit the new opportunities in its own interest?

The record leaves little doubt about the answer.
California Standard, getting into Middle Eastern
production in a big way but without adequate marketing outlets, teamed up internationally with Tex-
aco rather than with one of the "brother" companies, and invaded the New England market, traditional stronghold of Jersey and Socony, even at
the cost of depressing gasoline prices. The others
were not long in following California's example,
and by now the various Standard companies have
completely broken away from the 1911 marketing
areas and are busily stealing markets from each
other as well as from the non-Standard companies.

Meanwhile Indiana Standard which in the early
days, no doubt at Rockefeller behest, had excluded
itself from the foreign field began to hunger for
the fantastic profits which the international cartel
companies were making on their Middle Eastern
operations. Indiana therefore joined the Italians
and Japanese, as well as certain smaller American
independents, in scabbing on the cartel by offering
Iran and other Middle Eastern producers a 25-75
profit split rather than the standard 50-50.

It is possible that the old Standard companies
may still be subject to Rockefeller influence, perhaps even control: publicly available information
is not conclusive one way or the other. But if they
are, one can only infer that the Rockefellers have
decided that the best way to promote their interests
is to allow, or perhaps encourage, each of the companies to promote its interests. In these circumstances the issue of Rockefeller control becomes
irrelevant to the behavior of the companies or the
modus operandi of the system of which they form
constituent parts. This is the point which we wish
to take into account in constructing our model: we
abstract from whatever elements of outside control
may still exist in the world of giant corporations
because they are in no sense essential to the way
it works.

This does not of course mean that each giant
corporation operates in isolation, that there are no
alliances and alignments, no agreements and groupings. On the contrary, these forms of action—
like their opposites, competition and struggle—
are of the very essence of monopoly capitalism.
All that we are asserting is that the relevant line-
ups are determined not by ties to outside control
centers but by the rational calculations of inside
managements. In the oil industry, for example,
Standard Companies are as ready and willing to
ally themselves with or fight against non-Standard
companies as with or against other Standard companies. It all depends on where the maximum profit lies.

But we are getting ahead of our story.

III

What pattern of behavior can we expect from
huge, management-controlled, financially independent corporations?

Formal economic theory has largely ignored this
question, continuing to operate with the assumption
of the profit-maximizing individual entrepreneur

who has occupied the central role in theories of the capitalist system since well before the time of Adam Smith. Retaining this assumption amounts in effect to making another: that in all respects that matter to the functioning of the system the corporation acts like an individual entrepreneur.

If one stops to think about it, this seems unlikely on the face of it. Furthermore, while economic theorists have largely ignored the corporation, other social scientists have devoted much time and energy to its study. So far as we know, none of them has ever supported the proposition that the modern corporation is merely an enlarged version of the classical entrepreneur. On the other hand, there is a voluminous literature dating back to the turn of the century and reaching its culmination in the famous work of Berle and Means which argues most emphatically that the modern corporation represents a qualitative break with the older form of individual enterprise and that radically different types of behavior are to be expected from it. According to Berle and Means:

> It is conceivable—indeed it seems almost inevitable if the corporate system is to survive—that the "control" of the great corporations should develop into a purely neutral technocracy, balancing a variety of claims by various groups in the community and assigning to each a portion of the income stream on the basis of public policy rather than private cupidity.[4]

What Berle and Means described as "conceivable" a quarter of a century ago is taken for granted as an accomplished fact by many present-day observers of the business scene. Thus Carl Kaysen, in a paper delivered at the 1956 annual meeting of the American Economic Association, speaks of "the wide-ranging scope of responsibility assumed by management" as one of the "characteristic features of behavior" of the modern corporation, and proceeds as follows:

> No longer the agent of proprietorship seeking to maximize return on investment, management sees itself as responsible to stockholders, employees, customers, the general public, and, perhaps most important, the firm itself as an institution . . .

From one point of view, this behavior can be termed responsible: there is no display of greed or graspingness; there is no attempt to push off onto workers or the community at large part of the social costs of the enterprise. The modern corporation is a soulful corporation.[5]

According to this view, which is certainly very widespread nowadays, the maximization of profits has ceased to be the guiding principle of business enterprise. Corporate managements, being self-appointed and responsible to no outside group, are free to choose their aims and in the typical case are assumed to subordinate the old-fashioned hunt for profits to a variety of other, quantitatively less precise but qualitatively more worthy, objectives.

The implications of this doctrine of the "soulful corporation" are far-reaching. The truth is that if it is accepted, the whole corpus of traditional economic theory must be abandoned and the time-honored justification of the existing social order in terms of economic efficiency, justice, etc., simply falls to the ground. This has been most effectively pointed out by Edward S. Mason:

> But if profit maximization is not the directing agent, how are resources allocated to their most productive uses, what relation have prices to relative scarcities, and how do factors get remunerated in accordance with their contribution to output? Assume an economy composed of a few hundred large corporations, each enjoying substantial market power and all directed by managements with a "conscience." Each management wants to do the best it can for society consistent, of course, with doing the best it can for labor, customers, suppliers, and owners. How

---

[4] The Modern Corporation and Private Property, New York, 1932, p. 356.

[5] Carl Kaysen, "The Social Significance of the Modern Corporation," American Economic Review, May 1957, pp. 313-314. See also M. J. Rathbone, President of Standard Oil of New Jersey, in the Saturday Review, April 16, 1960: "Managements of large companies must harmonize a wide span of obligations: to investors, customers, suppliers, employees, communities and the national interest. Thus the large organization may actually have a narrower range for its decision-making than the small, closely held corporation which is not so much in the public eye and hence not so exposed to criticism."

do prices get determined in such an economy? How are factors remunerated, and
what relation is there between remuneration
and performance? What is the mechanism,
if any, that assures effective resource use,
and how can corporate managements "do
right by" labor, suppliers, customers, and
owners while simultaneously serving the
public interests?[6]

Economists have made no attempt to answer
these questions, and indeed it is doubtful whether
it even makes sense to ask them in relation to an
economy such as Mason postulates, that is to say,
one made up of or dominated by a few hundred soulful corporations. Prices and incomes would be
indeterminate, and there would be no theoretically
definable tendencies toward equilibrium. To be
sure, economic life in such a society might settle
down into routines and patterns which could be analyzed by historians, sociologists, and statisticians,
but it seems reasonably clear that today's economic
theorists would be out of a job.

One school of thought, associated especially with
the name of Herbert A. Simon of Carnegie Institute
of Technology, seems already to have drawn these
conclusions and is attempting to study the big corporation and its implications by means of what
Simon calls "organization theory." According to
this theory, corporations do not try to maximize
anything but merely to achieve "satisfactory" results. Thus, to the maximizing behavior which
was assumed to characterize the old-fashioned
entrepreneur, Simon contrasts what he calls the
"satisficing" behavior of modern corporate managements. At the annual meetings of the American
Economic Association in 1956, a paper by Simon
expounding this view was answered by James Earley
of the University of Wisconsin who had been engaged for a number of years on a study of the management policies of a sample of large and successful American corporations. Summing up a wealth
of carefully collected and analyzed empirical material, Earley had little difficulty in disposing of
Simon's theory; what is more significant from our
point of view is that he went on to give a most useful and illuminating description of how modern
corporate managements really behave. This statement is so good that it seems worthwhile to rescue

large parts of it from the untitled obscurity of the
Economic Association's Papers and Proceedings.
After noting some points of agreement and others
of minor disagreement with Simon, Earley proceeds
as follows:

I have more serious reservations concerning what appears to be the major economic
theorem Simon arrives at; namely, that the
business enterprise looks for merely satisfactory solutions of its problems and specifically seeks merely satisfactory profits.
That his approach has led so directly to this
conclusion is one of the facts that makes me
especially doubt that it is a satisfactory one.
Whatever may be true of individuals or of
other types of organization, I cannot square
Simon's "satisficing" behavior with the behavior of the large-scale American business
firm. I agree that the conventional notion
of profit maximization and of general "optimization" must be modified. I contend this
is carrying the change much too far. Let
me briefly catalogue the main types of evidence that lead me to reject the "satisficing"
postulate.

(1) As a part of my research, I have
made a study of recent management literature, both general and specialized, one of
my hypotheses in doing so being that this
literature will reveal the frames of reference and mores of advanced business management. A striking characteristic of this
literature (except where public relations
is an evident objective) is its systematic
focus on cost reduction, the expansion of
revenue, and the increase of profits. There
is, of course, much reference to standards
and to the need of remedying unsatisfactory
situations. The drive is always toward the
better and frequently the best, not just the
good. Like Samuel Gompers' ideal union
leader, the exemplary man of management
seems to have "More!" for at least one of
his mottoes.

(2) Secondly, my questionnaire studies
of the practices and policies of leading so-
called "excellently managed" companies lead
me toward generally similar conclusions.
I have published the major results of the
first of these studies and will not review
them here.[7]

_____
[6] Edward S. Mason, "The Apologetics of 'Managerialism,'" The Journal of Business, January
1958, p. 7.

_____
[7] The author's reference here is to James S.

(3) The third fact that makes me doubt Simon's postulate as applied to the firm is the rapidly growing use of economists, market analysts, other types of specialists, and management consultants by our larger businesses. The main function of most of these people is to help the firm reduce costs, find superior methods, choose the most profitable alternatives, and uncover new profit opportunities. As these sophisticated gentlemen gain in influence in business councils—and I confidently believe they will—profit oriented rationality is likely to be more and more representative of business behavior.

(4) Most of all I am impressed by the rapid development of analytical and managerial techniques that both stimulate and assist the business firms to find the least costly ways of doing things and the most profitable things to do. Operations research and mathematical programming are only the more fancy of this growing genus. There are also greatly improved forms of accounting and budgeting, improved methods of market analysis, refinements in business forecasting, and interesting types of nonmathematical programming. The unifying character of these new techniques is that they seek to apply the principles of rational problem-solving to business planning and decision making.

Let me conclude by briefly sketching the notion of business behavior that seems to be emerging from my own studies. It falls somewhere between the old postulate of profit maximization and Simon's "satisfactory profit." It fully recognizes the limited informational and computational resources of the firm. It also incorporates his suggested concept of the "aspiration level" and a modified principle of "viability." My behavioral postulate could best be briefly described as "a systematic temporal search for highest practicable profits."

The theory underlying it runs, very briefly as follows:

The major goals of modern large-scale business are high managerial incomes, good profits, a strong competitive position, and growth. Modern management does not view these goals as seriously inconsistent but rather, indeed, as necessary, one to the other. Competitive strength and even survival, management believes, require large innovative and substantial growth expenditures in the rapidly changing technical and market conditions of the present day. Since growth by merger is hazardous and frequently impossible, large and more or less continuous capital expenditures are necessary. For well-recognized reasons, management wishes to minimize outside financing, so the funds for most of these expenditures must be internally generated. This requires high and growing profits above dividend levels. So, too, do high managerial rewards. High and rising profits are hence an instrument as well as a direct goal of great importance.

With these goals and needs in view, advanced management plans for profit through time, using coordinated programs stretching as far ahead as practicable. The profit targets incorporated in these programs are sufficient to finance not only good dividends but also desired innovative and growth expenditures. The programs are revised frequently, as experience accrues and new opportunities are discovered.

The tendency toward profit maximization (i.e., highest practicable profit) appears in this system along several dimensions. In the process of revising and reformulating programs, more expensive and less profitable activities are pruned or dropped and cheaper or more profitable ones are added. Less costly processes and the more profitable product and market sectors serve as the standards toward which others are expected to converge or be replaced. By steadily selecting those methods and sectors that promise better returns, these standards are kept high and, if possible, rising. Finally, the overall profit and growth targets of the enterprise as a whole are raised through time, unless adversity prevents.

These goals and programs and standards, it is true, represent at any time certain "aspiration levels," and the efforts to satisfy them receive prime attention. But the two major points about them are that (1) they are likely to be hard to reach and (2) they will ordinarily recede (i.e., grow larger)

Earley, "Marginal Policies of 'Excellently Managed' Companies," The American Economic Review, March 1956.

through time. Even in good times the firm's aspiration levels, therefore, are fairly taut, and they are highly elastic upward. On the other hand, there is great resistance to adjusting profit and other standards downward so that in bad times the business firm tries even harder to make the highest practicable profits.

I readily agree that I have sketched the behavior of what might be called the "exemplary firm" rather than the firm that is quantitatively representative of the present business population. But my main point is that the management techniques and the expertise that can validate my notion are developing rapidly, are increasingly being made available to business, and are being rapidly adopted by leading firms. Consequently, I suspect, the examplary firm will be the representative firm of the future. If so, its behavior will be more rather than less appropriately analyzed by some of our time-honored theoretical notions, such as profit maximization. . . . [8]

Two aspects of this admirable statement call for comment. First, it introduces a healthy corrective to what Earley calls "the conventional notion of profit maximization and general 'optimization.'" This conventional notion has been tied to a more or less explicitly stated assumption that the maximizing entrepreneur has complete knowledge of all alternatives open to him and of the consequences of choosing any combination of them. Given this assumption, he can always select the combination of alternatives which yields an absolute maximum. Further, if it is assumed that his knowledge remains equally complete in the face of changing conditions, it follows logically that he can always make instantaneous and appropriate adjustments to new circumstances. What is involved here is an assumption of omniscience on the part of the entrepreneur, which, far from being a useful abstraction, is of course an absurdity. In practice, to be sure, economists have usually given a more sensible meaning to the maximization principle, but by failing expressly to repudiate the omniscience postulate, by failing to spell out what is and what is not involved in the assumption of profit maximization, they have left themselves

vulnerable to attacks of the kind mounted by Simon. It is therefore valuable to have Earley's carefully considered statement. By stressing the "limited informational and computational resources of the firm," he makes clear that no assumption of complete knowledge is involved, and his entire argument is based on the rejection of any idea of an absolute maximum or optimum. The firm (whether individual entrepreneur or corporation makes no difference) always finds itself in a given historical situation, with limited knowledge of changing conditions. In this context it can never do more than improve its profit position. In practice, the search for the greatest increase in profits which is possible in the given situation, subject of course to the elementary proviso that the exploitation of today's profit opportunities must not ruin tomorrow's. This is all there is to the profit maximization principle, but it also happens to be all that is necessary to validate the "economizing" behavior patterns which have been the very backbone of all serious economic theory for the last two centuries.

The second aspect of Earley's statement which we want to emphasize, and the one most relevant to our present purpose, is the convincing demonstration that the big corporation, if not more profit-oriented than the individual entrepreneur (he quite properly leaves this question open), is at any rate better equipped to pursue a policy of profit maximization. The result is much the same: the economy of large corporations is more, not less dominated by the logic of profit-making than the economy of small entrepreneurs ever was.

It might be thought that this is enough to dispose of the soulful corporation and at the same time to justify the procedure of those economists who have altogether ignored the rise of the corporate form of enterprise and continued to reason in terms of the individual entrepreneur. This is not so, however, and for two reasons: First, the alleged soulfulness of the corporation relates not only to its attitude toward the acquisition of profits but also to its attitude toward the utilization of profits, and there is still much to be said on the latter subject. Second, there are undoubtedly differences between individual enterprise and corporate enterprise which have little to do with the goal of profit maximization but which still are of great importance for economic theory. But before we take up these topics it will repay us to probe somewhat more deeply into the motivational and behavioral patterns of corporate managements.

[8] American Economic Review, May 1957, pp. 333-335.

IV

The big corporation came into its own in the second half of the nineteenth century, first in the fields of finance and railroads, spreading to industry around the turn of the century, and later invading most other branches of the national economy. In the typical case, the early corporate giants were organized by—or, as a result of merger, failure, or other emergency, soon fell under the control of—a class of financier-promoters who have become famous in American history as "robber barons," "moguls," or "tycoons"—all terms reflecting the popular feeling that the American Big Businessman of that period resembled the feudal lord in his predatory habits and lack of concern for the public welfare.

The center of the business world in those days was not the corporation but the tycoon, who typically controlled a collection of corporations in various lines of activity.[9] A very wealthy man, the tycoon nevertheless did not believe in tying up his funds permanently even in corporations under his own control. The corporation's assets for the most part represented "other people's money" which the tycoon managed with a view to his own profit, not theirs. Apart from methods such as stealing, fraud, milking one company for the benefit of another, etc.—all celebrated in the muckraking literature of the day—his primary interest lay in capital gains made through buying securities cheap and selling them dear, an objective which could be promoted at times by building up a company and at others by wrecking it. To quote Veblen, who may be regarded as the classical theorist of this kind of business enterprise:

> With a fuller development of the modern closeknit and comprehensive industrial system, the point of chief attention for the business man has shifted from the old-fashioned surveillance and regulation of a given industrial process, with which his livelihood was once bound up, to an alert redistribution of investments from less to more gainful ventures, and to a strategic control of the conjunctures of business through shrewd investments and coalitions with other business men.[10]

The present-day corporation manager is a very different type from the tycoon of fifty years ago. In one respect he represents a return to pre-tycoon days; his chief concern is once again the "surveillance and regulation of a given industrial process with which his livelihood is bound up." On the other hand, in another respect he is the antithesis of classical entrepreneur and tycoon alike: they were both individualists par excellence, while he is the leading species of the genus "organization man."

There are many ways to describe the contrast between tycoon and modern manager. The former was the parent of the giant corporation, the latter is its child. The tycoon stood outside and above, dominating the corporation. The manager is an insider, dominated by it. The loyalty of the one was to himself and his family (which, in its bourgeois form, is essentially an extension of self); the loyalty of the other is to the organization to which he belongs and through which he expresses himself. To the one the corporation was merely a means to enrichment; to the other the good of the company has become both an economic and an ethical end. The one stole from the corporation, the other steals for it.[11]

---

[9] The word "tycoon" entered the language around the middle of the nineteenth century as a title which foreigners (incorrectly) applied to the Japanese Shogun.

[10] Thorstein Veblen, The Theory of Business Enterprise, New York, 1904, p. 24.

[11] Popular sentiment condones the latter but not the former. This is presumably the reason for the widespread impression, which has by now attained the status of axiomatic truth among those who describe and comment on the American scene, that the businessman of today is a highly moral person by comparison with his predecessor of a half century ago. There seems to be no good reason for accepting this view; indeed, the extent of executive criminality in furtherance of company aims which was revealed by the late E. H. Sutherland in his important but much neglected work White Collar Crime (New York, 1949) would seem clearly to point to the opposite conclusion. What undoubtedly has changed is the pattern of executive criminality, though no one, including Sutherland himself, seems to have appreciated the importance of this fact to an understanding of recent American history. See also J. G. Fuller, The Gentlemen Conspirators (New York, 1962): this is the story of the famous price-fixing case in the heavy electrical equipment industry.

All of this has been aptly summed up by a modern manager who is the grandson of one of the most famous entrepreneurs of the past. In a speech before the American Newspaper Publishers' Association on April 28, 1955, Henry Ford II said:

The modern corporate or joint-venture capitalism has largely replaced tycoon capitalism. The one-man-band owner-manager is fast being replaced by a new class of professional managers, dedicated more to the advancement of the company than to the enrichment of a few owners.

Actually, managers are not professionals in the sense that doctors and lawyers are—there are no recognized standards, training, etc.—but on the main point Mr. Ford is unquestionably right. The tycoon was interested in self-enrichment: he was an individualist. The modern manager is dedicated to the advancement of the company: he is a "company man."[12]

None of the foregoing is intended to imply that the tycoon has altogether vanished from the American scene. The long inflation of the 1940's and 1950's produced a whole crop of promoters and operators conforming exactly to the sociological type of the tycoon. But nowadays they operate around the periphery and in the interstices of the American economy, and they are looked down upon with a mixture of disdain and contempt by the real Big Businessmen of today, the managers of the giant corporations. In this connection we are fortunate to have a record of a direct confrontation of

the two types. The latter-day tycoon is Cash McCall, hero of the novel of the same name by Cameron Hawley, himself a Big Businessman turned writer. The corporate manager is Frank Abrams, retired board chairman of Standard Oil Company of New Jersey, in terms of assets America's largest industrial corporation. The confrontation was arranged by Business Week, which queried a number of businessmen of varying backgrounds about their reactions to Cash McCall and his methods of operation.[13]

Cash McCall is a man of almost superhuman skill and daring who possesses an infallible Midas touch. He specializes in buying companies, doctoring them up, and selling them at a big profit. For this purpose he has a string of high-powered retainers—lawyers, management consultants, spies, etc. He has no interest in holding onto or developing any of the properties which come into his control, and for this reason he is contrasted throughout the book with the "company man" (the term is Hawley's) whose first loyalty is to the company he works for and who is represented as becoming increasingly the normal American businessman. Here is the gist of Frank Abrams's opinion of Cash McCall (the insertions and omissions are Business Week's):

The individualist seems [in Hawley's book] to be the man of ideas who performs miracles in reorganization, and the company man the plodder who makes little or no contribution to the larger scheme of things. My experience is quite to the contrary. The company man, I have found, is the man who likes to serve a good cause to the best of his ability, and is content to prosper with [his company]. The individualist is quite apt to be a self-seeker . . . he will switch allegiance from company to company, and seems mainly concerned with personal power and the trappings of wealth.

My business experience has been . . . relatively free of the tax manipulations and promotional shenanigans that seem the chief concern of the principal characters of this

---

[12] Mr. Ford's statement was later borrowed and characteristically embellished by a Big Business public relations man. J. C. McQueen, Manager of Employee and Plant Community Relations at the Evandale Plant of General Electric, at the Tenth Annual Teachers' Institute of the Cincinnati Public Schools, August 29, 1956, made a speech in which he repeated without attribution the above statement of Henry Ford II from "The modern corporate or joint-venture capitalism" through "class of professional managers." The final clause, however, reads as follows: "dedicated to serving the balanced best interests of all contributors to and claimants on the goods and services of the business." (Mimeographed release.) Here we meet the soulful corporation again—and also get a glimpse of its origins in the fertile minds of the public-relations fraternity.

---

[13] "How Good an Operator Is Cash McCall?" Business Week, December 17, 1955. Among those queried, Cash McCall's most enthusiastic supporter was Louis E. Wolfson, perhaps the best publicized of the real-life Cash McCalls of the postwar decade.

book. Perhaps I have been insulated from
some of the facts of smaller business life, a
and if so I can now, in retirement, appreciate how fortunate I have been.

This is the voice of the genuine aristocrat, one
who is firmly established in his station in life,
secure and confident. He is proud to identify himself with his company, to share in its prosperity.
He has little use for individualists: they are unre-
liable and their insecurities lead them into the
vulgarities of power-grabbing and conspicuous
display. Above all, he is conscious of living in the
world of Big Business, the rulers of which, like
the feudal nobility of old, have learned to live gra-
ciously, "insulated from the facts of smaller business life."

This last phrase speaks volumes about present-
day American society. Cash McCall is no petty
shopkeeper. He owns one of the largest hotels in
Philadelphia and occupies a whole floor of it; he
flies his own private plane and maintains a great
country estate; he spends millions of dollars on
the impulse of the moment. By Hollywood standards, in fact, Cash McCall is the very model of
a Big Businessman. And yet to Frank Abrams—
who may or may not have as much money as Cash
McCall is supposed to have—all this is merely vulgar display and cheap shenanigans. To the aristocracy of company men, Big Business is Standard
Oil and a few score similar corporate giants which
collectively control the nation's economic destiny
—all the rest is unceremoniously relegated to the
limbo of "smaller business." "In the United States
today," writes one of the aristocrats, a Vice President of the Pittsburgh Plate Glass Company, "135
corporations own 45 percent of the industrial assets. These are the companies to watch. Here
lies managerial power."[14] Clearly, the exercise
of power is matched by the consciousness of power.[15]

---

[14] Leland Hazard, "What Economists Don't Know
About Wages," Harvard Business Review, January-
February 1957, p. 56.

[15] No attempt can be made here to explore the
ramifications and implications of the transformation of the Big Businessman from tycoon to company
man. Nevertheless, we cannot leave the subject
without noting that it has made its mark on serious
literature (Cash McCall is to be rated rather as
a tract for the times in novel form). "In the fifty-
four years since Frank Norris created the prototype

V

Big corporations, then are run by company men.
What kind of people are they? What do they want
and why? What position do they hold in the class
structure of American society?

There is a widespread impression, and much
literature to support and propagate it, that the managements of big corporations form some sort of
separate, independent, or "neutral" social class.
This view we have already encountered in an elementary form in the "neutral technocracy" of Berle
and Means and the "soulful corporation" of Carl
Kaysen; it is developed more elaborately in such
works as James Burnham's The Managerial Revolution and Berle's The 20th-Century Capitalist
Revolution. Most of the variants of this theory
have interesting and enlightening insights to contribute, but in our view they all share a common
defect: the basic idea is wrong.

---

of the modern capitalist in The Pit," writes David
Dempsey, "the approach of American novelists
toward the world of business has undergone a complete revision. Norris, and subsequently Dreiser,
saw the rise of the corporation as a one-man affair;
their focus was on the individual who dominated
business for his own ends, but whose actions affected society at large. Norris' wheat speculator
Curtis Jadwin, like Dreiser's nineteenth-century
capitalist, Frank Cowperwood, is molded in the
classic tradition of the hero who builds an empire
at the cost of his own integrity. Since few American corporations at present are dominated by a
single individual, the novelist has been compelled
to reorient—actually, to invert—his point of view.
Today, it is the corporation itself . . . that has
become the villain; it is the individual caught in
the corporate structure, rather than the public,
who is the victim. . . ." Review of From the Dark
Tower by Ernest Pawel, New York Times (Sunday
Book Section), June 23, 1957.

In one important respect, this analysis seems
to us not quite accurate. The crux of the matter
is not that "few American corporations at present
are dominated by a single individual." There are
plenty of them, even among the biggest. The point
is that the company man, even when he rises to a
dominant position in his company, as often happens,
is a very different type and plays a very different
role from the old-fashioned tycoon. For the tycoon,
the company is merely a means, while to the company man it has become an end.

The fact is that the managerial stratum is the most active and influential part of the propertied class. All studies show that its members are largely recruited from the middle and upper reaches of the class structure; they overlap with what C. Wright Mills calls the "very rich"; with few and negligible exceptions, they are wealthy men in their own right, quite apart from the large incomes and extensive privileges which they derive from their corporate connections.[16] It is of course true, as we have emphasized, that in the typical big corporation the management is not subject to stockholder control, and in this sense the "separation of ownership from control" is a fact. But there is no justification for concluding from this that managements in general are divorced from ownership in general. Quite the contrary, managers are among the biggest owners; and because of the strategic positions they occupy, they function as the protectors and spokesmen for all large-scale property. Far from being a separate class, they constitute in reality the leading echelon of the property-owning class.

This is not to argue that managers have no distinctive interests qua managers. Like other segments of the propertied class, they do. But the conflicts of interest that arise in this way are between managers and large property owners. The clearest case in point has to do with dividend policy.

It is generally assumed that the desire of managers, noted earlier, to generate the largest feasible volume of internal corporate funds leads to an interest in a low dividend payout rate, while stockholders' concern to maximize their disposable cash income leads to an interest in a high payout rate. Actually, this is much too simple. Most managers are themselves big owners of stock (in their own and other companies) and as such have the same interest in dividends as other big stockholders. This interest is neither in a minimum nor a maximum payout rate but somewhere in between: stockholdings should yield a reasonable cash income (for managers this is particularly important as a guarantee of family security after they retire or die); on the other hand, they should also steadily appreciate in value. The first requirement calls for dividends, the second for plowing back of earnings. Nevertheless, the special managerial interest in a low payout rate does exist and is undoubt-

edly important. But the point to be emphasized is that this makes managers the allies of the very largest stockholders for whom a minimum payout rate is also a desideratum. The reason of course is that the very rich save a large part of their incomes in any case, and it is to their advantage for the corporations in which they own stock to do the saving for them rather than pay out dividends from which to do their own saving. Corporate saving results in an increase in the value of their stock. If at any time they need the cash, either to spend or for some other investment, they can sell part or all of their shares, realizing the increment of value in the form of a capital gain taxable at the maximum rate of 25 percent. On the other hand, if they receive more in the form of dividends they have to pay taxes at the much higher rates applicable to their brackets, which of course cuts down their effective rate of saving.

Pressure for higher payout rates generally comes from small stockholders. Only rarely is it effectively exerted on managements via the formal corporate voting machinery, but this does not mean that the small stockholder is without influence. Socially the seven million or so small stockholders in the United States are an important group: they are quite likely to be solid citizens, leaders of public opinion with local political influence. Since the tiny upper echelon of the propertied class (including its leading element, the managers of the big corporations) is always politically vulnerable, it naturally wants to have the support and loyalty of the small stockholder. A moderate, and perhaps even more important a steady, dividend policy is the most effective way of insuring this support.

In practice, dividend policies are the outcome of a compromise between the desire of managements and large stockholders for a low payout rate and the desire of small stockholders for a high rate. Moreover, as would be expected, there is considerable variation from one company to another. Those which are largely owned by a few rich individuals or families tend to have the lowest payout rates; while the highest rates of all are likely to be paid by companies which both have a large number of small stockholders and are also situated in what may be called "public-relations-sensitive" areas of the economy. As would also be expected, managements as a rule hold the upper hand in determining the terms of the compromise, maintaining payout rates of 50 percent or less in most management-controlled industrial corporations. When profits rise, moreover, managements deliberately

---

[16] By far the best treatment of these subjects will be found in C. Wright Mills, The Power Elite, especially Chapters 6, 7, and 8.

delay the adjustment of dividends to the new profit level, so that in time of prosperity the actual as distinct from the target payout rate tends to decline.[17] All of which testifies to the combined power of management and the very rich: the two are in fact integrated into a harmonious interest group at the top of the economic pyramid.

VI

The company man is dedicated to the advancement of his company. This does not mean, however, that he is any more or less homo economicus, any more or less selfish, any more or less altruistic than either the tycoon or the individual owner-entrepreneur before him. All of these conceptions are at best irrelevant and at worst misleading. The problem is not one of "psychology" of any kind but of the selective and molding effects of institutions on the personnel that operates them. It might seem that this is too elementary to require mention, but unfortunately it is not possible to take for granted such a degree of enlightenment among economists. Economic theory is still heavily permeated by the "psychologizing" tradition of nineteenth-century utilitarianism, and economists need continually to be reminded that this tradition leads only to confusion and obscurantism.

To be a going concern, a social order must instill in its members the ambition to be a success in its own terms. Under capitalism the highest form of success is business success, and under monopoly capitalism the highest form of business is the big corporation. In this system the normal procedure for an ambitious young man must be to work himself up to as near the top as possible of as big a corporation as possible.[18] Once he enters a given corporation, he devotes himself to two ends: ascending the managerial ladder and advancing the relative status of his company in the corporate world. In practice these two ends are indistinguishable: the young man's rise in the company

depends on his contribution to improving the position of the company. This is the crux of the matter, and this is why we can say without qualification that the company man is dedicated to the advancement of his company: he is dedicated to the advancement of his company precisely to the extent that he is dedicated to advancing himself.

This remains true even after he has reached the top of a given company. If he makes a good record, he may be "called" to a larger company. And even if he is not, or has no hope of being, he is still just as much interested in improving the position of the company he heads; for standing, prestige, and power in the business world are not personal attributes but rather are conferred on the individual businessman by the standing, prestige, and power of his company and by his position in that company.

These propositions are vividly illustrated in Cash McCall. Grant Austen, one of the main characters, is owner and president of a small company. During the Second World War the company becomes enormously profitable, but Austen soon discovers that his position in the business world remains unchanged. "Earnings leaped to a level where he could have paid himself an annual salary of $100,000 —the hallmark of a Big Business president—but Grant Austen knew from his increased contact with the world of Washington, New York and Detroit that the Suffolk Moulding Company was a painfully small example of what was referred to as Small Business. His standing in the world of industry was the sociological equivalent of an underprivileged sharecropper." His daughter is refused admission to an exclusive girls' school on the pretext that there are no openings. "Grant Austen knew better. There were other men whose daughters had applied afterward and been accepted. There was only one possible explanation—he wasn't a big enough man to count. The Chadwick School was like so many of the men he met in Pullman club cars—they had never heard of the Suffolk Moulding Company. Being president of a small company didn't mean a thing." The best week of Grant Austin's married life is spent at a National Association of Manufacturers convention in New York where he and his wife give a dinner party. "Their guests were other presidential couples, all of whom outranked them in net worth, but Miriam held her own. . . . During the days while he was attending convention sessions, she managed to get acquainted with two women whose husbands were both officers of companies that had their securities listed on the New York Stock Exchange." The end of Austen's

---

[17] For more complete quantitative data, see the excellent study of John Lintner, "Distribution of Incomes of Corporations Among Dividends, Retained Earnings, and Taxes," American Economic Review, May 1956.

[18] "The way to achieve and retain greatness is always to be striving for something more." Osborn Elliott, Men at the Top, New York, 1959, p. 40. This book contains much useful information on American business leaders.

business career drives home the main point with an ironic twist. Harassed and frustrated by the problems of small business, he finally decides to sell out. He gets two million dollars more than the company is worth—only to discover that now all at once, unattached to any company, he is a nobody even in those business circles which had formerly accepted him as an equal.

But size is not the only index of corporate status: this is an oversimplification. Other important indexes are rate of growth and "strength" as measured by such standards as credit rating and the price of a company's securities. Thus, assuming equal size, one company will rank ahead of others if it is stronger and growing more rapidly; and strength and rapid growth may even offset a big size differential if the larger company is stagnant or declining. The primary objectives of corporate policy—which are at the same time and inevitably the personal objectives of the corporate managers —are thus strength, rate of growth, and size. There is no general formula for quantifying or combining these objectives—nor is there any need for one. For they are reducible to the single common denominator of profitability. Profits provide the internal funds for expansion. Profits are the sinew and muscle of strength, which in turn gives access to outside funds if and when they are needed. Internal expansion, acquisition, and merger are the ways in which corporations grow, and growth is the road to size. Thus profits, even though not the ultimate goal, are the necessary means to all ultimate goals. As such, they become the immediate, unique, unifying, quantitative aim of corporate policies, the touchstone of corporate rationality, the measure of corporate success. Here is the real—the socio-structural as distinct from individual-psychological—explanation of the kind of profit-maximizing behavior so ably described by Earley in the passage quoted on pages 24-26.

Nothing has yet been said about whether corporate executives strive to maximize their salaries and/or personal incomes. [19] It is probably safe to

assume that they do, for two reasons. For one thing, there is a selective process at work which tends to draw the people who are most interested in making money into business and to divert those less interested into other pursuits. As Veblen said, "men whose aim is not an increase of possessions do not go into business."[20] And second, within any given business milieu, relative salary or income is an important badge of standing. William H. Whyte, Jr., inquiring into executives' attitudes toward taxes, found the following to be true:

> Unhappy as executives are about high taxes, to them the key aspect of salary is not its absolute but its relative size. And the relative size does depend on the income before taxes. The part of the pay stub that shows gross salary may be cause for hollow laughter, but it is still the part that is critical, and the man who gets $30,000 a year finds very little comfort in pondering the thought that his $37,000-a-year rival takes home only $892 more than he does. [21]

There can thus hardly be any doubt that corporate managers do normally strive to maximize personal income. But nothing in the theory of corporate behavior would be changed if we were to make the opposite assumption: that company men are unconcerned about the size of their incomes, that they go into business and work hard at it because they like to rather than for the money it brings in. There certainly are some businessmen who feel this way; and indeed they might all be of this type, and might be paid accordingly, without changing anything in their behavior as company men.

One way of clarifying this is by an analogy. A professional baseball player makes his living by playing ball. He may detest the life and stay with it solely for the money. Or he may love the game and be quite willing to play for nothing if necessary. It makes no difference at all when he gets out on the playing field. There his objectives are no longer dictated by his personal feelings and preferences;

---

[19] The two are of course not identical. Mainly for tax reasons, the corporate world has devised a variety of methods for compensating executives in addition to the old-fashioned salary and bonus. Taken over the whole life of the executive, these "fringe benefits" may be even more important than salary. "In these days of profit-sharing benefits, retirement plans, and stock options," says an advertisement of the Guaranty Trust Company in

Business Week of November 24, 1956, "the present and future capital assets of the average business executive are far greater than his bank balance and salary check seem to indicate."

[20] The Theory of Business Enterprise, p. 20.

[21] The Organization Man, New York, 1958, pp. 144-145.

they are laid down for him in the baseball rule book. Whatever his likes and dislikes, whatever his inner urges, his actions must be directed to the single, measurable aim of getting more runs than the other team. If he won't or can't play the game according to the book, he is dropped from the team and loses his job. If his contribution to his club's success is inadequate, he is benched or sent down to the minor leagues.

Baseball, it is said, is America's national game. It would be more accurate to say that business is America's national game: there are many more people engaged in it and the stakes are much higher. But the two operate on similar principles. In baseball the objective is to get to the top of the league; day-to-day policies are directed toward winning games by getting more runs than opposing teams; players are judged by their cumulative day-to-day performance. In business the aim is to get to the top of the corporate pyramid; day-to-day policies are directed to making the most possible profits; as in baseball, men are judged by their cumulative day-to-day performance. In both, those who refuse to play according to the rules get thrown out. Those whose performance is substandard sink toward the bottom. In neither are personal motivations important except insofar as they may contribute to effectiveness in action, and in this respect they play their part along with many other factors such as physique, intelligence, skill, training, and the like.

To sum up: Business is an ordered system which selects and rewards according to well understood criteria. The guiding principle is to get as near as possible to the top among corporations. Hence the need for maximum profits. Hence the need to devote profits once acquired to enhancing financial strength and speeding up growth. These things become the subjective aims and values of the business world because they are the objective requirements of the system. The character of the system determines the psychology of its members, not vice versa.

One corollary of this analysis requires particular emphasis. "At the historical dawn of capitalist production," Marx wrote, "avarice, and desire to get rich, are the ruling passions. . . . Accumulate! Accumulate! That is Moses and the prophets."[22] But he was careful to point out that this ruling passion was not an emanation of human nature but rather was the product of the system in which it played so crucial a role:

[The capitalist] shares with the miser the passion for wealth as wealth. But that which in the miser is a mere idiosyncrasy, is, in the capitalist, the effect of the social mechanism of which he is but one of the wheels. Moreover, the development of capitalist production makes it constantly necessary to keep increasing the amount of the capital laid out in a given industrial undertaking, and competition makes the immanent laws of capitalist production to be felt by each individual capitalist, as external coercive laws. It compels him to keep constantly extending his capital, in order to preserve it, but extend it he cannot, except by means of progressive accumulation.[23]

We have come a long way since the historical dawn of capitalist production, and even since Karl Marx wrote Das Kapital. Nowadays the avaricious capitalist, grasping for every penny and anxiously watching over his growing fortune, seems like a stereotype out of a nineteenth-century novel. The company man of today has a different attitude. To be sure, he likes to make as much money as he can, but he spends it freely, and the retirement benefits and other perquisites which he gets from his company enable him to take a rather casual attitude toward his personal savings. Noting the contrast between the modern businessman and his earlier counterpart, one might jump to the conclusion that the old drive has gone out of the system, that the classical picture of capitalism restlessly propelled forward by the engine of accumulation is simply inappropriate to the conditions of today.[24]

---

[22] Capital, Volume 1, Chapter 22, Section 4.

[23] Ibid.

[24] Schumpeter made this very mistake. "The bourgeoisie worked primarily in order to invest, and it was not so much a standard of consumption as a standard of accumulation that the bourgeoisie struggled for and tried to defend against governments that took the short-run view. With the decline of the driving power supplied by the family motive, the businessman's time-horizon shrinks, roughly, to his life expectation. And he might now be less willing than he was to fulfill that function of earning, saving and investing even if he saw no reason to fear that the results would but swell his tax bills. He drifts into an anti-saving frame of mind and accepts with an increasing readiness anti-saving theories that are indicative of a short-run philosophy." J. A. Schumpeter, Capitalism,

We can now see that this is a superficial view. The real capitalist today is not the individual businessman but the corporation. What the businessman does in his private life, his attitude toward the getting and spending of his personal income— these are essentially irrelevant to the functioning of the system. What counts is what he does in his company life and his attitude toward the getting and spending of the company's income. And here there can be no doubt that the making and accumulating of profits hold as dominant a position today as they ever did. Over the portals of the magnificent office building of today, as on the wall of the modest counting house of a century or two ago, it would be equally appropriate to find engraved the motto: "Accumulate! Accumulate! That is Moses and the Prophets."

VII

The replacement of the individual capitalist by the corporate capitalist constitutes an institutionalization of the capitalist function. The heart and core of the capitalist function is accumulation: accumulation has always been the prime mover of the system, the locus of its conflicts, the source of both its triumphs and its disasters. But only in the infancy of the system could accumulation be said to exhaust the obligations of the capitalist. With success came also responsibilities. In the words of Marx:

> When a certain stage of development has been reached, a conventional degree of prodigality, which is also an exhibition of wealth, and consequently a source of credit, becomes a business necessity to the "unfortunate" capitalist. Luxury enters into capital's expenses of representation. [25]

These expenses of representation have traditionally taken the form of conspicuous waste on the one hand and philanthropy on the other. Both have always had what would nowadays be called a public-relations purpose: the one to dazzle and overawe the public, the other to secure its loyalty and affection. Both have been borne by the capitalist in his private capacity.

_____
Socialism, and Democracy, New York, 1942, pp. 160-161. That none of this applies to the corporate capitalist seems to have escaped Schumpeter altogether.

[25] Capital, Volume 1, Chapter 22, Section 4.

One of the most striking changes in the American scene in recent years has been a marked decline of both types of expenditure by the aristocracy of the business world. The great estates of Newport and Southampton, the regal yachts of the Morgans and the Astors, the debutante parties costing half a million dollars or more—one now reads more about these things in history books than in the society pages of the daily paper. The Big Businessman of today (Texas oilmen excepted, as they should be) lives if not modestly at least in decent obscurity: the last thing he wants is to make a big splash with his wealth. Similarly, individual philanthropy seems to play a decreasingly prominent role—so much so that one of the country's biggest businessmen, writing about the problems of the corporate world, feels justified in titling one of his chapters "The Vanishing Philanthropist," [26]

These developments do not mean, however, that capital's expenses of representation have somehow been abolished. Like other aspects of the capitalist function, responsibility for meeting capital's expenses of representation has been institutionalized. Nowadays it is the corporation itself that has to maintain a high standard of living before the public, and it does so by erecting grandiose headquarters buildings, providing its functionaries with offices which grow plushier by the year, transporting them in fleets of company-owned jet planes and Cadillacs, granting them unlimited expense accounts, and so on and on. [27] Most of this is the sheerest kind of

_____
[26] Crawford H. Greenewalt, The Uncommon Man: The Individual in the Organization, New York, Toronto, London, 1959, pp. 113 ff.

[27] Consider the new sixty-story Chase Manhattan Bank building. "Tall enough at 813 feet to throw the early morning sun back at itself," says a brochure issued by the bank under the title A New Landmark for New York, "the Chase Manhattan Bank building represents the fulfillment of an architectural ideal and a high water mark in modern management. It was designed not just to function but to express—its soaring angularities bespeaking an era rather than a transient need. . . . When the building was in an embryonic state, it was decided that the decorative element which would best complement the stark simplicity of its modern architecture was fine art. Accordingly, the bank recruited the services of a committee of art experts to select works which would contribute to a warm and stimulating environment in which the employees would work and at the same time express the bank's concern with those things man holds dearest. The

conspicuous waste, correlated negatively, if at all, with productive efficiency; yet no corporation with serious claims to Big Business standing would dream of neglecting this aspect of its operations. Size, success, strength—the desiderata of corporate policy—must be not only achieved but also displayed for all the world to see. The need to dazzle and overawe is as great as ever, and the costs which it entails have certainly grown along with the growth of capital. What have changed are the form and method of conspicuous waste, not the purpose or content.

Much the same can be said about philanthropy. This too is being institutionalized, and though up to now foundations have taken the lead, the corporations themselves are playing an increasingly important role, especially in the field of providing private support for institutions of higher learning.[28] Doubtless those observers are right who see here a trend that will continue into the indefinite future; the end may well be that the cost of nearly all private philanthropy will be directly borne by corporations.

It is in this area of philanthropy, and the public-relations efforts which accompany it and are closely related to it, that we find a genuine kernel of

———————
works chosen to adorn private offices and reception areas range from the latest in abstract impressionism to primitive Americana and connote the bank's rich role in American history as well as its global interests. . . . 1 Chase Manhattan Plaza is really many things in one—a product of an age when reaching for the stars is no longer a figure of speech and men pierce the ocean depths as blithely as they cross the street—a bench mark in architectural history—a staggering complex of machinery—an art gallery unlike any other in the world—a towering symbol of Chase Manhattan's confidence in the future of the storied financial district." All Americans can share a legitimate pride in this monument to what man holds dearest, the more so since as taxpayers they pay about half its cost.

[28] One should not assume that this is all pure philanthropy. "Business corporations," writes William M. Compton, President of the Council for Financial Aid to Education, "are not benevolent institutions. But they can be 'benevolent' when considered benevolence is in the interests of their owners." Association of American Colleges Bulletin, March 1954. Presumably Mr. Compton knows from personal experience how corporations feel about these matters. Or to cite again Crawford

truth in the "soulful corporation" idea. In criticizing this notion earlier, we rejected the view in Kaysen's paper "The Social Significance of the Modern Corporation" that profit maximization has ceased to be the guiding principle of corporate conduct. But when Kaysen says that the modern corporation's "responsibilities to the general public are widespread" and lists among them "leadership in local charitable enterprises, concern with factory architecture and landscaping, provision of support for higher education, and even research in pure science," there is no reason to cavil. Having maximized their profits, corporations do feel called upon to engage in activities of this sort and almost certainly will do so to an increasing extent. If these are emanations of the corporate soul, then the existence of that metaphysical entity can be taken to be a fact. But it is a familiar soul, not a new one. Escaping from the dying body of the capitalist philanthropist, it has migrated to the capitalist corporation. For the system as a whole, there has been no net increase of soulfulness.

VIII

We have tried to show that the giant corporation of today is an engine for maximizing profits and accumulating capital to at least as great an extent as the individual enterprise of an earlier period. But it is not merely an enlarged and institutionalized version of the personal capitalist. There are major differences between these types of business enterprise, and at least two of them are of key importance to a general theory of monopoly capitalism: the corporation has a longer time horizon than the

———————
Greenewalt, President of Du Pont: the continued progress of American industry depends on the nation's having "a balanced research program, which means that it must supplement its applied research with an amount of fundamental research sufficient to provide the basic information upon which all scientific progress depends. . . . A substantial amount of such research is now being done by industry. The major responsibility, however, must rest with our universities, for only they can provide the atmosphere in which truly fundamental scientific inquiry can flourish. The problem is not so much one of persuasion as of finance; it is here that industry, by supporting academic fundamental research, can at the same time serve its stockholders and supply a public need." The Uncommon Man, pp. 137-138.

individual capitalist, and it is a more rational cal-
culator. Both differences are fundamentally related to the incomparably larger scale of the corporations's operations.

The corporation is in principle immortal and
inculcates in its functionaries a long time horizon,
not because of its special legal form (after all, a
corporation can be wound up just as easily as a
proprietorship) but because what it "incorporates"
is a vast and complex capital investment the value
of which depends on its being maintained as a going
concern. Similarly, the size of the corporation's
operations enforces a far-reaching specialization
and rationalization of the managerial function.
Perhaps the best analogy to an executive's job, "
writes Crawford H. Greenewalt, President of the
Du Pont Company, "is that of the symphony con-
ductor under whose hand a hundred or so highly
specialized and yet very different skills become
a single effort of great effectiveness. "[29]   And as
to the rationalistic ethos of the big corporation
there could hardly be more eloquent testimony than
the rapid spread of methods (and the personnel to
work them) of the kind so strongly emphasized in
the statement by Earley quoted on pages 24-26—
cost accounting, budgeting, data processing, management consulting, operations research, and
much else besides.

The long corporate time horizon and the rationalization of management generate certain characteristic attitudes and modes of behavior. Of these
perhaps the most important are (1) a systematic
avoidance of risk-taking, and (2) an attitude of
live-and-let-live toward other members of the
corporate world. In both respects the change from
the old-fashioned individual enterprise is so great
in quantity as to amount to a change in quality.

(1) With regard to risk-taking, the difference
is not so much that the individual capitalist was
inherently more of a gambler than the corporation
(though very likely he was) but rather that he had
neither the capability nor the habit of calculating
risks. He was like the little fellow who keeps on
playing the numbers game either not knowing or
not caring about the certain odds against him; while
the big corporation is like the professional gambler
who takes good care that the odds are in his favor.
The time horizon factor also plays a role here:
the corporation, being under no pressure to realize quick returns and disposing over ample resources, approaches a new development with care

and circumspection and does not make a final commitment until the relevant investigations and preparations have been carried out. Finally, and in
a sense ironically, the corporation knows how to
use for its own ends the very weaknesses of the
small enterprise which it has outgrown. When a
new industry or field of operations is being opened
up, the big corporation tends to hold back deliberately and to allow individual entrepreneurs or small
businesses to do the vital pioneering work. Many
fail and drop out of the picture, but those which
succeed trace out the most promising lines of development for the future. It is at this stage that
the big corporations move to the center of the
stage. Referring to the electric appliance field
which he knew from long experience, T. K. Quinn,
formerly a Vice President of General Electric,
wrote: "I know of no original product invention,
not even electric shavers or heating pads, made by
by any of the giant laboratories or corporations,
with the possible exception of the household garbage grinder. . . . The record of the giants is
one of moving in, buying out and absorbing the
smaller creators. "[30]   Though no general information on this subject seems to be available, there
is reason to believe that Mr. Quinn's statement
holds true of many other industries.

(2) The attitude of live-and-let-live which characterizes Big Business likewise derives from the
magnitude of the corporation's investment and from
the calculating rationality of its management. By
and large, this attitude is reserved for other big
corporations and does not extend to the smaller bus
businessman. For example, the big three automobile companies behave toward one another in a
way that Schumpeter appropriately called "corespective, "[31] while their behavior to the scores of

---

[29] The Uncommon Man, p. 64.

[30] T. K. Quinn, Giant Business: Threat to Democracy, New York, 1953, p. 117. After this
chapter was published in the July-August 1962
issue of Monthly Review, we received a letter from
Mr. Morrison Sharp of Racine, Wisconsin, which
reads in part as follows: "Mr. Quinn might consult
either his own legal department, or the Racine
Chamber of Commerce, or even the In-Sink-Erator
Company of Racine, which invented and perfected
the household garbage grinder. Common gossip
has it that the giant GE makes its own brand-name
machine under rights from the In-Sink-Erator
Company after the settlement of a long and successful lawsuit. " Alas for illusions!

[31] Capitalism, Socialism, and Democracy, p. 90n.

thousands of dealers who sell their products to the public is notoriously overbearing and dictatorial. The reason, of course, is that each of the big ones recognizes the strength and retaliatory power of the other big ones and as a matter of deliberately calculated policy avoids provoking them. But corespective behavior is by no means limited to competitors. If one big corporation is not a competitor of another, it is quite likely to be either a customer or a supplier; and in this realm of corporate relations the sovereign principle is reciprocity, which enjoins corespective behavior as surely as competition does. In addition, the Big Business community is numerically small, comprising perhaps 10,000 or so people for the entire country, and its members are tied together by a whole network of social as well as economic ties. Conscious of their power and standing in the larger national community, they naturally tend to develop a group ethic which calls for solidarity and mutual help among themselves and for presenting a common front to the outside world.

It wasn't always so. In the early days when Big Business was emerging from the jungle of small-scale competition, corespective behavior was rare indeed. Even the railroads had to go through a series of exhausting rate wars before they finally got it into their corporate heads that roadbeds and tracks and locomotives and cars would go on being used to carry passengers and freight whatever might happen to security owners or rival managements. The original tycoons, faced with the consequences of cutthroat competition, sought a way out through a policy of ruthless monopolization. The victims of this drive, however, were numerous and not without influence. By entering into a temporary alliance with dissatisfied farmers and workers, they succeeded in getting the antitrust laws passed, which, though far from achieving their avowed aim of preserving (or restoring) free competition, nevertheless put very real roadblocks in the way of full monopolization. For this reason, as well as others of a technological and economic nature, there were few cases in which one corporation or even one financial interest group succeeded in establishing effective control over an entire market.

It was under these circumstances the Big Businessmen began to learn the virtues of corespective behavior. The process of learning was hastened as the highly individualistic tycoon passed from the scene and the company man gradually took his place as the typical representative of corporate business.

Today there are probably fewer genuine monopolies than there were at the turn of the century, but there is also infinitely less cutthroat competition. And this brings us straight to the problem of the interaction of the corporate giants.

Part 4

MILITARY-INDUSTRIAL COMPLEX

IS THERE A MILITARY INDUSTRIAL COMPLEX WHICH PREVENTS PEACE?: CONSENSUS AND COUNTERVAILING POWER IN PLURALISTIC SYSTEMS*

Marc Pilisuk and Thomas Hayden

Introduction

The term "military-industrial complex" is very much in the literature. If its most sinister depictions are correct, then the peace researcher who works with the hope that his research may actually improve chances for world peace is wasting his time. A research finding, like a bit of knowledge, is always double-edged in what it portends for application. The project which tells us the surest steps to peace, tells us with equal certainty the steps which must be bypassed if peace is shunned. If there exists an omnipotent elite, committed to militarism, then there is simply no basis for hope that voices for peace have gotten, or can get, an influential channel into inner policy circles. If, on the other hand, the pluralist thesis can be said to apply in full even to basic policy directions of preparedness for war or for peace, then some influential decision makers must be eagerly awaiting the research findings on paths to peace with intentions to press for their immediate application.

Because we agree with neither of the above positions, because we believe that most research workers in this area tend either to ignore or to over-rate the potential consequences of their work to peace, and because we feel that consideration of the conditions which dictate major directions of policy is essential for an evaluation of any contribution to peace research, we are bringing the concept of the "military-industrial complex" to both the microscope and the scalpel. The implications of this inquiry point to a research approach which does have relevance to the decision process and to the most central agencies of social change, and resistance to change, within American society.

*From Marc Pilisuk and Thomas Hayden, "Is There a Military Industrial Complex Which Prevents Peace?: Consensus and Contervailing Power in a Pluralistic System," Journal of Social Issues, Vol. XXI, No. 3, pp. 67-113. Reprinted by permission.

The New Concern

Not since the 30's has there been such a rash of attention to military-industrial power as there is today. Then, as now, the President himself raised the spectre of improper military influence. FDR, on the eve of a Senate investigation of the munitions industry, said flatly that the arms race was a "grave menace . . . due in no small measure to the uncontrolled activities of the manufacturers and merchants of the engines of destruction and it must be met by the concerted action of the people of all nations." (Raymond, 1964, p. 262; also Congressional Quarterly Weekly Report, 6, pp. 265-278.) While Dwight Eisenhower did not sound as militant as Roosevelt, and while he never adopted FDR's 1932 campaign pledge to "take the profits out of war," he did resume a popular tradition with his warning about the "unwarrented influence" of the military-industrial complex. It may be a significant measure of the times that one President could make such warnings in his very first campaign for office, while the other couched it among several other going-away remarks.

The 30's serve as a prelude to the 60's, too, in the area of congressional investigation of militarism. Then it was Senator Gerald P. Nye investigating the fabulous World War I profits of U.S. Steel and Hercules Powder and discovering, with horror, the instrumental role of munitions-makers and other commercial interests in beginning the war. Nye revealed, for example, that the American ambassador in London informed President Wilson in 1917 that probably "the only way of maintaining our pre-eminent trade position and averting a panic is by declaring war on Germany" (Raymond, p. 264). As Roosevelt was more aggressive than Eisenhower, so also were Nye, Borah and other popular Senators more aggressive than their present counterparts in the 60's. But, nevertheless, similar issues are now being raised in congressional committees. The most shocking of these may be found in the hearings of Senator John McClellen's committee on Pyramiding of Profits and Costs in the Missile Procurement Program. This report pointed out the likely danger that the government "can be placed in the unenviable position of reluctant acquiescence to the demands and conditions set by the contractor," and that "profits were pyramided on other profits without any relationship at all to the effort being expended by those making the profit." In what might have been front page scandal in any area but national defense, the committee documented two mechanisms by which millions upon millions of dollars of excess profit have been reaped by the defense industries. The mechanisms are: a) claiming profits on work subcontracted to other firms (which in turn subcontract portions of their work to others and charge a profit on the sub-subcontracted work, too), and b) overestimating the subcontracting costs (on incentive type contracts) thereby reaping huge profit rates by undercutting the original estimates. However, the contrast with the 30's is clear; Senator McClellen only wants to improve the efficiency of what he calls "these necessary monopolies." (U.S. Senate, Committee on Government Operations, report of the Permanent Subcommittee on Investigations, Pyramiding of Profits and Costs in the Missile Procurement Program, March 31, 1964.) A more far-reaching investigation, under the direction of Senator Clark, deals with the convertibility of the defense empire to civilian job-creating tasks. He claims that 1) the new defense emphasis on electronics and on research and development, and the monopolization of defense by a few companies and geographic areas, considerably reduces the potential effect of defense as an economic stabilizer; and 2) that certain firms, especially those in the aerospace industry, are suffering an overcapacity crisis that spurs them to insist on more missiles than the nation needs. (U.S. Senate, Committee on Labor and Public Welfare, report of the Subcommittee on Employment and Manpower, Convertibility of Space and Defense Resources to Civilian Needs: A Search for New Employment Potentials, 88th Congress, 2d Session, 1964.) Senator Clark's hearings, too, are mild in contrast to the 30's. Even milder, however, was the recent survey report of Senator Hubert Humphrey, who says it is "nonsense" to believe American industry is opposed to disarmament. (U.S. Senate, Committee on Senate Foreign Relations, Subcommittee on Disarmament, The Economic Impact of Arms Control Agreements, Congressional Record, October 5, 1962, pp. 2139-2194.)

Another measure of interest in military-industrial power is the number of popular and technical books dealing with the subject. In the 30's, the widely read books were Davenport's Zaharoff,

High Priest of War, Engelbrecht and Haneghen's Merchants of Death and Selde's Iron, Blood and Profits. Two decades then passed before the work of C. Wright Mills began to attract broad attention to the subject of organized militarism. Including Mills' pioneering books, there have been at least 21 major books published in this area during the past several years. Many of them are by journlists (Cook, Coffin, Raymond, Swomley, Wise and Ross); some by economists (Benoit, Boulding, Melman, Peck, Perlo, Scherer); sociologists (Etzioni, Horowitz, Janowitz, Mills); political scientists (Meisel, Rogow); novelists (Bailey, Burdick, Knebel, Sutton); and at least one physical scientist (Lapp).

Whatever the objective referent, if any, of a "military-industrial complex" may be, it is undeniable that the concept occupies an important role in the political consciousness of many persons, on a scale without precedent since the 30's. It is a telling fact that the new literature, with the exceptions of Mills, Cook and Perlo, still lacks the bite of the old, and that the proposed solutions are quite "modest." In the 30's a typical popular solution, proposed by the Nye Committee but never implemented, was the nationalization of the munitions industries. By the 60's the reverse has happened; most military research, development, and production is done by private companies subsidized by the Federal government. The loci of military-political-industrial cooperation are so pervasive and frequent that it becomes a hair-splitting task to identify specifically any "merchants of death." Also, the scale of potential destruction has so increased, the nature of warfare strategy so changed, and the existence of the military in peacetime so accepted, that it seems quaint to associate defense contractors with bloody hands. Furthermore, the assumed threat of communist expansion has become the ultimate justification of the post-war military buildup, whereas in the past such buildups could be attributed more clearly to industrial profit and power motives. Probably reasons such as these explain both the long silence and the modest character of the current resurgence in discussion of these matters.

But these reasons account partially for the inadequacy of analysis as well. The question, "Does there exist a military-industrial complex which prevents peace?" at first seems debatable in straightforward yes-or-no terms. Indeed, it might have been answerable in the 20's or 30's but not in the post-war period. When there is permanent intermingling and coordination among military, industrial, and governmental elites, and whenever greater war-preparedness can be justified by reference to the communist movement, it becomes a much "stickier" question. Because it is sticky, the easiest conclusion to support is that a "complex" simply does not exist as an omnipresent obstacle to policy change. Indeed, this belief has become the accepted norm for "informed" discussion of interests vested in the perpetuation of military preparedness. The next most easily supported conclusion would be that we have become trapped in the hell-fires of militarism by a sinister but concealed elite of military-industrial leaders, which through its puppets, pulls the strings on every major policy decision. This latter theory is non-conformist, radical, and smacks too closely of classical conspiracy theory to be palatable to most scholars. Indeed, the dominant attitude (explicit or tacit) in most of the new literature is that there exists no military-industrial complex capable of preventing peace. It is claimed that the military-industrial complex operates as a sub-group within the limits of an essentially civilian society. In this view the complex is seen as making an interest-conscious equation of its own interests with those of the nation as a whole. But, it is argued, this tendency of power aggrandizement is checked by countervailing interest blocks in the society. Moreover, the "complex" is not seen as having a corrosive effect on democratic processes; even if it is conceded that military and technological expertise or well-financed public relations give the "complex" unusual privilege and visibility, this is no different in principle, from certain other influential groups, all of which are limited by the web of constraints but comprise a pluralist society. Usually, it is added that the internal differences in the "complex" such as differences among the separate services or between the military and the industrial procurement sectors, tend to restrict further its ability to impose a policy "line" on the United States. These points of view appear in scattered form throughout the literature. A few examples are cited to demonstrate this.

Wise and Ross call their brilliantly-rich study of the CIA The Invisible Government without realizing the theoretical problems immediately raised by such a title. Does the CIA, and the broader "intelligence community" actually have the tools and, more importantly, the prerogatives of sovereignty (for its own operations) associated with the concept of "government"? If this is the case, then the conventional pluralist argument would be perforated decisively, because it rests on the assumption that no power centers are unaccountable to democratic review. The nature of the evidence used in the book, however, precludes an objective answer to this question. Using case studies primarily, although there also are chapters on the CIA structure, the authors are concerned with such issues as: the contradictions between sinister CIA practices and professed U.S. policy objectives; the tendency of the CIA to support only conservative or reactionary governments; the danger that the CIA can influence specific policy objectives of the U.S. government, as in the case of the U-2 interference with the 1960 Paris summit meeting; the progressive acceptance in America of subversive techniques as part of a "necessary Cold War strategy." But it is explicitly maintained that the "invisible government" is subordinate, at least so far, to the visible one in general as well as in nearly every specific case. At worst, it has an undefined "quasi-independent" status which should be brought under somewhat greater congressional and executive review (p. 352). Also, the authors suggest fewer statements of misinformation and "more discreet silence" by the government "in difficult circumstances" (p. 356). Accepting the broad lines of government policy, but realizing the dilemmas of such a stance, the authors conclude:

> The secret intelligence machinery of the government can never be totally reconciled with the tradition of a free republic. But in a time of Cold War, the solution lies not in dismantling this machinery, but in bringing it under greater control. The resultant danger of exposure is far less than the danger of secret power. If we err as a society, let it be on the side of control (356).

New York Times reporter, Jack Raymond, is much less forboding in his Power at the Pentagon, but assumes the same framework of government control over the defense establishment. He goes further, however, to point that "the United States could embrace militarism under civilian as well as military auspices." With the same popular democratic values as Wise and Ross (the better journalists remain pugnaciously committed to the civil liberties), he believes that the traditional arguments against military dominance must be broadened to challenge civilian, or bureaucratic, dominance as well.

The military apparatus must not be an automated juggernaut whose operations we take for granted. We ought to raise hell with it constantly, ask questions, demand truthful answers. (334)

This point of view is reflected also in periodic statements by political leaders as disparate as Dwight Eisenhower and Hubert Humphrey. Eisenhower's speech, as mentioned, was instrumental in spurring and legitimizing later discussions. His point of view was that the military-industrial complex might exercise "unwarranted influence":

In the councils of government, we must guard against the acquisition of unwarranted influence, whether sought or unsought, by the military-industrial complex. The potential for the disastrous rise of misplaced power exists and will persist. . . . Only an alert and knowledgeable citizenry can compel the proper meshing of the huge industrial and military machinery of defense with our peaceful methods and goals, so that security and liberty may prosper together. (Eisenhower's Farewell Address)

Humphrey's Subcommittee report claimed that by and large U.S. industries not only could, but would be delighted to shift to full peacetime production of goods and services.[1] According to Humphrey, the military-industrial complex that President Eisenhower warned against "is one which appears to be centered in a few hands and in a few key places." Where Raymond attempted to use fragmentary evidence, mostly personal interviews and citations of particular instances, and Eisenhower cited no evidence at all, Humphrey is more like Wise and Ross in his attempt to generalize from studies of a "slice" of military-industrial organization. That is, even were we to accept his evidence as a valid representation of industrial reality, it still neglects the interrelation of industry with military and political interests. It isolates a part from the whole, then makes claims about the nature of the whole.

While extremely interesting and useful, it takes

the word of contractors as a valid measure of the desirability and feasibility of conversion. No doubt such words are critically important, but they constitute only a piece of objective reality. It is with such pieces that the existence of an obstructing elite is denied.

Disarmament and the American Economy, edited by Benoit and Boulding, is a collection of essays and studies by several separate individuals. That many of these individuals have connections in the worlds of defense, industry, and government probably reflects the degree to which these worlds command the intellectual resources of modern America. It is a book which received considerable attention in policy-making circles when it appeared last year. It is considerably more lenient in its interpretation of a military-industrial complex, merely pointing out that a few vested interests of long duration are among the structural obstacles to a disarmament pact. These obstacles, according to Emile Benoit, can be overcome rather easily by economic growth in sectors which could more lucratively employ those presently in defense-related work. Prosperity becomes the lubricant for change. But this approach glosses over the existence of propensities to place short-run security over long-run prosperity, and so avoids delineating the kind of political forces which might oppose economic change. As the authors themselves admit, their volume is abstracted from politics. In plainer fact, this abstracting process considerably dissolves any military-industrial complex which might exist. What is left is a pooh-poohing of the threat of a complex, plus the claim that increased overall demand, and therefore new employment opportunities, will make "structural adjustments" manageable:

[The massive defense complex] does not mean that disarmament is impossible or that the possibilities of peace are threatened by the vested interests of an holy alliance of generals and war contractors. It does mean that to redefine the content of many defense jobs will be a far easier and more constructive solution than to abolish them. (291)

While the authors address themselves only to the question of what the economy can do if disarmament should somehow come about, they are obviously aware of the potential socio-political consequences of removing the threat of the more foreboding economic consequences of disarmament which have sometimes been suggested. Perhaps

---

[1] Senator Humphrey's investigation consisted of an inquiry sent by mail to a sample of major industrial defense contractors asking about their willingness to shift to non-defense areas if cutbacks were necessitated by progress toward arms reduction. For some unexplicable reason the results were classified but the Senator's statement indicated apparent readiness to make the shift.

the authors assume that only through a new con-consensus, sweetened by economic opportunities, can there be a chance for disarmament. That, however, is allowing the problem of social change to be defined by the hope for disarmament. Such an approach may well be a utopian one, and tends to the pole opposite Wise and Ross among the be-lievers in civilian control.

Easily the most well-researched book of this kind is The Weapons Acquisition Process by Peck and Scherer, both at Harvard Business School. This book is by and for persons with a sophisti-cated business viewpoint. After several hundred pages of detailed data and analysis, it concludes that the weapons acquisition process is honest and efficient. However, it too is relatively "above" the politics of the defense economy. Much politics, they find, is ritualistic, with "little impact at the operating levels where the source selection de-cision is made" (382). Where they believe poli-tics do enter, for instance when competing pro-ducers of the Bomarc and Nike-Hercules take out full-page advertisements, they defend its practice. While President Eisenhower warned against the "munitions lobby," in the Bomarc-Nike-Hercules case Peck and Scherer believe that "selling" the Government is symptomatic of a healthy tendency.

> Both contractors and sponsoring agencies, which are often the contractors' allies, be-lieve their weapons programs are essential to the national defense. If this sincerity does not come from pride in invention, it soon develops as a result of constantly liv-ing with the idea. This zeal serves a use-ful function, since it fortifies the partici-pants' . . . personal contact with "the right people" and is an effective means of getting ideas accepted. Similarly, creating public demand for a program through advertising and feature articles is a way of winning over or bypassing balky decision-makers. (243)

This book thus explicitly defends the "advocates" who exaggerate their weapons' capabilities, "what-ever the effect of this (military-industrial) com-plex upon grand strategy" (243).

Whether such salesmanship or advocacy is as ethical as it is effective is a question not raised in the Peck and Scherer book. One of our own in-terviews with the vice-president of a defense con-tracting firm specializing in Research and Devel-opment, sites the positive ethical value of develop-ing and promoting strategic conceptions of military function (which include the use of the weapon sys-tem being worked upon). Such promotion is an absolutely essential buttress to the military ser-vices which are incapable of constructing their own strategic doctrines. The system manager con-cept, a concept used by some prime contractors to justify profit pyramiding, in testimony before the McClellen Committee, seems to suggest that promotion of the concept of the entire weapon sys-tem is part of the contractor's service to the mili-tary and as such is not only ethical but deserving of compensation.

None of these denials of irresponsible military-industrial power marshall very significant evidence to support their views. There are examples given of specific conflicts between civilian and military groups which were lost by the military (e.g., the dropping of General Walker, the refusal to be first to break the moratorium on testing). There are examples given of heated divisions between the services over what military strategy should be pursued (the arguments over conventional warfare in the late 50's and the more recent RS 70 contro-versy). There are sociological studies which re-veal underlying diversities within single corpora-tions, between competing corporations, and within the demographic and institutional character of each branch of the armed services.[2] And, throughout, there are citations of American pluralism as an automatic check system against any elite group.[3]

At a more general level, these fragments of evidence point toward three grounds for denying that a military-industrial complex prevents peace:

1) it is held that the scope of decisions made by any interest group is quite narrow and cannot be said to govern anything so broad as foreign policy.

---

[2] See Janowitz for a good sociological study of in-terservice differences.

[3] For the thesis that a "peacefare state" counter-weighs the "warfare state," see Klaus Knorr's re-view of Fred J. Cook in the Journal of Conflict Re-solution, VII, 4 (December, 1963). The "pluralist position," which usually is that the social system has semi-automatic checking mechanisms against tyranny, appears as basic in discussions not only of the military, but of economics and politics as well. See Robert Dahl, Who Governs?"; John K. Gal-braith, American Capitalism; Seymour Martin Lip-set, Political Man; Talcott Parsons, The Social System.

2) it is held that the "complex" is not mono-lithic, not self-conscious, and not coordinated, the presumed attributes of a ruling elite.

3) it is held that the military industrial complex does not wield power if the term "power" is defined as the ability to realize its will even against the resistance of others and regardless of external conditions.

These formulations, to repeat, are made neither explicitly nor consistently in the new literature. But they crystallize the basic questions about definition which the new literature raises. Moreover, they are quite definitely the major contentions made by academic criticisms of power elite theory. The more widely read of these academic critics include Daniel Bell, Robert Dahl, and Talcott Parsons. Since their critiques are mainly directed at the work of C. Wright Mills, it is with Mills that we will begin to analyze the theories which claim there is a military-industrial complex blocking peace.

The Thesis of Elite Control

Mills is by far the most formidable exponent of the theory of a power elite. In his view, the period in America since World War II has been dominated by the ascendance of corporation and military elites to positions of institutional power. These "commanding heights" allow them to exercise control over the trends of the business cycle and international relations. The Cold War set the conditions which legitimize this ascendance, and the decline and incorporation of significant left-liberal movements, such as the CIO, symbolizes the end of opposition forces. The power elite monopolizes sovereignty, in that political initiative and control stem mainly from the top hierarchical levels of position and influence. Through the communications system the elite facilitates the growth of a politically indifferent mass society below the powerful institutions. This, according to the Mills argument, would explain why an observer finds widespread apathy. Only a small minority believes in actual participation in the larger decisions which affect their existence and only the ritual forms of "popular democracy" are practiced by the vast majority. Mills' argument addresses itself to the terms of the three basic issues we have designated, i.e., scope of decision power, awareness of common interest, and the definition of power exerted.

By scope, we are referring to the sphere of society over which an elite is presumed to exercise power. Mills argues that the scope of this elite is general, embracing all the decisions which in any way could be called vital (slump and boom, peace and war, etc.). He does not argue that each decision is directly determined, but rather that the political alternatives from which the "Deciders" choose are shaped and limited by the elite through its possession of all the large-scale institutions. By this kind of argument, Mills avoids the need to demonstrate how his elite is at work during each decision. He speaks instead in terms of institutions and resources. But the problem is that his basic evidence is of a rather negative kind. No major decisions have been made for 20 years contrary to the policies of anti-communism and corporate or military aggrandizement; therefore a power elite must be prevailing. Mills might have improved his claims about the scope of elite decisions by analysing a series of actual decisions in terms of the premises which were not debated. This could point to the mechanisms (implicit or explicit) which led to the exclusion of these premises from debate. But this and other means he might have found more satisfying evidence of the common, though perhaps tacit, presuppositions of seemingly disparate institutions. He then might have developed a framework analyzing "scope" on different levels. The scope of the Joint Chiefs of Staff, for instance, could be seen as limited, while at the same time the Joint Chiefs could be placed in a larger elite context having larger scope. Whether this could be shown awaits research of this kind. Until it is done, however, Mills theory of scope remains open to attack, but, conversely, is not subject to refutation.

Mills' theory also eludes the traditional requirements for inferring monolithic structure, i.e., consciousness of elite status, and coordination. The modern tradition of viewing elites in this way began with Mosca's The Ruling Class in a period when family units and inheritance systems were the basic means of conferring power. Mills departs from this influential tradition precisely because of his emphasis on institutions at the basic elements. If the military, political, and economic institutional orders involve a high coincidence of interest, then the groups composing the institutional orders need not be monolithic, conscious, and coordinated, yet still they can exercise elite power.[4]

[4] See James H. Meisel, The Myth of the Ruling Class, for the best availabel discussion of this innovation in theorizing about elites.

This means specifically that a military-industrial complex could exist as an expression of a certain fixed ideology (reflecting common institutional needs), yet be "composed" of an endless shuffle of specific groups. For instance, our tables show 82 companies have dropped out of the list of 100 top defense contractors, and only 36 "durables" have remained on the list in the years since 1940. In terms of industry, the percentage of contracts going to the automobile industry dropped from 25 percent in World War II to 4 percent in the missile age. At the same time, the aircraft companies went from 34 to 54 percent of all contracts, and the electronics industry from 9 to 28 percent (Peck and Scherer, 1962). Mills' most central argument is that this ebb-and-flow is not necessarily evidence for the pluralists. His stress is on the unities which underlie the procession of competition and change. The decision to change the technology of warfare was one which enabled one group to "overcome" another in an overall system to which both are fundamentally committed. Moreover, the decision issued from the laboratories and planning boards of the defense establishment and only superficially involved any role for public opinion. The case studies of weapons development by Peck and Scherer, in which politics is described as a marginal ritual, would certainly buttress Mills' point of view.

Making this institution analysis enables Mills to make interesting comments on his human actors. The integration of institutions means that hundreds of individuals become familiar with several roles: General, politician, lobbyist, defense contractor. These men are the power elite, but they need not know it. They conspire, but conspiracy is not absolutely essential to their maintenance. They mix together easily, but can remain in power even if they are mostly anonymous to each other. They make decisions, big and small, sometimes with the knowledge of others and sometimes not, which ultimately control all the significant action and resources of society.

Where this approach tends to fall short, is in its unclarity about how discontinuities arise. Is the military-industrial complex a feature of American society which can disappear and still leave the general social structure intact? Horst Brand has suggested a tension between financial companies and the defense industries because of the relatively few investment markets created by defense (1962). Others are beginning to challenge the traditional view that defense spending stimulates high demand and employment. Their claim is that the concentration of contracts in a few states, the monopolization of defense and space industry by the largest 75 or 100 corporations, the low multiplier effect of the new weapons, the declining numbers of blue-collar workers required, and other factors, make the defense economy more of a drag than a stimulant (Melman et al., 1963; Etzioni, 1964). Mills died before these trends became the subject of debate, but he might have pioneered in discussion of them if his analytic categories had differentiated more finely between various industries and interest groups in his power elite. His emphasis was almost entirely on the "need" for a "permanent war economy" just when that need was being questioned even among his elite.

However, this failure does not necessarily undermine the rest of Mills' analysis. His institutional analysis is still the best means of identifying a complex without calling it monolithic, conscious and coordinated. Had he differentiated more exactly he might have been able to describe various degrees of commitment to an arms race, a rightist ideology constricting the arena of meaningful debate, and other characteristics of a complex. This task remains to be done, and will be discussed at a later point.

Where Mills' theory is most awkward is in his assertions that the elite can, and does, make its decisions against the will of others and regardless of external conditions. This way of looking at power is inherited by Mills, and much of modern sociology, directly from Max Weber. What is attributed to the elite is a rather fantastic quality: literal omnipotence. Conversely, any group that is not able to realize its will even against the resistance of others is only "influential" but not an elite. Mills attempts to defend this viewpoint but, in essence, modifies it. He says he is describing a tendency, not a finalized state of affairs. This is a helpful device in explaining cracks in the monolith—for instance, the inability of the elite to establish a full corporate state against the will of small businessmen. However, it does not change the ultimate argument—that the power elite cannot become more than a tendency, cannot realize its actual self, unless it takes on the quality of omnipotence.

When power is defined as this kind of dominance, it is easily open to critical dispute. The conception of power depicts a vital and complex social system as essentially static, as having within it a set of stable governing components, with precharted interests which infiltrate and control every outpost of decision-authority. Thereby, internal accommodation is made necessary and significant change, aside from growth, becomes impossible. This conception goes beyond the idea of social or economic determinism. In fact, it defines a "closed social system." A "closed system" may be a dramatic image, but it is a forced one as well. Its defender sees events such as the rise of the labor movement essentially as a means of rationalizing modern capitalism. But true or false as this may be, did not the labor movement also constitute a "collective will" which the elite could not resist? An accommodation was reached, probably more on the side of capital than labor, but the very term "accommodation" implies the existence of more than one independent will. On a world scale, this becomes even more obvious. Certainly the rise of communism has not been through the will of capitalists, and Mills would be the first to agree. Nor does the elite fully control technological development; surely the process of invention has some independent, even if minor, place in the process of social change.

Mills' definition of power as dominance ironically serves the pluralist argument, rather than countering it. When power is defined so extremely, it becomes rather easy to claim that such power is curbed in the contemporary United States. The pluralists can say that Mills has conjured up a bogeyman to explain his own failure to realize his will. This is indeed what has been done in review after review of Mills' writings. A leading pluralist thinker, Edward Shils, says that Mills was too much influenced by Trotsky and Kafka:

> Power, although concentrated, is not so soncentrated so powerful, or so permeative as Professor Mills seems to believe . . . . There have been years in Western history, e.g. in Germany during the last years of the Weimer Republic and under Nazis when reality approximated this picture more closely. . . . But as a picture of Western societies, and not just as an ideal type of extreme possibilities which might be realized if so much else that is vital were lacking, it will not do. (Shils, 1961)

But is Mills' definition the only suitable one here? If it is, then the pluralists have won the debate. But if there is a way to designate an irresponsible elite without giving it omnipotence, then the debate may be recast at least.

This fundamental question is not answered in the other major books which affirm the existence of a military-industrial complex. Cook's The Warfare State and Perlo's Militarism and Industry are good examples of this literature which is theoretically inferior to Mill's perplexing account.

Cook's volume has been pilloried severely by deniers of the military-industrial complex. At least it has the merit of creating discussion by being one of the few dissenting books distributed widely on a commercial basis. It suffers, however, from many of the same unclarities typical of the deniers. Its title assumes a "warfare state" while its evidence, although rich, is only a compilation of incidents, pronouncements, and trends, lacking any framework for weighing and measuring. From his writing several hypothesis can be extracted about the "face of the Warfare State," all of them suggestive but none of them conclusive: 1) the Department of Defense owns more property than any other organization in the world:[5] 2) between 60 and 70 percent of the national budget is consistently allocated to defense or defense related expenditures: 3) the Military and Big Business join in an inevitable meeting of minds over billions of dollars in contracts the one has to order and the other to fulfill: 4) the 100 top corporations monopolize three-fourths of the contracts, 85 percent of them being awarded without competition; 5) as much as one-third of all production and service indirectly depends on defense; 6) business and other conservative groups, even though outside of the Defense establishment, benefit from the warfare emphasis because it keeps subordinate the welfare-state which is anathema to them (pages 20-24, 162-202).

Cook's work, much more than Mills' is open to the counter-argument that no monolithic semi-conspiratorial elite exists. Even his definitions of vested interests are crude and presumed. Moreover, he suffers far more than Mills from a failure to differentiate between groups. For instance, there is nothing in his book (written in 1962) which would explain the economic drag of defense spending,

---

[5] Swomley (1964) accounts for Department of Defense holdings equivalent in size to eight states of the U.S.A. Kenneth Boulding, including personnel as well as property criteria, calls the Department of Defense the world's third largest socialist state. (Personal discussion, 1963.)

which Cook perceptively observed in a Nation article, "The Coming Politics of Disarmament" in 1963. One year he wrote that Big Business was being fattened off war contracts, but the next year the "prolonged arms race has started, at last, to commit a form of economic hara-kiri." "Hara-kiri" does not happen spontaneously; it is a culmination of long-developing abnormalities. That Cook could not diagnose them before they became common in congressional testimony illustrates the lack of refinement in his 1962 analysis. Cook's failure lies in visualizing a monolith, which obscures the strains which promote new trends and configurations.

It is in this attention to strains that Perlo's book is useful. He draws interesting connections between the largest industrial corporations and the defense economy, finding that defense accounts for 12 percent of the profits of the 25 largest firms. He adds the factor of foreign investment as one which creates a further propensity in favor of a large defense system, and he calculates that military business and foreign investments combined total 40 percent of the aggregate profits among the top 25. He draws deeper connections between companies and the major financial groups controlling their assets.

This kind of analysis begins to reveal important disunities within the business community. For instance, it can be seen that the Rockefellers are increasing their direct military investments while maintaining their largest foreign holdings in extremely volatile Middle Eastern and Latin American companies. The Morgans are involved in domestic industries of a rather easy-to-convert type, and their main foreign holdings are in the "safer" European countries, although they too have "unsafe" mining interests in Latin America and Africa. The First National City Bank, while having large holdings in Latin American sugar and fruit, has a more technical relation to its associated firms than the stock-owner relation. The Mellons have sizeable oil holdings on Kuwait, but on the whole are less involved in defense than the other groups. The DuPonts, traditionally the major munitions makers, are "diversified" into the booming aerospace and plutonium industries, but their overseas holdings are heavily in Europe. Certain other groups with financial holdings, such as Young and Eaton interests in Cleveland, have almost no profit stake in defense or foreign investments. On the other hand, some of the new wealth in Los Angeles is deeply committed to the aerospace industry.

Perlo makes several differentiations of this sort, including the use of foreign-policy statements by leading industrial groups. But he does not have a way to predict under what conditions a given company would actively support economic shifts away from the arms race. These and other gaps, however, are not nearly as grave as his lack of analysis of other components of the military-industrial complex.[6] There is no attempt to include politicians, military groups and other forces in a "map" of the military-industrial complex which Perlo believes exists. This may be partly because of the book's intent, which is to document profiteering by arms contractors, but for whatever reason, the book is not theoretically edifying about the question we are posing. Nor does it refute the pluralist case. In fact, it contains just the kind of evidence that pluralist arguments currently employ to demonstrate the absence of a monolith.

Revising the Criteria for Inferring Power

After finding fault with so many books and divergent viewpoints, the most obvious conclusion is that current social theory is currently deficient in its explanation of power. We concur with one of Mills' severest critics, Daniel Bell, who at least agrees with Mills that most current analysis concentrates on the "intermediate sectors," e.g., parties, interest groups, formal structures, without attempting to view the underlying system of "renewable power independent of any momentary group of actors" (Bell, 1964). However, we have indicated that only formidable analysis of the underlying system of renewable power, that of Mills, has profound shortcomings because of its definition of power. Therefore, before we can offer an answer of our own to the question, "Is there a military-industrial complex which blocks peace?", it is imperative to return to the question of power itself in American society.

We have agreed essentially with the pluralist claim that ruling-group models do not "fit" the American structure. We have classified Mills' model as that of a ruling-group because of his

---

[6] In an earlier book, The Empire of High Finance (1957), he documented the close relations of the major financial groups and the political executive. He did not, however, carry this analysis to congressmen and senators, nor did he offer sufficient comparative evidence to demonstrate a long-term pattern.

Weberian definition of power, but we have noted also that Mills successfully went beyond two traps common to elite theories, viz., that the elite is total in the scope of its decisions, and that the elite is a coordinated monolith.

But we perhaps have not stressed sufficiently that the alternative case for pluralism is inadequate in its claim to describe the historical dynamics of American society. The point of our dissent from pluralism is over the doctrine of "counter-vailing power." This is the modern version of Adam Smith's economics and of the Madisonian or Federalism theory of checks-and-balances, adapted to the new circumstances of large-scale organization. Its evidence is composed of self-serving incidents and a faith in semi-mystical resources. For instance, in the sphere of political economy, it is argued that oligopoly contains automatic checking mechanisms against undue corporate growth, and that additionally, the factors of "public opinion" and "corporate conscience" are built-in limiting forces.[7] We believe that evidence in the field, however, suggests that oligopoly is a means of stabilizing an industrial sphere either through tacit agreements to follow price leadership or rigged agreements in the case of custom-made goods; that "public opinion" tends much more to be manipulated and apathetic than independently critical; that "corporate conscience" is less suitable as a description than Reagan's terms, "corporate arrogance."

To take the more immediate example of the military sphere, the pluralist claim is that the military is subordinate to broader, civilian interests. The first problem with the statement is the ambiguity of "civilian." Is it clear that military men are more "militaristic" than civilian men? To say so would be to deny the increasing trend of "white-collar militarism." The top strategists in the Department of Defense, the Central Intelligence Agency and the key advisory positions often are Ph.D.'s. In fact, "civilians" including McGeorge Bundy, Robert Kennedy, James Rostow and Robert McNamara are mainly responsible for the development of the only remaining "heroic" form of combat: counter-insurgency operations in the

jungles of the underdeveloped countries. If "militarism"[8] has permeated this deeply into the "civilian" sphere, then the distinction between the terms becomes largely nominal. Meisel's description is imaginative and alluring:

> What we still honor with the name of peace is only the domestic aspect of a world-wide industrial mobilization let up at intervals by the explosions of a shooting war. . . . The industrial revolution in its class-struggle aspect is becoming externalized, projected upon the industrial field, that it is being relegated, so to speak, from barricade to barracks. . . . The armies, navies, and air forces of our time (are) the embodiment of the industrial revolution in its aggressive form (Meisel, 1962, pp. 157-158).

While the more traditional military men have not taken kindly to the takeover of military planning by civilian professors, the takeover has, none-the-less, gone far. More than 300 universities and non-profit research institutions supply civilian personnel to, and seek contracts from, the Department of Defense. Approximately half of these institutions were created specifically to do specialized strategic research. Probably the most influential of the lot of these civilian centers is the Rand Corporation.

Consistent with its Air Force origins, Rand's civilian army of almost 1,000 professional researchers and supporting personnel derives most of its support from Air Force Project Rand Studies. Rand charges the Air Force six percent of the estimated cost of the contracts which the Air Force farms out to private industry as a result of work done at Rand. This brings the Air Force contribution to Rand to over 80 percent where it has been for the past few years. When a large Ford Foundation Grant permitted Rand's reorganization in May of 1948, the organization was granted virtual autonomy from the Air Force and from Douglas Aviation which were its original parents. Such autonomy seemed necessary both to draw independent intellectuals into the establishment and to promote the image of objectivity in its research. The charter establishes a non-profit corporation to "further and promote scientific, educational and

---

[7] For this argument, see A.A. Berle, The Twentieth Century Capitalist Revolution and J.K. Galbraith, American Capitalism. For sound criticisms, but without sound alternatives, see Mills and Perlo's books. Also see Michael Reagan, The Managed Economy (1963) and Berland Nossiter, The Mythmakers (1964) for other refutations of the counter-vailing power thesis.

---

[8] We are defining the term as "primary reliance on coercive means, particularly violence or the threat of violence, to deal with social problems."

charitable purposes, all for the public welfare and security of the United States of America." The actual measure of Rand autonomy should not be taken solely from its dependence upon Air Force money. In actual practice, Rand scholars have differed with the Air Force and on issues quite important to the Air Force. The turns of the cold war strategies from massive retaliation through finite deterrence and limited war, through counter-force, and on into controlled response had never, until 1961 and 1962 involved major reductions in any type of weaponry other than the post Korean War automotive cutbacks. Automotives were, however, a largely civilian market industry. The first place where the strategic innovations served not only to rationalize existing weaponry (in the more specialized defense industry) or to call for accelerated development in additional areas, but also to call for "cost effectiveness" or cutting back in a favored weapon area, came at the expense of the Air Force. In short order the Skybolt and the RS 70 met their demise. For a time, Harvard economist Charles Hitch (then with Rand, now Defense Department comptroller) and perhaps the entire battalion of systems analysts at Rand were personally unpopular with Air Force brass. The Air Force was particularly incensed over the inclination and ability of Rand personnel to consult directly with the Defense Department and bypass the Air Force. Rand, incidentally, maintains a permanent Washington office which facilitates such confrontation. This is not exactly what Air Force spokesmen intend when they see Rand serving the function of giving "prestige type support for favored Air Force proposals to the Department of Defense and the Congress" (Friedman, 1963). The controversy shows that there is obviously no monolithic influence in defense policy. It shows also that civilian and military factions are involved and that, in this instance, even the combined influential interests of traditional Air Force leaders and industrial aircraft contractors could not hold sway over the civilian analysts. The case also illustrates the weakness of the pluralist argument. The controversy, involving sums of money exceeding the total requested for President Johnson's war on poverty, did not threaten to starve either the Air Force or the aircraft industries. Indeed, it was a controversy among family members all sharing the same source of income and the same assumptions regarding the need for maximal military strength in the cold war. While Rand scientists played the role of civilian efficiency experts in this particular controversy, Rand experts have clearly played the role of military expansionists in civilian clothing at other times. Albert Wohlstetter and Herbert Dinerstein, Rand experts on military strategy and Soviet policy, deserve major credits for the creation of the mythical "missile gap" and for the equally unreal-preemptive war strategy for the Soviet Union during the period from Sputnik, in October of 1957, until the issue of inadequate military preparedness helped bring the New Frontier to Washington. Among the possible consequences of the U.S. missile build-up to overcome the mythical gap may well have been the Soviet resumption of nuclear tests in defiance of the moratorium, an act which completed a rung of the spiralling arms race which in turn nourishes all factions, civilian and military, who are engaged in military preparedness. We do not wish to labor the point that Rand experts have at times, allowed the assumptions of their own ideology to form the basis of their rational analyses of Soviet capability and intentions. The point we wish to stress here is merely that the apparent flourishing of such civilian agencies as Rand (it earned over 20 million dollars in 1962 with all the earnings going into expansion and has already spawned the non-profit Systems Development Corporation with annual earnings exceeding 50 million dollars) is no reflection of countervailing power. The doctrine of controlled response under which the RS 70 fell was one which served the general aspirations of each of the separate services; of the Polaris and Minuteman stabile deterrent factions, of the brushfire or limited war proponents, guerrilla war and paramilitary operations advocates, and of the counterforce adherents. It is a doctrine of versatility intended to leave the widest range of military options for retaliation and escalation in U.S. hands. It can hardly be claimed as victory against military thought. The fighting may have been intense but the area of consensus between military and civilian factions was great.

The process of "civilianizing" the military is not restricted to the level of attitudes but extends to the arena of social interaction. Traditionally, the military has been a semi-caste quite apart from the mainstream of American life. But that changed with World War II; as Mills points out:

Unless the military sat in on corporate decisions, they would not be sure that their programs would be carried out; and unless the corporation chieftains knew something of the war plans, they could not plan war production . . . the very organization of the economics of war made for the coincidence of interest and the political mingling among economic and military chiefs (Mills, 1965, p. 212).

One relatively early statement (January, 1944), by Charles E. Wilson, shows that the intermeshing of military and industrial leaders was, at least on the part of some, a self-conscious and policy-oriented enterprise. Wilson proposed a permanent war economy led by the Commander and Chief, and the War Department in cooperation with an industrial partner whose response and cooperation must be free from such political accusations as the "merchants of death" label. The program would not be a creature of emergency but rather an interminable measure to eliminate emergencies. "The role of Congress," Wilson added, "is limited to voting the funds" (Swomley, 1959). Now, twenty years later we can report a personal interview with a mid-western Congressman, a fourteen-year veteran, suggesting some truth to Wilson's projection.

It is not possible for a congressman to know, according to veteran Congressman George Meader, whether defense cutbacks are feasible. The whole area is very complicated and technical and congress has very few military experts in its membership or on its research staffs. When budget time comes about the Department of Defense sends literally hundreds of experts to report before committee hearings. We have to take the word of the people who know. This paraphrased statement regarding the rubber stamping of more than 60 percent of the national budget was made by a congressman who claims a perfect record in opposition to the growth of governmental bureaucracy and to federal spending. If we were to examine the dozen or so congressional "experts" to whom Congressman Meader makes reference we find among them a number of high ranking reserve officers and a number representing districts or states economically dependent upon either military bases, or defense contracts, or both.

The same kind of planning requirements for modern war forced an overlapping of politicians with military and businessmen. There too, the very nature of world war, and especially cold war, integrated military, political and economic concepts of strategy, making the military officer much more than a cog. A variety of recent studies demonstrate the outcome of these developments. The

1959 hearings and survey by the House Armed Services Subcommittee disclosed that over 1400 retired officers with the rank of major or higher (including 261 of general or flag rank) were in the employ of the top 100 defense contractors [Hebert Subcommittee of the House Armed Services Committee, 1959]. Coffin listed 74 Senators and Representatives with continuing status in the armed forces (Coffin, 1964). By 1957, 200 active (not reserve) generals or admirals were on assignment to "non-military" departments of the government or to international or interservice agencies. An added 1300 colonels or naval officers of comparable rank, and 6000 lower grade officers were similarly assigned (Swomley, 1959). Janowitz studied an historical sample of over 760 generals and admirals, administered questionnaires to about 600 current Pentagon staff officers, and interviewed 113 career officers. He found an "elite in transition" toward civilian and managerial habits: 1) the basis of authority and discipline is changing from authoritarian domination to greater reliance on manipulation, persuasion and group consensus; 2) the skill differential between civilians and soldiers is narrowing because of the need for technical specialties in the military; 3) officers are being recruited from a broader status and class base, reflecting the demand for more specialists; 4) the source of prestige recognition is shifting from military circles to the public at large; 5) this growth makes the officer define himself more and more as a political, rather than a technical, person with concerns about national security concepts and affairs (Janowitz, 1960, pp. 3016, 442-452). These trends clearly demonstrate that the traditional American separation of military and civilian is outmoded. The new, blurred reality has not been successfully defined.

The main point here is that the pluralist argument relies on "counter-vailing forces" which are more mythical than real. The Wise and Ross book shows indisputably that at least during certain instances the Executive is not countervailing the CIA. Moreover, who is countervailing the "military-civilian" Executive centered in the Pentagon and the White House? What Knorr sees as a "peacefare state" countervailing the "warfare state" is merely its white-collar brother. The symbolic figure of the Arms Control and Disarmament Agency demonstrates this reality vividly. One side of the ACDA figure is a diplomat with tie and attache case; the other side is a warrior dedicated to the pursuit of stabilizing control measures which might assure national advantages in a never ending cold war.

within their scope which are essentially unaccountable in the democratic process. These groups are too uneven to be described with the shorthand term "class." Their personnel have many different characteristics (compare IBM executives and the Southern Dixiecrats) and their needs as groups are different enough to cause endless fights, as for example, small vs. big business. No one group or coalition of several groups can tyrannize the rest as is demonstrated, for example, in the changing status of the major financial groups, particularly the fast-rising Bank of America which has been built from the financial needs of the previously-neglected small consumer.

However, it is clear that these groups exist within consensus relationships of a more general and durable kind than their conflict relationships. This is true, first of all of their social characteristics. The tables above combine data from Suzanne Keller's compilation of military, economic, political and diplomatic elite survey materials in Beyond the Ruling Class (1963) and from an exhaustive study of American elites contained in Warner, et al., The American Federal Executive (1963). Data on elites vary slightly from study to study because of varying operational definitions of the elite population. However, the data selected here are fairly representative and refer exclusively to studies with major data collected within the decade of the fifties. (See Tables 1, 2, 3.)

The relevant continuities represented in this data suggest an educated elite with an emphasis upon Protestant and business-oriented origins. Moreover, the data suggest inbreeding with business orientation in backgrounds likely to have been at least maintained, if not augmented, through marriage. The consistencies suggest orientations not unlike those which are to be found in examination of editorial content of major business newspapers and weeklies and in more directly sampled assessments of elite opinions.[10]

The second evidence of consensus relationships, besides attitude and background data indicating a pro-business sympathy, would come from an examination of the practice of decision making. By analysis of such actual behavior we can understand which consensus attitudes are reflected in decision-making. Here, in retrospect, it is possible to

discover the values and assumptions which are defended recurrently. This is at least a rough means of finding the boundaries of consensus relations. Often these boundaries are invisible because of the very infrequency with which they are tested. What are visible most of the time are the parameters of conflict relationships among different groups. These conflict relationships constitute the ingredients of experience which give individuals or groups their uniqueness and varieties, while the consensus relations constitute the common underpinnings of behavior. The tendency in social science has been to study decision-making in order to study group differences; we need to study decision-making also to understand group commonalities.

Were such studies done, our hypothesis would be that certain "core beliefs" are continuously unquestioned. One of these, undoubtedly, would be that efficacy is preferable to principle in foreign affairs. In practice, this means that violence is preferable to non-violence as a means of defense. A second is that private property is preferable to collective property. A third assumption is that the particular form of constitutional government, which is practiced within the United States is preferable to any other system of government. We refer to the preferred mode as limited parliamentary democracy, a system in which institutionalized forms of direct representation are carefully retained but with fundamental limitations placed upon the prerogatives of governing. Specifically included among the areas of limitation are many matters encroaching upon corporation property and state hegemony. While adherence to this form of government is conceivably the strongest of the domestic "core values," at least among business elites, it is probably the least strongly held of the three on the international scene. American relations with, and assistance for, authoritarian and semi-feudal regimes occurs exactly in those areas where the recipient regime is evaluated primarily upon the two former assumptions and given rather extensive leeway on the latter one.

The implications of these "core beliefs" for the social system are immense, for they justify the maintenance of our largest institutional structures: the military, the corporate economy, and a system of partisan politics which protects the concept of limited democracy. These institutions, in turn, may be seen as current agencies of the more basic social structure. We use the term "social structure" as Robert S. Lynd does as the stratification of people identified according to kinship, sex, age,

---

[10] For some interesting work bearing upon the attitudes of business and military elites see (Angell, 1964; Bauer et al., 1963; Eells and Walton, 1961; and Singer, 1964).

division of labor, race, religion, or other factors which differentiate them in terms of role, status, access to resources, and power. According to Lynd:

> This structure established durable relations that hold groups of people together for certain purposes and separate them for others. Such social structures may persist over many generations. Its continuance depends upon its ability to cope with historical changes that involve absorption of new groupings and relations of men without fundamental change in the structure of the society of a kind that involves major transfer of power (Lynd, 1959).

The "renewable basis of power" in America at the present time underlies those institutional orders linked in consensus relationships: military defense of private property and parliamentary democracy. These institutional orders are not permanently secure, by definition. Their maintenance involves a continuous coping with new conditions, such as technological innovation and with the inherent instabilities of a social structure which arbitrarily classifies persons by role, status, access to resources, and power. The myriad groups composing these orders are even less secure because of their weak ability to command "coping resources," e.g., the service branches are less stable than the institution of the military, particular companies are less stable than the institutions of corporate property, political parties are less stable than the institution of parliamentary government.

In the United States there is no ruling group. Nor is there any easily discernible ruling institutional order, so meshed have the separate sources of elite power become. But there is a social structure which is organized to create and protect power centers with only partial accountability. In this definition of power we are avoiding the Weber-Mills meaning of omnipotence and the contrary pluralist definition of power as consistently diffuse. We are describing the current system as one of overall "minimal accountability" and "minimal consent." We mean that the role of democratic review, based on genuine popular consent, is made marginal and reactive. Elite groups are minimally accountable to publics and have a substantial, though by no means maximum, freedom to shape popular attitudes. The reverse of our

system would be one in which democratic participation would be the orienting demand around which the social structure is organized.

Some will counter this case by saying that we are measuring "reality" against an "ideal," a technique which permits the conclusion that the social structure is undemocratic according to its distance from our utopian values. This is a convenient apology for the present system, of course. We think it possible, at least in theory, to develop measures of the undemocratic in democratic conditions, and place given social structures along a continuum. These measures, in rough form, might include such variables as economic security, education, legal guarantees, access to information, and participatory control over systems of economy, government, and jurisprudence.

The reasons for our concern with democratic process in an article questioning the power of a purported military-industrial complex are twofold. First, just as scientific method both legitimizes and promotes change in the world of knowledge, democratic method both legitimizes and promotes change in the world of social institutions. Every society, regardless of how democratic, protects its core institutions in a web of widely shared values. But if the core institutions should be dictated by the requisites of military preparedness, then restrictions on the democratic process, i.e., restrictions in either mass opinion exchange (as by voluntary or imposed news management) or in decision-making bodies (as by selection of participants in a manner guaranteeing exclusion of certain positions), then such restrictions would be critical obstacles to peace.

Second, certain elements of democratic process are inimical to features of militarily oriented society, and the absence of these elements offers one type of evidence for a military-industrial complex even in the absence of a ruling elite. Secretary of Defense Robert McNamara made the point amply clear in his testimony in 1961 before the Senate Armed Services Committee:

> Why should we tell Russia that the Zeus development may not be satisfactory? What we ought to be saying is that we have the most perfect anti-ICBM system that the human mind will ever devise. Instead the public domain is already full of statements that the Zeus may not be satisfactory, that it has deficiencies. I think it is absurd to release that level of information. (Military Procurement Authorization Fiscal Year 1962)

Under subsequent questioning McNamara attempted to clarify his statement that he only wished to delude Russian, not American, citizens about U.S. might. Just how this might be done was not explained.

A long established tradition exists for "executive privilege" which permits the President to refuse to release information when, in his opinion, it would be damaging to the national interest. Under modern conditions responsibility for handling information of a strategic nature is shared among military, industrial, and executive agencies. The discretion regarding when to withhold what information must also be shared. Moreover, the existence of a perpetual danger makes the justification, "in this time of national crisis" suitable to every occasion in which secrecy must be justified. McNamara's statement cited above referred not to a crisis in Cuba or Viet Nam but rather to the perpetual state of cold war crisis. And since the decision about what is to be released and when, is subject to just such management the media became dependent upon the agencies for timely leaks and major stories. This not only adds an aura of omniscience to the agencies, but gives these same agencies the power to reward "good" journalists and punish the critical ones.

The issues involved in the question of news management involve more than the elements of control available to the President, the State Department, the Department of Defense, the Central Intelligence Agency, the Atomic Energy Commission or any of the major prime contractors of defense contracts. Outright control of news flow is probably less pervasive than voluntary acquiescence to the objectives of these prominent institutions of our society. Nobody has to tell the wire services when to release a story on the bearded dictator of our hemisphere or the purported brutality of Ho Chi Minh. A frequent model, the personified devil image of an enemy, has become a press tradition. In addition to a sizeable quantity of radio and television programming and spot time purchased directly by the Pentagon, an amount of service, valued at $6 million by Variety, is donated annually by the networks and by public relations agencies for various military shows (Swomley, 1959). Again, the pluralistic shell of an independent press or broadcasting media is left hollow by the absence of a countervailing social force of any significant power.

The absence of a countervailing force for peace cannot, we have claimed, be demonstrated by an absence of conflicting interests among powerful sectors of American society. Indeed, such conflicts are ever-present examples of American pluralism. Demonstrating the absence of a discussion of the shared premises, among the most potent sectors of society, would go far in highlighting the area of forced or acquiescent consensus. But even the absence of debate could not complete the case unless we can show how the accepted premises are inconsistent with requisites of a viable peace-time social system. It is to this question: of the compatibility of the unquestioned assumptions of American society with conditions of peace, that we now turn. The "core beliefs" which we listed as unchallenged by any potent locus of institutionalized power are:

a) Efficacy is preferable to principle in foreign affairs (thus military means are chosen over non-violent means);

b) Private property is preferable to public property; and

c) Limited parliamentary democracy is preferable to any other system of government.

What characteristics of a continuing world system devoid of military conflict fly in the face of these assumptions?

We identify three conditions for enduring peace which clash with one or more of the core beliefs. These are: 1) the requirements for programming an orderly transition and the subsequent maintenance of a non-defense economy within a highly automated and relatively affluent society; 2) the conditions for peaceful settlement of internal disputes within underdeveloped countries and between alien nations and commercial interests; and 3) the conditions under which disparities in living standards between have and have-not nations can be handled with minimum violence.

If one pools available projections regarding the offset programs, especially regional and local offset programs, necessary to maintain economic well-being in the face of disarmament in this country, the programs will highlight two important features. One is the lag time in industrial conversion. The second is the need for coordination in the timing and spacing of programs. One cannot reinvest in new home building in an area which has just been deserted by its major industry and left a ghost town. The short-term and long-term offset values of new hospitals and educational facilities will differ in the building and the utilization stages and regional offset programs have

demonstrable interregional effects (Reiner, 1964).
Plans requiring worker mobility on a large scale
will require a central bank for storing job information and a smooth system for its dissemination.
Such coordination will require a degree of centralization of controls beyond the realm which our
assumption regarding primacy of private property
would permit.

Gross intransigence can be expected on this
issue. Shortly after Sperry Rand on Long Island
was forced to make major cutbacks of its professional and engineering staff to adapt to the ter-
mination of certain defense contracts, the union
approached Sperry's management with the prospect
of collaborating in efforts to commence contingency
plans for diversification. The response, by Carl
A. Frische, President of Sperry Gyroscope, a
division of Sperry Rand, remains a classic. There
must be no "government-controlled mechanisms
under the hood of the economy." He suggested,
with regard to such planning, that "we let Russia
continue with that." (Long Island Sunday Press,
February 23, 1964.) Sperry is an old-timer in
defense production. Its board of directors average
several years older than the more avant garde
board of directors of, say, General Dynamics.
But the prospect of contingency planning will be
no more warmly welcomed in the newer aeroframe
industry (which is only 60% convertible to needs of
a peace-time society), (McDonagh and Zimmerman,
1964). Private planning, by an individual firm for
its own future does occur, but, without coordinated
plans, the time forecast for market conditions remains smaller than the lag time for major retool-
ing. A lag time of from six to ten years would not
be atypical before plans by a somewhat over-spe-
cialized defense contractor could result in retool-
ing for production in a peace-time market. In the
meantime, technological innovations, governmental fiscal or regulatory policies, shifts in consumer
preferences, or the decision by other firms to enter that same market could well make the market
vanish. Moreover, the example of defense firms
which have attempted even the smaller step toward
diversification presents a picture which has not
been entirely promising (Fearon and Hook, 1964).
Indeed, one of several reasons for the failures in
this endeavor has been that marketing skills necessary to compete in a private enterprise economy
have been lost by those industrial giants who have
been managing with a sales force of one or two retired generals to deal with the firm's only customer. Even if the path of successful conversion by
some firms were to serve as the model for all individual attempts, the collective result would be
poor. To avoid a financially disastrous glutting of
limited markets some coordinated planning will be
needed.

The intransigence regarding public or collabor-
ative planning occurs against a backdrop of a soon-
to-be increasing army of unemployed youth and
aged, as well as regional armies of unemployed
victims of automation. Whether one thinks of work
in traditional job market terms or as anything
worthwhile that a person can do with his life, work
(and some means of livihood) will have to be found
for these people. There is much work to be done
in community services, education, public health,
and recreation, but this is people work, not product work. The lack of a countervailing force prevents the major reallocation of human and economic resources from the sector defined as preferable by the most potent institutions of society. One
point must be stressed. We are not saying that
limited planning to cushion the impact of arms reduction is impossible. Indeed, it is going on and
with the apparent blessing of the Department of
Defense (Barber, 1963). We are saying that the
type of accommodation needed by a cutback of $9
billion in R & D and $16 billion in military pro-
curement requires a type of preparation not consistent with the unchallenged assumptions.

Even the existence of facilities for coordinated
planning does not, to be sure, guarantee the success of such planning. Bureaucratic institutions,
designed as they may be for coordination and control, do set up internal resistance to the very co-
ordination they seek to achieve. The mechanisms
for handling these bureaucratic intransigencies usually rely upon such techniques as bringing participants into the process of formulating the decisions
which will affect their own behavior. We can conceive of no system of coordinated conversion planning which could function without full and motivated
cooperation from the major corporations, the larger
unions, and representatives of smaller business and
industry. Unfortunately, it is just as difficult to
conceive of a system which would assure this necessary level of participation and cooperation. This
same argument cuts deeper still when we speak of
the millions of separate individuals in the "other
America" whose lives would be increasingly "administered" with the type of centralized planning
needed to offset a defense economy. The job assignment which requires moving, the vocational
retraining program, the development of housing

projects to meet minimal standards, educational enrichment programs, all of the programs which are conceived by middle-class white America for racially mixed low income groups, face the same difficulty in execution of plans. Without direct participation in the formulation of the programs, the target populations are less likely to participate in the programs and more likely to continue feelings of alienation from the social system which looks upon them as an unfortunate problem rather than as contributing members. Considering the need for active participation in real decisions, every step of coordinated planning carries with it the responsibility for an equal step in the direction of participatory democracy. This means that the voice of the unemployed urban worker may have to be heard, not only on city council meetings which discuss policy on the control of rats in his dwelling, but also on decisions about where a particular major corporation will be relocated and where the major resource allocations of the country will be invested. That such decision participation would run counter to the consensus on the items of limited parliamentary democracy and private property is exactly the point we wish to make.

Just as the theoretical offset plans can be traced to the sources of power with which they conflict, so too can the theoretical plans for international governing and peace-keeping operations be shown to conflict with the unquestioned beliefs. U.S. consent to international jurisdiction in the settlement of claims deriving from the nationalization of American overseas holdings or the removal of U.S. military installations is almost inconceivable. Moreover, the mode of American relations to less-developed countries is so much a part of the operations of those American institutions which base their existence upon interminable conflict with Communism that the contingency in which the U.S. might have to face the question of international jurisdiction in these areas seems unreal. Offers to mediate, with Cuba by Mexico, with North Viet Nam by France, are bluntly rejected. Acceptance of such offers would have called into question not one but all three of the assumptions in the core system. International jurisdictional authority could institutionalize a means to call the beliefs into question. It is for this reason (but perhaps most directly because of our preference for forceful means) that American preoccupation in those negotiations regarding the extension of international control which have taken place, deal

almost exclusively with controls in the area of weaponry and police operations and not at all in the areas of political or social justice.[11]

The acceptance of complete international authority even in the area of weaponry poses certain inconsistencies with the preferred "core beliefs." Non-violent settlement of Asian-African area conflicts would be slow and ineffective in protecting American interests. The elimination, however, of military preparedness, both for projected crises and for their potential escalation, requires a faith in alternate means of resolution. The phasing of the American plan for general and complete disarmament is one which says in effect: prove that the alternatives are as efficient as our arms in protection of our interests and then we disarm. In the short term, however, the effectiveness of force always looks greater.

The state of world peace contains certain conditions imposed by the fact that people now compare themselves with persons who have more of the benefits of industrialization than they themselves. Such comparative reference groups serve to increase the demand for rapid change. While modern communications heighten the pressures imposed by such comparisons, the actual disparities revealed in comparison speak for violence. Population growth rates, often as high as three percent, promise population doubling within a single generation in countries least able to provide for their members. The absolute number of illiterates as well as the absolute number of persons starving is greater now than ever before in history. Foreign aid barely offsets the disparity between declining prices paid for the prime commodities exported by underdeveloped countries and rising prices paid for the finished products imported into these countries (Horowitz, 1962). All schemes for tight centralized planning employed by these countries to accrue and disperse scarce capital by rational means are blocked by the unchallenged assumptions on private property and limited parliamentary democracy. A recent restatement of the principle came in the report of General Lucius Clay's committee on foreign aid. The report stated that the U.S. should not assist foreign governments "in projects establishing government owned industrial and commercial enterprises which compete with existing private endeavors." When Congressman Broomfield's amendment

---

[11]An objective account of the major negotiations related to disarmament which have taken place may be found in Frye (1963).

Table 1

Social Characteristics of American Elites

Elite	Nativity % Foreign Born	Rural–Urban % Urban Born	Religion % Protestant	Education % College Grads.
Military	2%	30–40%	90	73–98%
Economic	6	65	85	61
Political	2	48	81	91
Diplomatic	4	66	60	81
U.S. Adult Males	7	42	65	7

Towns of 2,500 or more.
30 years of age or older.
Taking the services separately.
1910 U.S. Population.

The majority of foreign-born and second-generation come from Northwestern Europe.
The proportion of foreign-born from these areas is significantly lower for the general
male population.

The difference between "political" and "diplomatic" and "economic" indicated
that Congress, in the 1950's was more conservative—especially in its small business
and non-integrationist attitudes—than the federal executive or the corporation
leaders. The sharp difference between "military" and the rest lumps military policy-
makers with lower level personnel, thus underemphasizing the new trend cited by
Janowitz.

Table 2

Father's Occupation

	Civilian federal executives	Military executives	Business leader's	Total U.S. male pop. 1930
Unskilled Laborer	4%	2%	5%	33%
Skilled Labor	17	12	10	15
White-Collar (clerk or sales)	9	9	8	12
Foreman	5	5	3	2
Business Owner	15	19	26	7
Business Executive	15	15	23	3
Professional	19	18	14	4
Farm owner or manager	14	9	8	16
Farm tenant or worker	1	1	1	6
Other	1	1	2	2

Table 3

Business and Executive Origins of Wives of Elites

Occupation	Political executives		Foreign-service executives		Military executives		Civilian federal executives		Business leaders	
	Father	Spouse's father	Father	Spouse's father	Father	Spouse's father	Father	Spouse's father	Father	Spouse's father
Minor executive	10%	10%	11%	11%	15%	12%	11%	11%	11%	7%
Major executive	6	5	9	9	5	7	4	4	15	8
Business owner	21	25	19	24	19	22	20	23	26	28
Professional	24	19	25	23	18	19	19	16	14	15
Military executive					9	11				

ACDA's narrow conception ... much a function of its internal ... ability as it is a matter of the ... it by a reluctant Congress. It ... ability not only in its apparent c ... ...ntial- ly technical questions for study ... also in its manner of study. One favored study technique is to collapse large socially significant questions into several questions answerable by short-term studies and suited for study by the grossly oversimplified techniques of policy appraisal employed by those same operations research corporations which serve, and live upon, defense contracts. These organizations have traditionally produced quick answers embedded in rationalistic models which ring with scientism and jargon. Strategy and Conscience, a powerfully written book by Anatol Rapoport, documents the manner in which the rationalist models employed in such strategic studies frequently conceal (often unknowingly) gross assumptions of the nature of the cold war. The point here is that if these are the same assumptions which necessitate a high level of military preparedness, then it matters little whether the studies are commissioned by civilian or military authorities.

Consensus

All that countervailing power refers to is the relationship between groups who fundamentally accept "the American system" but who compete for advantages within it. The corporate executive wants higher profits, the laborer a higher wage. The President wants the final word on military strategies, the Chairman of the Joint Chiefs does not trust him with it. Boeing wants the contract, but General Dynamics is closer at the time to the Navy Secretary and the President, and so on: what is prevented by countervailing forces is the dominance of society by a group or clique or a party. But this process suggests a profoundly important point; that the constant pattern in American society is the rise and fall of temporarily-irresponsible groups.[9] By temporary we mean that, outside of the largest industrial conglomerates, the groups which wield significant power to influence policy decisions are not guaranteed stability. By irresponsible we mean that there are many activities

---

[9] The term used in recent hearings by Senator Philip A. Hart refers to industrial organizations like Textron, which have holdings in every major sector of American industry.

foreign aid resulted in cancellation of a U.S. promise to India to build a steel mill in Bokaro, Broomfield stated the case succinctly: "The main issue is private enterprise vs. state socialism." (The Atlantic, September, 1964, p. 6.) Moreover, preference for forceful solutions assures that the capital now invested in preparedness will not be allocated in a gross way to the needs of underdeveloped countries. Instead, the manifest crises periodically erupting in violence justify further the need for reliance upon military preparedness.

We agree fully with an analysis by Lowi (1964) distinguishing types of decisions for which elite-like forces seem to appear and hold control (redistributive) and other types in which pluralist powers battle for their respective interests (distributive). In the latter type the pie is large and the fights are over who gets how much. Factional strife within and among military industrial and political forces in our country are largely of this nature. In redistributive decisions, the factions coalesce, for the pie itself is threatened. We have been arguing that the transition to peace is a process of redistributive decision.

Is there, then, a military-industrial complex which prevents peace? The answer is inextricably imbedded into the mainstream of American institutions and mores. Our concept is not that American society contains a ruling military-industrial complex. Our concept is more nearly that American society is a military-industrial complex. It can accommodate a wide range of factional interests from those concerned with the production or utilization of a particular weapon to those enraptured with the mystique of optimal global strategies. It can accommodate those with rabid desires to advance toward the brink and into limitless intensification of the arms race. It can even accommodate those who wish either to prevent war or to limit the destructiveness of war through the gradual achievement of arms control and disarmament agreements. What it cannot accommodate is the type of radical departures needed to produce enduring peace.

The requirements of a social system geared to peace, as well as the requirements for making a transition to such a social system, share a pattern of resource distribution which is different from the one the world now has. Moreover, these requirements for peace are, in significant measure, inconsistent with constraints set by the more enduring convergencies among power structures in the

United States. The same is true whether one speaks of allocation of material or of intellectual resources. Both are geared to the protection of the premises rather than to avenues of change. We are not saying that war is inevitable or that the changes cannot be made. We are saying that the American political, military, and industrial system operates with certain built-in stabilizers which resist a change in the system. If there is to be peace, as opposed to detente or temporary absence of war, marked changes will be needed. Whether this society can or will accommodate to such changes is a question which is fundamentally different from the questions posed by most studies conventionally grouped under the rubric of peace research. One difference which marks the question of capacity to accommodate is in the theoretical conception or model of the cold war which is assumed. And a second distinction lies in the manner in which the end product of the research may be suited to meet the social forces (as apart from the intellectual arguments) which promote long-term changes in policy.

Role of the Peace Scholars

In recent years, intellectual attention to the problem of peace has usually been directed to the problem of averting war. The context of this problem is that of the non-zero-sum game in which the players have both a joint common advantage (in averting nuclear war) and a bargaining problem in deciding upon the competitive distribution of other non-sharable advantages. Much of the intellectual attention from social scientists has been directed to problems of trust, controls, and assurances of good faith—problems relevant to protecting the common advantage. Meanwhile the strategists have tended to give relatively greater emphasis to the problem of competitive advantage. There have been clashes between these two groups of intellectuals but both share, and both assume that foreign adversaries also share, the assumption that nuclear war ought to be avoided. The question is one of means to that end and of risks to be taken.

In the question of permanent peace with its contingent institutions, there is no such fundamental agreement about the desirability of the end. In fact, we have argued that there exists a large area of consensus which precludes the very set of contingent institutions which may be needed for lasting peace. Without certain shared end values, research on the part of peace protagonists cannot be used as a rational wedge in policy debate. The clash is with a social system some of whose very bases of organization run counter to the requirements of stable peace. Under such circumstances, there are zero-sum components to the conflict. Some institutions and some status positions within the society must change and some may actually have to perish if certain newer ones are to thrive. Research in this area becomes what most researchers who are justly sensitive about their scientific objectivity dread—a part of a political struggle. Dorwin Cartwright has called power "the neglected variable" in studies of interpersonal behavior (Cartwright, 1959). The scarcity of good empirical studies of the power to effect or constrain national policies shows an even greater area of neglect. Whatever the reasons for this neglect, there seems a need to follow the course once set by Freud if we are ever to learn about, and eventually make changes in, this taboo area.

Another departure intended by the type of research we shall suggest may be seen by a brief comparison with a sample of questions now being tackled by inquiry into problems of peace. Look, for example, at each of the following questions:

How will detection and punishment be regulated in the event of violations in an arms control agreement? What system of jurisdiction and policing could replace national armed forces? What institutionalized channels could be created to replace war as an expression of individual or social aggression? What sequences of events have led to escalation of conflicts in the past and how can these sequences be altered? How will the electronics industry, or Southern California, get along without defense contracts? What sequence of arms reduction and what type of inspections and controls would prevent a successful surprise attack during the disarmament process? When are unilateral gestures likely to be reciprocated?

Taken together, these questions and variations of them comprise a remarkably wide slice of the entire peace research movement (as intellectually popular as it has become on financially sparse resources). The questions are doubtlessly important ones, but they hold in common a certain format of answers. Each project seeks, and some find, as an answer to its research, a scheme which —if it were enacted—would promote enduring peace. Why the plan is not enacted is usually not asked, if asked at all, then answered within the framework of basic assumptions which protect the status quo. The propensity of scholars seems often to be

an equation of their own ability to understand ways to treat a problem with the actual resolution of the problem. This may have been true for small pox but it is, so far, not true for over-population, and this understanding by itself falls many steps short of implementing the treatment for problems of war and peace. In the case of war and peace the discovery of answers could be irrelevant to their application—could be, that is, unless directed to foci of emergent power and change within the system. By and large, the efforts of the peace intellectuals have not been so directed.

We do not mean this as an indictment against the peace research movement. As an activity which institutionalizes means to support scholars who wish to devote their professional talents to the quest for peace, the movement is admirable. Moreover, it is a young movement still groping for its major task and hence capable of learning. But the nature of the current outputs by these scholars, the policy suggestions which they make as reflections of their intellectual inquiry, suggest a common denominator of difficulties.[12]

The better known among the proposals are associated with the names of Charles Osgood (GRIT), Stephan James (peace hostage exchange), Ralph Lapp and others (finite deterrence), J. David Singer (gradual accretion of U.N. custody for major weapons), John Strachey (militarily enforced peace through Soviet-American alliance), Morton Deutsch (suspicion-reducing and trust-building steps), Herbert Kelman (neutral international armies), Amitai Etzioni (gradual reduction of military programs to finite levels and reinvestment in economic offensives), Quincy Wright and others (building of interpersonal and organizational ties which transcend the cold war), S.I. Hayakawa (listening), Anatol Rapoport (ideological debate), Louis Sohn and others (world federal government), Jerome Frank and others (education in non-violence), Eric Fromm (major unilateral arms reduction), and so forth. Several of the authors of these and related proposals have provided us with the arguments necessary to demonstrate that each of the plans offered is "not feasible." Usually the basis for the judgment of not feasible lies in the intransigence of the very conditions which that particular plan was

---

[12] We wish to give credit to Philip Green's article in the Bulletin of the Atomic Scientists, November 1963, for a detailed critique of "peace proposals" from which we have borrowed.

designed to overcome. Psycho-logic and self-fulfilling prophecy prevents as well as necessitates a reversal in the arms race. Nationalism prevents as well as necessitates the growth of international friendships, armies, and governmental agencies. Without a theoretical model of what is or is not tractible in the social system, a marked tendency exists toward seeing the system and its basic assumptions as relatively immobile but for the cracks provided by one's own insight.

That the various proposals do not all agree on whether tensions or weapons must be first to go, or whether international institutions must precede or follow international allegiances, is not a critical problem. Each of the hypotheses presented in the plans may well be true but none may ever be tested. The specification of alternatives in the cold war is necessary. But just offering the alternatives does not serve to generate new goals for a society. Were the goals of our society appropriate to world peace all of these proposals, and many far more exotic than these, would already have been tried. Conversely, the military strategy proposals which have been either tried or subjected to serious policy consideration are not always more reasonable than the works of the peace scholars.

That the fault is not in the plans but in the absence of a market for them may be seen in a plan offered, in jest, by Anatol Rapoport which has much logical merit. Briefly, it suggests that two teams of high ranking officers of the two major powers, rather than civilian diplomats, be given the task of negotiating an agreement on general and complete disarmament. If the teams should fail, they are painlessly put to death and replaced by the next team, and so on. The plan assures a) that knowledge of the military requisites for national security will not be missing from consideration, b) that a demilitarization of society will come one way or another, and c) that those who advocate that we should be willing to die for our country would be given the opportunity to do so. What is missing here, as in each of the other plans, is the social force necessary to try the plan.[15]

---

[13] We have omitted reference to a number of substantial contributors among the scholars suggesting various peace policies. Some in particular bear mentioning because they have been associated with ideas which have tried to avoid the problems mentioned above. First, Seymour Melman in his emphasis upon detailed studies of industrial conversion for possible use by industrial organizations

The Research Task

What sort of research would be instrumental in the transformation of American ideologies and of the power structures in which they are encased? And where is the market for such research? We shall venture the beginnings of an answer in the suggestion of a type of research which is "politically relevant," i.e., which is related to the strategy of its own application. To do this we shall define a notion of power which determines major trends in policy. Second we shall discuss briefly the research task in identifying the potential for change in the current loci of power. And last, we shall sketch the emergence of a countervailing force, a market for the research findings.

What we have been calling the military-industrial comples is an informal and changing coalition of groups with vested psychological, moral, and material interests in the continuous development and maintenance of high levels of weaponry, in preservation of colonial markets and in military-strategic conceptions of international affairs. A survey of such a complex would probably delineate no useful boundaries except those coextensive with American society and its sphere of influence. Hence, a study of the relations of any group to the cold war could reveal a set of economic transactions and communication activities which give it a degree of centrality in the present consensus of power. A study of those groups with more focal

---

clearly intends to find a basis for breaking alliances of interest between military and industrial sectors. Second, Otto Feinstein's approach, tapping the institutional involvements in peace of such enduring groups as educators, clergy, and local political machines, is an idea with an intended market which is obvious. Third, Leo Szilard, H.S. Hughes, and others who have pioneered in the cultivation of a politically viable peace movement also have target populations in their designs. To this we must add plans for utilization of professional societies in exerting of political influence by scholars in several disciplines. Moreover, several of the very persons mentioned in the text have consciensiously sought a market for their proposals within and without governmental agencies. The efforts are laudable but with the possible exception of Melman, are not entirely relevant to our thesis that peace research could bear an intrinsic relationship to both the requisites of enduring peace and to the sources of power which have a stake in such a change.

postitions in the power complex would reveal a particular but diverse set of institutions, each somewhat unique in internal dynamics and in the peculiarities of its participation in the cold war. The essence of such study is in differentiating among the institutions for there will certainly be varying scope and depth of commitment. Likewise, some of the institutions, and perhaps many of the key individuals, will present a picture which is psychologically, economically, and politically convertible to the needs of peace.

Convertibility has several meanings. One useful standard will be objective economic adaptability. Can the group in question survive a basic policy shift? Some organized social groupings within the military services and major portions of the aerospace companies may not be viable in sustained peace. If 1,800 aircraft can service all scheduled airlines in the U.S. then 33,000 aircraft and most of all aviation production facilities belonging to the U.S. armed forces could present an overabundancy crisis (Convertibility of Space and Defense Hearings, 1964). But some firms will be able to emerge unscathed and many more could probably survive with any of a wide range of governmental offset programs. Individual viability may differ sharply from that of the institution. A study of stock holdings of the officers and directors of the major defense contracting firms could reveal the types of diversification from defense orientation which has already been occuring.

A second view of convertibility is strongly social psychological but with economic underpinnings. It deals with the condition under which the desirability of shift might outweigh the positive incentives which provide psychological sustenance within the current system. We distinguish several types of incentives which research could reveal. Profit, of course, is one incentive which keeps some major defense contractors content but the number wholly satisfied in this manner may be shifting with the introduction of new cost-accounting devices and competitive bidding by the Pentagon. A related incentive is foreign investment requiring military security. Companies with holdings in Latin America, Africa, and the Near East may be "objectively adaptable" to even total loss of these holdings. However, some, like the petroleum companies, habituated to insecure holdings and high profits, may not be planning for, or willing to accept, any alternative to the military maintenance of "friendly" regimes in underdeveloped countries. The incentive of governmen-

tal subsidy for technological advance is often mentioned among benefits of defense contracts. Marketable civilian goods emerge as side-products of research in electronics, aviation, and machine components. Research could reveal both beneficiaries and the neglected firms in this area. Moreover, it is not clear whether similar incentives could operate to draw firms out of the current system through governmental research offerings in the areas of automated hospital, library, educational or traffic control facilities.

Approaching the more clearly psychological incentives we consider ideological satisfaction. The gamut ranges from a chauvinistic dedication to exorcise devils from Godly America to basic beliefs in the ultimate nature of untested assumptions of the social structure. It includes devotion to "hard nosed," masculine, competitive market-place theories of "rational" self-interest in international relations and rationalizations of special privileges which have been defended to the point of firm belief. Ideological commitment to the arms race is far from uniform. We believe that sensitive interview studies would reveal pockets of cynicism and even guilt. They might well reveal dedication to particularistic goals at the expense of other power centers (e.g., dedication to Air Force preeminence), thus indicating strains amidst the convergencies of military, political and industrial coalitions. Further, the particular ideologies uncovered may not be consonant with the non-military goals or values of the individuals involved. This could suggest the places in which ideological transfer might occur to civilian research objectives or to the rigorous pursuit of international police operations.

A last type of incentive is vocational satisfaction. We know very little of the daily gratifications from the many vocational roles tied to national security. We do not know whether the lavish parties and status through personal contracts mark a peripheral or central attraction of elite adaptations. We do not know whether the opportunities for creative intellectual effort in technology and strategy are truly basic attractions or even whether such opportunities actually exist beyond job opportunity advertisements of the electronics, missile, and Research and Development corporations. Such knowledge could suggest the possibilities for vocational convertibility in peace time. We do know, however, that in the wax and wain of success and influence within the military-industrial system, there are appearing with increasing frequency groups of individuals who are descending in position and who may be prone to such reactions as.

a) intensified efforts for maintaining status (and the status quo) within the society, b) nationalistic or extremist affiliations which identify scapegoats and maintain group cohesion without realistic bases, and c) defections from positions central to the complex and realignment with forces of change.

We have concentrated our discussion upon the social-psychological convertibility of economic elites. A similar study could reveal analogous information about political and military elites. Professionalization of the military holds both positive and negative omens for convertibility. Study of the psychologically reasonable retirement opportunities for officers are of obvious importance.

Studies of political elites central to the preservation of military-industrial power pose difficulties of access but also offer the promise of exposing the communication channels through which influence is exerted. Campaign contributions to congressmen and promotional efforts to obtain prime contracts in one's area are both available data. Congressional roll-call votes on cold war issues can be studied, using contract dependency in the congressman's district and reserve officer status of the congressman, as independent variables. Military and industrial lobbying activities are valid objects for study and may be found related to invitations to give testimony on pending legislation. In the executive branch, data on presidential visitors are already compiled and published regularly. Data on stock holdings, vocational histories and voluntary associations of such influential groups as the Joint Chiefs of Staff or the Council of Economic Advisors could give insight into the recruitment mechanisms which indirectly determine the agenda for questions of major resource allocations.

In some institutions, focal to decisions affecting defense policy, it may be possible to discover positive feedback mechanisms which extend militarism (as in the alleged support by certain defense contracting firms of super-patriotic "educational" programs which press the need for greater force), (Westin, 1963).

The suggested questions are neither complete nor are they a research design, but rather a part of a strategy in the use of research to promote policy change. The findings from such studies would describe institutions which are a) ripe for defection from the consensus of military orientation, b) potentially capable of accommodation to the conditions of peace, and c) completely intran-

sigent. Depending again upon what studies of operations of influence would reveal, it may be possible to classify the intransigents in accordance with their ability to constrain decisions for peace, were such decisions forthcoming. Such visibility of interests and of power relationships is itself a tool of ascendance in groups which have the most at stake in a major reallocation of American resources. To indicate how such research might be used, and by whom, we will have to shift gears sharply and focus upon two theories of the nature of American poverty.

The New Consumers for Peace Research

One popular theory of poverty considers the American economy as fundamentally healthy and as capable of moderate equitable distribution as it is of high production. The theory in its more conservative form calls only for ever increasing productivity (of anything), for an adequate trickle down of the benefits of prosperity. The same theory in its liberal statement considers the poverty-stricken person to be one of the accidents of the system, a person whose deficiencies in skills, achievement orientation, middle-class values, education, and physical and psychological health can be met by federal programs intended to provide more counseling, health care, job training, etc. People thus rehabilitated, the theory goes, will then acquire their share of American affluence.

The contrasting theory attributes American poverty to basic defects in the system of resource allocation. It notes, for example, such effects of technology (including automation) as the dropping of 90% of the unskilled workers in the turnover from manned bombers to missiles. It notes that what increases in jobs have occurred in the last decade have been mainly in the public sector. And in rejecting the idea that poverty represents a set of separate misfortunes, it finds a series of shared interests among the impoverished and a necessity for the involvement of the poor in the design and the politics of a war on poverty. Hopefully, this gives fuller regard to the actual needs of the deprived rather than assuming the poor to be cases in need of restitution for their deficiencies in middle class orientations or achievements. In any event, the market for the research approach we propose depends upon the rationale and the modus operandi for application of this latter theory of poverty. We depart further from our original problem to provide this rationale in some detail.

A reasonable starting point for this departure may be found in Herbert J. Gans' seventeen proposals for government policy in the field of poverty (The Correspondent, Jan.-Feb., 1964). The categories are:

1. incentives to encourage entry into unfilled jobs;
2. the creation of helping technicians or sub-professionals;
3. incentives to encourage occupational shifts;
4. incentives for earlier entry into skilled occupations;
5. industry incentives to develop a secondary work force;
6. incentives to workers to reduce work hours;
7. elimination of involuntary workers from the labor force;
8. grants for currently unpaid volunteer work;
9. the professionalization of all occupations;
10. export of surplus American consumer goods;
11. "export" of American skilled workers;
12. employer incentives for the hiring of the unemployed;
13. temporary adjustment of the minimum wage law (downward);
14. encouragement of new business using unskilled labor;
15. a blue collar national service corp;
16. the elimination of income taxes among the low income population; and
17. direct income grants to the low income population.

These seventeen proposals for government policy to reduce the intolerable consequences of automation would go far, if adopted, to ease problems of domestic unemployment. But, as Gans himself suggests, the proposals are not likely to be adopted without certain antecedent political action by the poor or by some rather profound changes in middle-class values. Even if the policies were enacted they would do considerably more to aid the domestic picture on employment than to aid the picture on self-respect and personal worth. Even in our own acquisitive, market-oriented society where people measure themselves in terms of what others will pay for their services, there are times when having a job is insufficient. There are times when people identify strong goals for themselves—conquering an enemy, making a home, getting an education, eradicating poverty, etc. At such times self-esteem stems more from doing a job than

from holding one. In fact, the case in which holding a job adequately serves the need for individual self-respect is probably a special case deriving from anomic and segmentalized features of our society. Autonomous middle-class families get the college educations, the boats and suburban homes they desire on savings from the income of their own jobs. But what is more generally needed is the feeling that one's effort is meaningfully related to meeting felt needs or aspirations, however limited these may be. People receive palliatives for their purposeless lives by being given a title, a salary, and a set of inconsequential duties. But a true sense of purpose is a more likely by-product of working on a job which one feels inwardly has to be done. If that quality of "having to be done" derives from cultural or subcultural goals, then the job gains two important properties. First, it earns esteem in the eyes of peers, and second, it means, for the individual, that he is a participant in, rather than a pawn of, the decision-forces which affect his daily life. Without such participation self-respect is a hoax.

This may sound as though we are speaking only of the standards for optimal mental health among middle class intellectuals. We are not. A psychologist colleague shared experiences with us from his research in an experimental workshop for psychotic geriatric patients. The work involves real (though minuscule) pay for real work contracted from industrial concerns or hospitals. The rehabilitative value is phenomenal. Patients in the program not only regain reality contact but have volunteered heavy overtime work to meet rush orders and have taken over much of the quality control and training tasks of the workshop. But two problems have emerged. What if there were no contracts, and what do the rehabilitated do when released? In discussing this with our colleague, he offered the opinion that sorting buttons into piles of different colors—which could then be mixed up by attendants and returned to the patients to be sorted again—would not bring about the rehabilitative result; genuine participation is necessary. Even if therapeutic results could be achieved by a ruse, many professionals would, for preservation of their own integrity, be unable to carry it out. "I would sooner tell the patients there isn't any job for them to do," is the way one psychologist put it. "In the long run it would certainly fail." And the problem for these patients upon discharge is just this: there isn't any real job for them in the existing social structure. Reward for moonshining or increase in social security benefits may provide enough pocket money to meet food—and some medical— bills, but there is no personal worth in this. The appropriate place to start a program which will achieve self-respect for these and other deprived minorities is not with the excuses we can find to channel a part of the national income to them. The starting point should be the place where they can, with or without income, participate in tasks which mean something. The most relevant "something" at this point in history seems to be political protest. Such protest is necessary not only to achieve the eventual governmental sanction for income redistributing policy; it is necessary as well for the mental health of the participants. Furthermore, it may be essential to the maintenance or even partial preservation of democratic institutions in a cybernated society. At this point channelled and organized protest seems the most promising manner for participation in the selection of social goals.

While we are creating programs to bring income to the poor we must be careful that we do something to overcome the decision gap as well as the income gap. In automated industrial society, the number of individuals who are "with it," able and willing to comprehend the technical bases for decisions affecting the course of society, tends to be reduced. Along with the growth of a technically competent and politically "savvy" elite, there is a simultaneous growth in the number of lives affected and the reach of consequences of each decision made. One major effect of this separation of the poor from the decisions which affect their livelihood is the abdication of responsibility to fight for legitimate interests. When this responsibility is lost, people are living in a state of decay.

The seventeen proposals were grouped into three major headings: those dealing with upgrading of workers to fill jobs which are available from a semi-skilled to a subprofessional level; those dealing with the creation of new jobs; and those dealing with the elimination of poverty. The proposals might also be classified according to the directness of the policy to the target groups for whose benefit they are intended. One set of policy suggestions are for less direct fiscal incentives by which individuals and firms, acting privately, might find it less lucrative to automate people out of jobs or to work harder or longer, and more lucrative for them to train themselves and others, to vacation, and to expand (or reside) selectively where expansion would create jobs. In addition to fiscal in-

centives to entice job-increasing decisions, there is a set of policy proposals which involves the direct transmission of money, employment information, and skills to the have-nots. Some of the latter group of suggestions, like the idea of training subprofessional social workers, teachers, etc., to fill shortages in areas of poverty, are bold and promising ventures for the government. But what characterizes both sets of proposals is that they are programs by which a benevolent elite does things to improve the lot of culturally deprived and somewhat alienated minorities. This is clearly not enough. Is there no legitimate role for the poor in the war on poverty? And how effectively will the program upgrade the self-appraisal of the impoverished unless it is, at least partly, their program?

What we are suggesting is that however good it may be to exterminate rats in the Harlem tenements, it is better still if the action follows a tenant-led rent strike than if it is decided upon by benevolent city administrators. This is not to say that the city officials and the liberal elites should avoid working through legislative channels to create a socio-legal framework in which these people might function with dignity. The point is that if the rats were removed without protest there would still be hundreds of grievances for which protest was needed. And without some identification with the voice of protest, people will feel almost as inadequate without rats and with a few dollars as they felt when they were broke and shared their apartments with rats. One might argue that identification with any goals—including middle-class goals of the children in college, the newer car, and the suburban house—might be as good. But are there any goals, outside of political protest against poverty and injustice, which are relevant to poor people's existing needs?

The argument could still be made that a voice of protest is good and perhaps essential but that proposals for government policy are necessarily restricted to the non-protest arena. This seems not entirely true. In the area of defense spending, for example, the cold war receives a number of "fringe benefits" which are quite above and beyond the particular piece of research or hardware being purchased. A prodefense pressure group is subsidized at congressional levels and in the regions where contracts are at stake. The Department of Defense not only directs industry to meet its needs but manages to give industry the opportunity to help define what these needs, present and future, will be.

Somewhere in the defense contracts is the money which supports the defense industries' lobbyists, their retired generals, and their "educational programs" which return dividends to the cold war. Whether or not this type of governmental sponsorship of political activity was arrived at by accident or by design, it is a good model for the anti-poverty warriors in government to follow. The effect of Defense Department fiscal policies on contract recipients has not only been in the provision of money for services rendered; it has also provided a sense of righteous, patriotic pride among the more rabid cold warriors, a rationale for their own existence which is a congruent part of the strategic rationale they have helped to create for the nation's pursuits. And isn't this a direct analogue of the conditions necessary to bring a sense of worth to impoverished groups? If so, then government proposals for the economic upgrading of people will have to find ways to leak resources into community-centered protest movements. Groups which have traditionally worked intimately with people in the ghettos will have to find channels of support for their organizational activities. This is vital if those who work less directly for people in these areas are to have effect.

The cultural bridge between planners and "planned for" is wide. Few planners know the have-nots closely enough to appreciate the resistance with which their plans will be met. The elites who make the paper calculations which result in an Appalachia program would not have the stomach for a week's visit with area residents. If the fondest expectations of the planners were to come true, one could envision a society in which the best operations researchers, organizers, and other scientists, now employed in defense and aerospace, were managing a vast data processing network. At the control centers, continuously revised projections regarding the availability of prospective jobs, present training facilities, and unemployed people would make possible calculations of where the unemployed (and potentially unemployed) person would go and what he would do to find and qualify for either real work or "make-work" of some sort. If the stakes are high enough, if his meal ticket depends upon it, he will show up to get new data about himself punched onto his card and he may overcome some subcultural resistances of mobility and make the move designed for him. But he will be frustrated in his dealings with a multi-level (and therefore slow) buck-passing bureaucracy. He will not have developed concerns

for the well-being of other people. He will still feel and be a pawn of remote forces, and he will be a recipient rather than a participant in the fruits of his society.

Some traditional concepts of the welfare state wither under the very conditions of automation which have made them salient. If welfare is to coexist with meaningful participation in a democratic society, the voice of protest will have to be nurtured. If we do not have the stomach to communicate directly with impoverished lower-class people, on their terms, we will have to find ways to support others who will do this. Without institutions for communication there will be little chance for upgrading human dignity.

The operating code of groups like SNCC, SDS, and Mobilization for Youth involves two principles for action. The first is to listen and gain rapport with their clients so that the leads for projects are taken from the needs presented. The second is to identify the power structures which do have the capacity for making decisions in the area of protest. The level of protest is continually revised from protest against the single landlord or shopkeeper, to protest to the city agencies which do not enforce housing codes, to protest against the mayor or city officers. Then it moves toward the local "business development councils" and the realtors' associations, the business chains, and the banking interests which often support these other groups, and on into the urban political machines. As the movement has gained in experience it has come, with increasing frequency, to bypass the private discriminating barber shop or the single building owner. While maintaining close client contact by residency in the midst of the slum area, the student workers have become increasingly adept at the use of industrial and elite registries from Who's Who in Commerce and Industry, through the large number of registries indicating stock, bond, and property holdings of the directors and officers of local corporations, or guidebooks to the identities of individuals of local power in the area of banking, transportation, private light, power, and utilities. They have become adept at discovering the business ties of local political elites. They have become equally adept at identifying police and managerial affiliations with extremist groups and union leaders and school principals who detest equal-status contact with spokesmen for the deprived. Records of county clerks, of tax assessors, and court records have also been used to spot the local powers and learn more about them.

Sometimes the threat of exposure has proven effective as in the case of steel companies moving rapidly for appeasing the Birmingham demonstrators immediately after SNCC distributed leaflets in front of the New York stock exchange discussing corporate involvements in the Birmingham situation. More frequently the young organizers have found that when they can identify the powers which really could make the changes they desire, their opposition becomes a formidable and unyielding one. That this voice of the poor has stepped on sensitive toes seems evident in the willingness of Northern newspapers to echo the charges of their Southern counterparts that the movement must be infiltrated by communists. Ultimately they run into the problem that the mayor himself cannot do something significant about their slum area even if he wished to, for he himself is a small part of a political system putting its major allocations of time and effort into military programs. Ultimately the power structures which they will uncover will be that diverse set of military, political, and economic institutions whose convergent interests form the present allocation policies. As their movement reaches this point, the research contribution we have suggested becomes relevant. There are potential alliances of interest with the more convertible segments of the complex. There are more intransigent elements whose operating procedures may make them vulnerable to exposure. There will be certain elections and certain pieces of legislation which cut more deeply than others into the points of cohesion within the complex. Knowing these points allows for concentration upon them.

This emergent movement of the organized lower income and no-income groups is thus the market for one brand of peace research. As a movement it has a potential for growth which was lacking in the middle-class peace movement, for its basis is omnipresent, unmet needs. Organizations of the aged and of the underprivileged young are already forming as potential converging forces.

It is important to note that the thrust of the movement is aimed not only at the horrendous misallocation of resources, but at the allocation process itself. We have not addressed ourselves to the question of what level of weaponry and what uses of it are good or necessary in the nuclear age. We have dealt only with the problem of the countervailing force necessary if a change such as general disarmament is even to be considered, or to be looked upon as genuinely desirable and worthy of intensified pursuit. And as the focus of the cold war moves toward areas of underdevelopment, it may be an important asset to have the organized poor demanding as much scrutiny over expenditures for military foreign aid as the business community has traditionally demanded for expenditures in economic aid.

Obviously, we have not answered our own question of whether there exists a military-industrial complex which can prevent peace. We have argued that the conditions of a stable peace will differ markedly from the conditions of temporary avoidance of war and that constellations of powerful and divergent interests coalesce on certain policies which work against social change. We have tried to show that the absence of monolithic decision power among these groups, while essentially correct, is a weak argument in the absence of a countervailing force for peace. We have attempted to prejudge—on scant and early evidence—the rise of a politically viable force with a critical stake in the decisions which move us toward peace and in the particular national and local programs which will offset the nation's defense efforts. We have hinted at the nature of social science research which could prove helpful to such a countervailing force.

There are, of course, numerous ways in which the social scientist can work through federal agencies to bring attention to the consequences of intellectual and scholarly efforts to the makers of policy decisions. Whether these decisions will in fact bring us closer to the transition to peace depends in large measure on the answer to the question we posed in our title. We stress here that the work of the social scientist could be a factor in the answer to that question.[14]

---

[14] This point is more fully developed in the original paper and in Pilsuk, M. "The Poor and the War on Poverty," The Correspondent, Summer, 1965.

References

Angell, Robert C. A study of social values: content analysis of elite media. The Journal of Conflict Resolution, VIII, 1964, 4, 329-85.

Bank Holding Companies: Scope of Operations and Stock Ownership. Committee on Banking and Currency. Washington: U.S. Government Printing Office, 1963.

Barber, Arthur. Some industrial aspects of arms control. The Journal of Conflict Resolution, VII, 1963, 3, 491-95.

Bauer, Raymond A., Pool, I., and Dexter, L. American business and public policy. Alberton, New York, 1963.

Bell, Daniel. The end of ideology. Glencoe: Free Press, 1959.

Benoit, Emile, and Boulding, K. E. (Eds.). Disarmament and the economy. New York: Harper, 1963.

Berle, Adolph A. The twentieth century capitalist revolution. New York: Harcourt, 1954.

Bluestone, Irving. Problems of the worker in industrial conversion. The Journal of Conflict Resolution, VII, 1963, 3, 495-502.

Brand, Horst. Disarmament and American capitalism. Dissent, Summer, 1962. 236-251.

Burdick, Eugene, and Wheeler, H. Fail-safe. New York: McGraw, 1962.

Burton, John. Peace theory. New York: Knopf, 1962.

Cartwright, Dorwin. Power: a neglected variable in social psychology, in Cartwright, D. (Ed.) Studies in social power. Ann Arbor: Research Center for Group Dynamics, 1959.

Catton, Bruce. The war lords of Washington. New York: Harcourt, 1948.

Coffin, Tristran. The passion of the hawks. New York: Macmillan, 1964.

Cohen, Bernard, C. The press and foreign policy. Princeton: Princeton University Press 1963.

Convertibility of Space and Defense Resources to Civilian Needs, 88th Congress, 2d Session, Vol. 2, Subcommittee on Employment and Manpower. Washington: U.S. Government Printing Office, 1964.

Cook, Fred J. The coming politics of disarmament. The Nation. February 6, 1963.

————. The warfare state. New York: Macmillan, 1962.

Dahl, Robert A. A modern political analysis. New York: Prentice Hall, 1963.

————. Who Governs? New Haven: Yale University Press, 1961.

Dillon, W. Little brother is watching. Boston, Houghton Mifflin, 1962.

Economic impacts of disarmament. U.S. Arms Control and Disarmament Agency, Economic Series 1, Washington: U.S. Government Printing Office, 1962.

Eells, Richard, and Walton, C. Conceptual foundations of business. Homewood, Illinois: Irwin Press, 1961.

Etzioni, Amitai. The hard way to peace. New York: Collier, 1962.

————. The moon-doggle. Garden City, New York: Doubleday, 1964.

Fearon, H. E., and Hook, R. C., Jr. The shift from military to industrial markets. Business Topics, Winter, 1964, 43-52.

Feingold, Eugene and Hayden, Thomas. What happened to democracy? New University Thought, Summer, 1964, 1, 39-48.

Fisher, Roger (Ed.). International conflict and behavioral science. New York: Basic Books, 1964.

Fishman, Leslie. A note on disarmament and effective demand. The Journal of Political Economy, LXX, 1962, 2, 183-186.

Foreign Assistance Act of 1964 (Parts VI and VII), Committee on Foreign Affairs. Hearings, 88th Congress, 2nd Session. Washington: U.S. Government Printing Office, 1964.

Friedman, S. The Rand Corporation and our Policy Makers, Atlantic Monthly, September, 1963, 61-68.

Frye, Wm. R. Characteristics of recent arms-control proposals and agreements. In Brennan, D. G. (Ed.), Arms control, disarmament, and national security. New York: Braziller, 1963.

Galbraith, J. K. American Capitalism. Boston: Houghton, 1956.

————. Poverty among nations. The Atlantic Monthly, October, 1962, 47-53.

Gans, Herbert J. Some proposals for government policy in an automating society. The Correspondent, 30, Jan.-Feb., 1964, 74-82.

Government Information Plans and Policies. Parts I-V, Hearings before a Sub-committee on Government Operations. 88th Congress, 1st Session, U.S. Govt. Printing Office: 1963.

Green, Philip. Alternative to overkill: dream and reality. Bulletin of the Atomic Scientists, November, 1963, 23-26.

Hayakawa, S. J. Formula for peace: listening. N.Y. Times Magazine. July 31, 1961.

Horowitz, David. World economic disparities: the haves and the have-nots. Center for Study of Democratic Institutions: Santa Barbara, 1962.

Horowitz, I. L. The war game: studies of the new civilian militarists. New York: Ballantine, 1963.

Humphrey, Hubert H. The economic impact of arms control agreements. Congressional Record. October 5, 1962, 2139-94.

Impact of Military Supply and Service Activities on the Economy. 88th Congress, 2nd Session. Report to the Joint Economic Committee. Washington: U.S. Government Printing Office, 1963.

Isard, Walter, and Schooler, E. W. An economic analysis of local and regional impacts of reduction of military expenditures. Papers Vol. 1, 1964 Peace Research Society International. Chicago Conference, 1963.

Janowitz, Morris. Military elites and the study of war. The Journal of Conflict Resolution, I, 1957, 1, 9-18.

———. The professional soldier. Glencoe, Ill.: The Free Press, 1960.

Keller, Suzanne. Beyond the ruling class. New York: Random House, 1963.

Knebel, Fletcher, and Bailey, C. Seven days in May. New York: Harper, 1962.

Knorr, Klaus. Warfare and peacefare states and the acts of transition. The Journal of Conflict Resolution, VII, 1963, 4, 754-62.

Lapp, Ralph E. Kill and overkill. New York: Basic Books, Inc., 1962.

Larson, Arthur. The internation rule of law. A Report to the committee on Research for Peace, No. 3, Institute for International Order, 1961.

Lasswell, Harold. Politics: Who gets what, when & how. New York: Meridian, 1958.

Lipset, Seymour M. Political man. Garden City: Doubleday, 1959.

Long Island Sunday Press, The. February 23, 1964.

Lowi, Theodore J. "American Business, Public Policy, Case-Studies, and Political Theory," World Politics, July, 1964, 676-715.

Lumer, Hyman. War economy and crisis. New York: International Publishers, 1954.

Lynd, Robert S., and Merrill, Helen. Middletown. New York: Harcourt, 1959.

Mannheim, Karl. Freedom, power, and democratic planning. London: Routledge and Kegan Paul, 1956.

McDonagh, James J., and Zimmerman, Steven M. A program for civilian diversifications of the airplane industry. In Convertibility of Space and Defense Resources to Civilian Needs. Subcommittee on Employment and Manpower. U.S. Senate, 88th Congress. Washington: U.S. Government Printing Office, 1964.

McNamara, Robert S. Remarks of the Secretary of Defense before the Economic Club of New York. Department of Defense Office of Public Affairs, Washington, November 18, 1963.

Meisel, James H. The fall of the republic. Ann Arbor: University of Michigan Press, 1962.

———. The myth of the ruling class. Ann Arbor University of Michigan Press, 1958.

Melman, Seymour (Ed.). A strategy for American Security, New York: Lee Offset Inc., 1963.

———. The peace race. New York: Braziller, 1962.

Merbaum, R. Rand: technocrats and power, New University Thought. December-January, 1963-64, 45-57.

Michael, Donald. Cybernation: the silent conquest. Center for the Study of Democratic Institutions Santa Barbara, 1962.

Milbrath, L. W. The Washington lobbyists. Chicago: Rand McNally, 1963.

Military Posture and Authorizing Appropriations for Aircraft, Missiles, and Naval Vessels. Hearings No. 36, 88th Congress, 2nd Session, U.S. Govt. Printing Office: 1964.

Military Procurement Authorization Fiscal Year 1962. Hearings before the Committee on Armed Services, U.S. Senate, 87th Congress, 1st Session, U.S. Govt. Printing Office: 1961.

Mills, C. Wright. The causes of World War III. New York: Simon & Schuster, 1958.

———. The power elite. New York: Oxford University Press, 1959.

Minnis, Jack. The care and feeding of power structures. New University Thought V. 4, Summer, 1964, 1, 73-79.

Nossiter, Berland. The Mythmakers: an essay on power and wealth. Boston: Houghton, 1964.

Osgood, Charles E. An alternative to war or surrender. Urbana: University of Illinois Press, 1962.

Parsons, Talcott. Structure and process in modern societies. Glencoe: Free Press, 1959.

———. The social system. Glencoe: Free Press, 1951.

Paul, J., and Laulicht, J. Leaders' and voters', attitudes on defense and disarmament. In Your

Opinion, V. 1, Canadian Peace Research Inst., Clarkson, Ontario, 1963.

Peck, M. J., and Scherer, F. M. The weapons acquisition process. Boston: Harvard University, 1962.

Perlo Victor. Militarism and industry. New York: International Publishers, 1963.

Piel, Gerard. Consumers of abundance. Center for the Study of Democratic Institutions, Santa Barbara, 1961.

Pilisuk, Marc. Dominance of the Military. Science, January 18, 1963, 247-48.

———. The Poor and the War on Poverty, The Correspondent, Summer, 1965.

Pyramiding of Profits and Costs in the Missile Procurement Program, Parts 1, 2 and 3. Committee on Government Operations, U.S. Senate. Hearings, 87th Congress, 2nd Session. Washington: U.S. Govt. Printing Office, 1962.

Pyramiding of Profits and Costs in the Missile Procurement Program, Report, 88th Congress, 2nd Session, Report No. 970. Washington: U.S. Government Printing Office, 1964.

Rapoport, Anatol. Fights, games, and debates. Ann Arbor: University of Michigan Press, 1960.

———. Strategy and conscience. New York: Harper, 1964.

Raymond, Jack. Power at the Pentagon. New York: Harper, 1964.

Reagan, Michael. The Managed Economy. New York: Oxford, 1963.

Reiner, Thomas. Spatial criteria to offset military cutbacks. Paper presented at the Univ. of Chicago Peace Research Conference, Nov. 18, 1964.

Report on the world today. The Atlantic, September, 1964, 4-8.

Rogow, Arnold A. James Forrestal. New York: Macmillan, 1963.

Satellite communications, 1964. (Part 1) Committee on Government Operations, Hearings, 88th Congress, 2nd Session. Washington: U.S. Government Printing Office, 1964.

Scherer, Frederick. The weapons acquisition process: economic incentives. Cambridge: Harvard Business School, 1964.

Shils, Edward. Professor Mills on the calling of sociology. World Politics, XIII, 1961, 4.

Singer, J. David. A study of foreign policy attitudes. The Journal of Conflict Resolution, VIII, 1964, 4, 424-85.

———. Deterrence, arms control and disarmament. Columbus: Ohio State University Press, 1962.

———. (ed), Weapons management in world politics. The Journal of Conflict Resolution, VII, No. 3, and Journal of Arms Control, Vol. 1, No. 4.

Stachey, John. On the prevention of war. New York: St. Martin's Press, 1963.

Strauss, Lewis L. Men and decisions. Garden City: Doubleday, 1962.

Sutton, Jefferson. The missile lords. New York: Dell, 1963.

Swomley, J. M., Jr. The growing power of the military. The Progressive, January, 1959.

———. The military establishment. Boston: Beacon Press, 1964.

Toward Full Employment: Proposals for a Comprehensive Employment and Manpower Policy in the U.S. A Report of the Committee on Labor and Public Welfare, United States Senate. Washington: U.S. Government Printing Office, 1964.

Toward world peace: a summary of U.S. disarmament efforts past and present. U.S. Arms Control and Disarmament Agency Publication 10: U.S. Government Printing Office, 1964.

Warner, Wm. Floyd, and Abegglen, J. D. Big business leaders in America. New York: Harper, 1955.

Warner, Wm. Floyd, Van Riper, P.P., Martin, N. H., and Collins, O. F. The American federal executive. New Haven: Yale University Press, 1963.

Watson-Watt, Sir Robert. Man's means to his end. London: Heinemann, 1962.

Westin, Alan. Anti-communism and the corporations. Commentary Magazine. December, 1963, 479-87.

Wise, David, and Ross, Thomas. The invisible government. New York: Random, 1964.

Wright, Quincy, Evans, Wm., and Deutsch, Morton (Eds.). Preventing World War III: some proposals. New York: Simon and Schuster, 1962.

WARFARE AND PEACEFARE STATES AND THE COSTS OF TRANSITION: A REVIEW

Emile Benoit and Kenneth E. Boulding, <u>Disarmament and the Economy</u>
Neil W. Chamberlain, <u>The West in a World Without War</u>
Fred J. Cook, <u>The Warfare State</u>
The Economist Intelligence Unit, <u>The Economic Effects of Disarmament</u>
United Nations, <u>Economic and Social Consequences of Disarmament</u>

Klaus Knorr

I

Mr. Cook's book <u>The Warfare State</u> (1962) deals with an important subject. His main thesis, reminiscent of the writings of the late C. Wright Mills, is rather simple. Since World War II, the United States has developed into a "Warfare State" that the military and the big business elite rule by means, first, of propaganda disseminated especially through the mass media of communication, managed by Madison Avenue, and, second, of the pocketbook appeal to the many enterprises and workers that have a vested interest in defense business. The avowed purpose of the Warfare State is to wage the Cold War and pursue the arms race; its real purpose is to protect the American status quo in terms of class and group interests. The consequences of the Warfare State will be the corruption of American society and, sooner or later, the outbreak of suicidal nuclear war.

Unfortunately, Mr. Cook has written a very bad book. I appreciate that it is not meant to be scholarly, but the fact that he is a journalist does not exempt him from using evidence responsibly and from avoiding distortion in his analysis and conclusions.

I also appreciate that I may be a biased reviewer. By all the counts listed in Mr. Cook's book, I am a supporting citizen of the Warfare State. To cite a few credentials, in 1957 I published a memorandum entitled "Is the American Defense Effort Enough?"—a question I answered in the negative. I have been, and am, a consultant to government agencies concerned with problems of national security. I have come to esteem a good number of generals and colonels, and among my

friends I count Herman Kahn and Henry Kissinger, whom Mr. Cook regards as "dedicated evangelists of the holy crusade against communism . . ." (p. 324). According to his standards, this should make me a "spearholder of the status quo" (p. 69), either a militarist or a dupe of the militarists.

If Mr. Cook had just written an atrocious book, I would not care to review it. He has, however, written a bad book on an important subject on which no good book exists, and it is for this reason that it may be worthwhile to document very selectively, of necessity, why it is a bad book.

According to Mr. Cook, the "military-industrial complex," dating from wartime collaboration, is ruled by the "ultra-conservative classes" (p. 351) and dominates American society (p. 351) and government, regardless of the party "in power" (p. 91), to the extent that the voting booth has become merely one of the "democratic trappings of our society" (p. 9). The military dominate the "complex." "In the Warfare State, the only word that counts a tinker's damn is the word of the Military" (p. 201). They control not only defense policy but also our foreign policy (pp. 195-6); indeed there is "hardly an area in our lives today in which the military influence is anything less than supreme" (p. 194).

Although Mr. Cook does not exonerate the Soviet leaders from co-responsibility for the arms race (e.g., pp. 163, 204, 249, 261), he has an amazingly exact date for the beginning of the Cold War—April 23, 1945, eleven days after the death of President Roosevelt and cites President Truman, Admiral Leahy, and Secretary Forrestal as the chief culprits. The rulers of the Warfare State succeeded quickly and completely in committing the United States to the "cul de sac of the Cold War" (p. 145), the arms race, and the inevitable doom of nuclear disaster (e.g., pp. 88, 355). Our rullers control us by keeping us in a perpetual state of fear (pp. 162-3), by conditioning our minds (largely by means of brainwashing for which, as taxpayers, we pay the bill), and—presumably lest

*From Klaus Knorr, "Warfare and Peacefare States and the Costs of Transition," Journal of Conflict Resolution, Vol. VII, December 1963, pp. 754-762. Reprinted by permission of the <u>Journal</u> and the author.

anyone attempt a breakthrough to reality—by appeal to self-interest in the jobs and profits afforded by our huge armament effort. Indeed, with the exception of a few discerning minds like Mr. Cook, Americans seem to have become a nation of boobs, or rather "sheep," as he suggests (p. 355). Thus the Warfare State—or, more tersely expressed, "insanity"—has become the "American way of life" (pp. 162, 349). This, in his view, is the mentality that made Buchenwald possible (p. 253).

Though Mr. Cook sees the military as top dog in the military-industrial complex, it seems to be the business elite that is the chief beneficiary of the Warfare State. Its ultimate raison d'etre is not to fight the Soviet Union but to protect business profits and, above all, to keep the United States from developing into a "Welfare State" (pp. 86, 170). At Bottom, the ultra-conservative classes have shackled and subverted American society because they are obsessed "by a paranoid phobia of change and revolution" (p. 351).

II

I will not attempt to refute Mr. Cook's thesis. The fair reader will conclude, at the very least, that exaggeration is not alien to his mode of expression. In my opinion, he has written a repulsive book for which he deserves to be censured even though, since it probably represents un crime passionel, he may claim extenuating circumstances. His performance is a pity, for there is, as President Eisenhower has warned us, a powerful "military-industrial complex," and we are badly in need of an empirical study—based, however, on painstaking and no doubt difficult research—of its size, structure, processes, and consequences. It may indeed be said, if one likes this sort of rhetoric, that we have a warfare state which is a subsystem of American society; that many, if not most of us, play a role in it; and that we must reconcile the claims of this role with those of the many other roles we play as members of mankind, of the United States, of a profession, family, political party, church, and many other groups. Professor Boulding, in his remarkable essay on "The World War Industry," points out that the producers of wealth (nonmilitary) and the destroyers of wealth (military) are "not, in fact, independent social species" (Benoit and Boulding, 1963, p. 6). However, most Americans are not members of either pure species. They are constituents of both the warfare and the peacefare state; and if the peacefare state ever subdues, and perhaps

does away with, the warfare state, this will result, I suspect, not so much from a vast preponderance of pure producers over pure destroyers than from a radical shift in the balance of effective claims that the two states are able to make on the average individual.

Warfare states do exist, here and elsewhere, because the international system and most of its actors are such that military aggression and war remain a fateful contingency; and, thus far at least, mankind has found no workable alternative to this system. As long as it does not, the United States in particular will be unable to do without maintaining an extensive warfare state. This country cannot hope to receive effective protection from the warfare states of other nations; rather, the military security of a great many less powerful countries is in fact dependent on American protection and the American warfare state.

III

Beyond question, therefore, Mr. Cook raises issues that are worrisome and demand attention and study. As long as we remain dependent on the warfare state, we are condemned "to wear a military scowl" (p. 355), a posture that represents a sharp break with national life before World War II (p. 35). But, contrary to Mr. Cook's thesis, it is precisely because the United States has not broken with its basically nonmilitary tradition, has not become a militarist nation, has not as a nation succumbed to the warfare state, that the leaders of the warfare state are often compelled to overdramatize international crises and exaggerate the threats confronting this country (see pp. 107 ff.) in order to make a fundamentally reluctant citizenry support the claims of the warfare state. This practice is apt to reduce the flexibility of action that our leaders require in the management of crises and conflicts—an unfortunate consequence tending to increase the risk of war. And there is the question of whether, over the longer run, the nation will not accept the warfare state as the ineluctable and dominating reality, accept what Professor Lasswell has called "the garrison state" (Huntington, 1962, ch. 3), and exhibit some of the properties depicted in Mr. Cook's lurid nightmare. He also is rightly disturbed about the hysteria to which large parts of the American public are susceptible in crisis situations (e.g., pp. 164 f.). Certainly, the kind of passion and rage at large during the Cuban crisis in 1962 makes it hard to achieve national security on a rational basis.

But these problems have been probed more subtly and perceptively by others—for instance, David Riesman (Riesman, 1963, pp. 14-7). He also is afraid of the cumulative impact on American public opinion of the constant accentuation of the dangers of Communist military and political power, of the Administration's problem of deterring the Americans as well as the Russians, and of the asymmetry that exists in this matter of popular pressures between the Soviet Union and the democratic world. Indeed, these conditions not only bespeak the danger of stimulating an excessive growth of the warfare state; they render the warfare state a less efficient instrument and thereby endanger national security. The warfare state, after all, functions best under a leadership that is cool as well as determined, flexible as well as strong, and with popular support that is resolute, enduring, and unsparing rather than volatile, at times frenzied, and possessed by an instability that originates in frustration over the neverending series of external troubles that refuse to be terminated by one furious and righteous blow. These characteristics do not seem to indicate the presence of the Lasswellian "garrison state," which involves a narrow rather than wide sharing of power and forms "the self-perpetuation of an elite specialized to the planning and implementation of coercive strategies of power" (Huntington, 1962, p. 59). Under conditions of chronic psychological mobilization in the United States, popular, if not populist, militancy does not rarely press hard on a government that, aware of the risks, prefers to move with controlled circumspection.

These grave issues deserve further exploration and increasing public ventilation. They also require empirical research on the nature and activities of the warfare state as it exists today. Professor Lasswell has supplied the conceptual framework. What remains to be done is to apply it to a study of the actual world we live in.

IV

Boulding is easily as pure a citizen of the peacefare state as Mr. Cook, but I vastly prefer his cool and refined conceptual world to Mr. Cook's sweaty fiction. The first part of Boulding's essay on the milorg system is clever, elegant, and amusing. Yet it hardly helps us in understanding the problems we face today. In a few passages he abandons his economic concepts and analogues—because they do not fit—and points up some of the tough problems that are liable to bedevil any transition from the warfare world to the peacefare world. One of the obstacles to disarmament, he notes, is the West's lack of confidence in waging ideological struggle; another, the problems presented by indirect aggression (p. 24).

However, the most interesting points relate to the payoffs expected from exchanging the peacefare for the warfare world. Boulding himself has no doubt about the worthwhileness of the payoff (pp. 18 ff.). But a lot of people do. Badly off as they know we are now, they are not sure that the peacefare world is better or that the passage to it is not full of peril. Boulding acknowledges some of the reasons for doubt. He indicates some of the advantages we would lose in terms of "cultural homogeneity and variety" and the "reduction of internal political problems to a manageable scale" (p. 15). He admits that there would be painful adjustments, including adjustments to the economic consequences of disarmament. He concedes that there is a problem of winding up all milorgs simultaneously. (If we do not manage an approximately simultaneous demobilization, one or some milorgs might regain "unconditional viability.") Conflicts would be transferred from the military to nonmilitary areas (p. 23 f.) and—this seems to me a crucial point—disarmament would be likely to involve a vast redistribution of power. Boulding states that the small countries would gain power at the expense of the larger ones (p. 23)—and, I would add, the nonnuclear powers, large or small, at the expense of the nuclear powers. It would also mean great gains in power of the many poor nations at the expense of the few wealthy ones, with consequences that are incalculable. Boulding suggests that "there must be some form of compensating payment" (p. 23) if the large countries are to accept general and complete disarmament. But, I am inclined to ask, who would enforce the compensatory arrangements once disarmament and the shift in power are complete? Between countries as well as within countries, the beneficiaries of disarmament are not necessarily the ones who would have to negotiate and bring it about.

V

The consequences of general disarmament on the international distribution of power is the central subject of Professor Chamberlain's study. He believes with Boulding that "the year of the bomb could prove to be a great watershed in human history" (Chamberlain, 1963, p. 80). According to his view, the inevitable spread of nuclear weapons to China and other nations makes any bilateral Soviet-American understandings on control ineffectual and will sooner or later compel nuclear disarmaments controlled and enforced by the United Nations (pp. 11 f.). Traditional sovereignty will come to an end at the very moment when this enforcement mechanism becomes effective. Military power and economic influence will cease as a basis of international power. They will be replaced by the "power to use the United Nations to one's own purposes" (p. 29). As a result, Western dominance will be superseded by the dominance of the underdeveloped Asiatic and African nations over the economically developed West, including Soviet Russia, and the Soviet-American conflict will be submerged by the governance of non-Western values. The chief consequence, according to Chamberlain, will be a compulsory redistribution of the world's wealth (p. 25). In effect, "the advanced, Westernized, industrialized societies would become resources" (p. 29), part of whose income would be distributed by means of a progressive tax system. The West would have no choice but to accept or to return to the frightening world of the nuclear arms race. Thus trapped, the West would decide to accept its tributary role. It would be securely "locked" into the new world organization (p. 29).

Chamberlain does not predict an uncomfortable future for the United States. The "draft on the economic capabilities of the West" (p. 37) would be limited by the capacity of the underdeveloped areas to absorb outside resources for the purpose of effective economic development (pp. 51 ff.). This would limit the draft to from 8 to 10 per cent of GNP, about the proportions of our gross income now going to the defense sector. "As a nation, our position in the world economy will roughly correspond to the position of our business leaders in the domestic economy today. The president of a large corporation is respected for his capabilities; he enjoys a fair amount of discretion in his daily work; he is permitted to live on a scale beyond that of most of society. But at the same time he works under considerable pressure and assumes much responsibility; the basic characteristics of the society in which he operates are determined chiefly outside of the environment which

he controls, and a large part of what he earns is taken away from him for the satisfaction of the wants of others" (pp. 79 f.). This does not, indeed, sound like too high a price to pay for the elimination of the destructive threat of nuclear war. By my standards, American business leaders do rather well. They have the opportunity for an active and interesting life, their post-tax incomes are quite high and their consumption level fairly sumptuous.

But I wonder whether Chamberlain's preview is realistic. He paints with an extremely broad brush. If disarmament would really engender the distribution of power he describes, why should the dominating majority of poor societies be so modest in its exploitation of the rich—especially since they may feel a great deal of pent-up resentment toward the West and the whites? Why must their take be limited by their absorptive capacity for economic growth? Why could it not go to raising consumption or to feeding the huge additions to their rapidly increasing populations? And why would they limit themselves to internationally redistributive finance? What, for example, if they wanted to redistribute population?

What I can see least of all is how the radical and clear-cut change in international power foreseen by Chamberlain would come about or, if it came about, how it would endure. Would the West and the Soviet Union negotiate disarmament with such startling prospects ahead? Once these kinds of consequences are contemplated, disarmament, as Chamberlain concedes, does not look so "rosy" (p. 83) and, unlike him, I do not believe that the United States has made a definite commitment to disarmament.

But supposing that nuclear disarmament and its enforcement did come about as predicted by Chamberlain, how effective would the anti-Western majority vote in the United Nations be? To be sure, any voting formula—except the inconceivable one of basing votes on wealth—would give the underdeveloped countries a majority, provided they formed a solid coalition against the developed Western nations. Yet how would this majority enforce its economic draft if the minority refused to pay? Who would be the tax collector and what would be his effective power over noncooperative countries such as the United States or the Soviet Union? It would take a huge U.N. force (or one prepared to employ nuclear arms against tax delinquents) to enforce collection. But who would finance such a force? It could only be the wealthy

West, including the U.S.S.R., and can one imagine these countries paying for large forces of Chinese, Indonesians, and Africans to occupy North America or Eastern Europe? And if noncooperation meant the breakdown of disarmament, would not some of the noncooperating countries prefer to rearm, and perhaps do so under conditions of arms control that they maintained and enforced among themselves?

Yet, fanciful as I think Mr. Chamberlain's predictions to be, he has identified and attacked problems that call for much more exploration than they have received. The difficulties they imply should not deter us. We might discover feasible solutions that are a definitely superior alternative to life under the shadow of the bomb. But the problems noted by Boulding and Chamberlain are unquestionably formidable. Their solution may well require "a world social contract" that, Boulding admits, is extremely difficult to achieve "under present conditions" (Benoit and Boulding, 1963, p. 18). Compared with the technical issues of arms control and inspection, these problems have not attracted much scholarly attention.

VI

One of the most potent impediments to the achievement of disarmament, according to Communist doctrine, is the dependence of the capitalist system on large armaments. Mr. Cook holds the same view. "The picture that emerges is that of a nation —the United States—whose entire economic welfare is tied to warfare" (Cook, 1962, p. 177). This thesis points to the relevance of the various works on the economic consequences of disarmament.

The books under review cause no surprise and offer no important new insights. This is partly so because Professor Benoit's long-awaited volume was preceded by several published progress reports on his work, and by the publication of other competent studies, such as the one undertaken by the United Nations (1962) and by the Intelligence Unit of the London Economist (1963). Furthermore, the studies are pretty much in agreement and confirm what economists have suspected all along.

If one assumes, as is reasonable, that general and complete disarmament would come about gradually over a number of years, and that reductions in defense spending would be offset in part by expenditures on an international arms control authority, then the magnitude of the economic problem is not formidable. It would be no larger than that experienced by national economies as a consequence of cyclical instability and economic development; and, as Professor Benoit points out, the aggregate adjustment indicated in his disarmament model is of the same size (relative to national income) as was the reduction in United States defense expenditures after the Korean War, from 1953 to 1960 (Benoit and Boulding, 1963, p. 272). The over-all requirement is one of maintaining a level of adequate demand, production, and employment by means of compensatory increases in private expenditures and nondefense public spending. There would, of course, be structural or frictional problems specific to states, localities, industries, and firms with a high dependence on defense outlays and, as Benoit observes (p. 285), the productive factors involved in defense contracts have become less mobile in recent years as a result of changes in defense technology and the increased emphasis on research and development. However, if aggregate demand is kept sufficiently high, and especially if the economy is growing, this problem is concluded to be essentially short-term, and capable of mitigation by various specific measures.

I do not mean to suggest that the books under review are not good and useful. Benoit's enterprise in particular can claim impressive results. This new literature gives us a better knowledge of the fine structure of the problems and of various methods of instrumenting the required remedial effort. Benoit's proposal of income tax holidays, for example, is ingenious (p. 294).

Yet the crucial problem posed by the economic dislocations of disarmament would be political. The economists know what needs to be done. But do our political leaders know it and, if they do, will the electorate permit them to act on this knowledge? Will the Administration in power propose and, above all, will the Congress enact an adequate combination of measures, and will they do so in time? I fail to see any reasons for optimism in this respect. Certainly the way our adjustment to the post-Korean cuts in defense expenditures was managed (cf. pp. 274 f.) does not inspire confidence.

Benoit and his associates recognize these obstacles. Benoit himself, for instance, is disturbed by the public "propensity to reduce the national debt out of defense savings" (p. 279). However, recognition of the problem by professional economists does not ensure its solution. Here seems to me to be another area for research for which the economic studies have paved the way, and which those interested in exploring the disarmament issue should undertake. The job would be one for political scientists and public opinion experts, not economists.

VII

The economic consequences of disarmament pose, I suspect, a further political question. Even if, in the event disarmament takes place, some such rational program as that outlined by Benoit and his associates were promptly adopted and duly executed, prestige, and comfort for a more or a great many people would suffer appreciable losses of employment, income, capital, less prolonged period of transition. These groups are employed in locations and occupations, or manage or own enterprises, now highly or completely dependent on the defense effort. It is all very well to argue that these "structural problems" can be solved over time. Aggregate analysis has its limitations. Will all these victims of transition be restored to the levels of income and prestige they now enjoy? (For instance, will this be true of the officer corps in the armed services or of the officials in the Department of Defense?) And will they be compensated for shortfalls in position and income, the discomforts of dislocation, and the uncertainties they will experience? In fact—and here we return to Mr. Cook—may they not experience anxieties now when confronted with the idea of disarmament? And would it be surprising if, subject to such anxieties, some of them preferred the warfare state —not in terms of putting their personal self-interest consciously above that of their country, but in ways protective of their self-respect; for example, by looking at the tough problems presented by disarmament and deciding that it is too risky for the nation? Few farmers, I am willing to bet, believe subsidized prices of farm products to be injurious to the country; and few members of labor unions regard as harmful to the economy practices that others describe as "feather-bedding." In this manner, the warfare state is probably anchored in self-interest, but I have no way of estimating the extent and weight of this factor (and neither has Mr. Cook).

If it ever comes to a national debate on the comparative merits of the warfare and peacefare states, its outcome should be relieved as much as possible of the impact that this factor might exert. This would seem to indicate the need for a sequel to Professor Benoit's work. What I have in mind is concentration on a few selected occupations (e.g., the military profession) and industries with a particularly high defense involvement, and the canvassing of special remedies adapted to their specific requirements by which their transition to the peacefare state could be made as painless as possible.

VIII

At first glance, one cannot help but be impressed by the large resources that nourish warfare states the world over. The United Nations experts estimate the total at roughly $120 billion a year, a figure equivalent to 8-9 per cent of the world's income, to one-half of the total resources set aside each year for gross capital formation, and to at least two-thirds of the entire national income of all the underdeveloped countries (United Nations, 1962, p. 3).

It is easy to imagine how much the peacefare state could do with these resources in terms of relieving poverty and improving education, health, and many other things. However, 85 per cent of military expenditures are made by seven countries, all—with the exception of mainland China—industrialized. Hence, unless Professor Chamberlain is right, the benefits from winding up the warfare state would accrue chiefly to the wealthy communities. And that means that the economic burden of the warfare state should be the least of our worries.

References

1. Benoit, Emile and Boulding, Kenneth E. (eds.). Disarmament and the Economy. New York: Harper & Row, 1963.

2. Chamberlain, Neil W. The West in a World Without War. New York: McGraw-Hill, 1963.

3. Cook, Fred J. The Warfare State. New York: Macmillan, 1962.

4. Economist Intelligence Unit. The Economic Effects of Disarmament. London: The Economist Intelligence Unit, 1963.

5. Huntington, Samuel P. (ed.). Changing Patterns of Military Politics. New York: The Free Press of Glencoe, 1962.

6. Knorr, Klaus. Is the American Defense Effort Enough? Memorandum No. 14, Princeton, N.J.: Center of International Studies, 1957.

7. Riesman, David. "Containing Ourselves: Some Reflections on the Enemy Within," The New Republic, April 6, 1963, pp. 14-7.

8. United Nations. Economic and Social Consequences of Disarmament. New York: United Nations, 1962.

Part 5

EDUCATIONAL COMPLEX

THE SEARCH FOR INTERNAL COHERENCE*

James A. Perkins

We have discussed the attributes of knowledge—its acquisition, transmission, and application—and discovered that they correspond to the three missions of the modern university: teaching, research, and public service. We suggested that the explosive power of knowledge might be traceable to an interaction of its attributes, and that in like manner the growth and current power of the university in the United States might derive from the fact that it, and perhaps it alone, had fully embraced its three missions.

We also observed that, in the midst of all this, the modern university appears threatened by its own success. There are some indications that the university may, in responding to society's urgent demands that it enlarge its research, teaching, and service functions, risk the fate which size and mindlessness imposed on the dinosaurs. It is a chilling thought, but I have hinted at my optimistic belief that we can avoid such a fate by the exercise of our reason and our organizing abilities.

We shall deal here with some of the more formidable problems which the university faces internally, within its own family on campus. Many of these problems have been created by the growth of the institution and also by the vast attending explosion in knowledge itself. Many of them are wrapped up, too, in the constant debate about the university's integrity, and that may be, therefore, a good place to start.

It is popular these days to talk about the compromising of university integrity, and to decry, in the words of one critic, the weakening of the university's "capacity to fulfill its function as the corporate agent of free inquiry." Presumably, integrity is something good the university once had and is now losing with every response to the forces that would change the status quo or compromise intellectual chastity with new social involvement.

I think we must be very careful that we do not turn integrity into a "dry-ice" word which freezes everything it touches. Certainly, it cannot be used to solidify the status quo and to resist change, for

change has long been the watchword of university development, and adaptation the key not only to its survival but to its enormous vitality and usefulness. Those who promulgated the Yale report of 1828 doubtless believed that to introduce engineering into the course of studies was to violate the university's integrity. If so, they were confusing the university's purposes with its traditions. Similarly, the addition of a law school to Princeton would surely not affect its integrity, whatever it might do to its traditions and its style.

University integrity, then, is involved not with preserving things as they are, but rather with maintaining the coherence of its various parts, and the harmony with which it is able to pursue its aims—whatever their specialized nature. Are the university's pursuits carried out to assure work of the highest order, with thoroughly professional standards and with clarity of purpose? Even more important, are the university's efforts in research, instruction, and public service undertaken in such a manner that each mission supports the other? We have already noted that these three missions are subtly and intricately meshed. It follows that the real integrity of the university is violated when large decisions in one area do not consider the impact on the other two. I would state it even more strongly: university integrity is compromised when decisions about any one of our three aspects of university activity fail to strengthen the others.

Keeping in mind these considerations which should influence the university's response to pressures for growth and change, let us look now at some of the factors which can help to inhibit the uncontrolled growth of the university—and which, to that end, can work in our favor.

With respect to research, the controlling factor is the increasing necessity for choosing among fields and areas where the university can expect to excel. Knowledge is growing so fast that no university can pretend to cover it all—at least not with any hope of maintaining high professional standards. Even a single department of physics or philosophy must decide to concentrate within its respective field. Uncontrolled growth may come, therefore, from an uncontrolled selection of areas for excellence and it follows that the university can and

*From James A. Perkins, The University in Transition, Princeton University Press, 1966, pp. 31-59. Reprinted by permission of Princeton University Press.

must choose among possibilities. The very nature of the knowledge explosion and the desire for highest standards will force choice and thus will act as a brake on uncontrolled growth.

It is wrong to say that this choice must not be influenced by outside considerations. On the contrary, there may be a pressing public need which attracts a university's attention, or an opportunity to draw superior talent to the campus, perhaps even combined with the availability of funds. Let me add quickly that the funds alone cannot be the determinant. But their availability may insure the highest standards for the activity to be financed— if it is the right activity. Whether it be in high-energy physics or comparative linguistics, if the activity fits into the university scene, the presence of funds should not be a barrier to the addition, nor its acceptance a violation of integrity. It is the casual, unreflective, opportunistic development of interests for the sole purpose of attracting funds and prestige which obviously violates integrity.

While research must operate under the restraints of choice and excellence in the disciplines, instruction must operate under the restraints of student numbers and student selection.

We must remember that the most important factor in the pressure for university growth is the increased percentage of the age group that is demanding access to higher education. The figure is now well on its way to 50 per cent. But there is a great difference of opinion as to what the trends may be in the future. Some believe 50 per cent will represent something of a plateau. Others believe that there may actually be an accelerated increase after that figure is reached as more young people move out of a minority status.

If those who predict a relatively slow growth are correct, the pressure from increasing numbers will begin to lose some of its steam in the foreseeable future. Then the system as a whole will be relieved, though the prestige universities will hardly feel it. As the Negro spiritual puts it, "No resting place down there." Such universities may find restrictions on further growth arising from student reaction to an overcrowded campus. As more colleges and universities achieve higher standards, there may well be a disposition to pass up those whose size is, from the social or even intellectual point of view, forbidding. There are already signs of such a development, aided and abetted by avowed government policy to promote geographic equality. But, alas, neither Cornell nor Princeton is large enough to be very much benefited by this prospective development either.

More important than any prospective leveling-off of enrollments, however, is the rapid emergence of alternatives to the university, primarily in private and state-supported systems of junior and four-year colleges. Certainly the absence of enough satisfactory alternatives has been responsible for some of the excessive enrollments in our universities—though we have not suffered anything like the growth of such institutions as the University of Mexico, with over 80,000 enrolled students, or Buenos Aires, with over 60,000, both of which are operating in systems where there are no alternatives at all. Now in the United States there are many alternatives—the junior and four-year colleges; courses given through educational TV, with off-campus testing programs; and various types of correspondence, radio, and taped curricula—all of which are beginning to drain off some of the demand for university attendance. Obviously, the universities have a profound stake in the successful development of these alternative measures, and for this reason they should lend their weight and prestige to assure that these measures are successful. Their own preservation will be at stake.

In its public service undertakings, the university may also find some natural restraints working to limit growth, although it is true that the demands of our fast-growing technological society are voracious and are becoming more so along the whole growing edge of social change: there is almost no problem in our society that does not increasingly require expert advice. It is also true that expert advice can be found most frequently and in greater variety in the university than in any other institution; indeed, hardly any field of knowledge in the university has not felt the heady experience of being publicly useful.

But the unique contribution of the university in all of this is knowledge, not operating skills, and this should be a limiting factor of great importance. The government and particularly the corporation have been organized in our society to get things done, and it is to these institutions that society normally looks for operational responsibility. The university social scientists can provide the economic case for a state sales tax, for example, but they should not be expected to collect the money. It is legitimate for a university engineer to design a bridge, but not to involve the university in building it. And it is often to the university's credit that its agronomists are called upon to discuss the corn-hog price ratio, but it makes no sense for the university to participate in the mechanics of that complicated business. The fact that lines can be and are drawn between advice on how to do something and assistance in doing it thus constitutes a limiting force which aids the university in its need to preserve its balance and its unity.

Turning from these factors which may impose certain general restrictions on the growth of university missions, we face a whole range of internal decision-making which affects the size and shape as well as the direction of the institution. I have already suggested that the essential criteria to guide this internal decision-making grow from the interrelatedness of the university's missions, and that the university's capability in each area must be strengthened by decisions regarding the other two. Let us see how this is so, by examining the ways in which each mission of the university must be specifically related to the others—if integrity is to be preserved.

Few would contest the proposition that research and instruction are intimately connected. Volumes have been written supporting the proposition that university-level instruction can best be accomplished by faculty members who themselves are working at the frontiers of knowledge. The teacher-researcher is the ideal. The argument is rarely over any conflict between the functions; it most generally involves questions of degree and emphasis.

But the university gives too little attention to those courses of instruction that mesh with the university's research responsibilities. If we wish the ideal professor to teach and undertake research at the same time, then it must follow that the nature of the teaching and the research must be conditioned by the fact that they are to be carried on by the same person. If the teaching and the research are not in some way coordinated, we will have faculty members who are attempting to lead coherent lives while their research is headed in one direction and their teaching in another.

Unfortunately, this is precisely what happens in most universities. The undergraduate curriculum, particularly in the first two years, is based on the familiar doctrine of general education. This theory holds that the student, irrespective of his future specialty, should be exposed early to a common body of knowledge—at the least, to an introductory course in each of the divisions of the humanities, the social sciences, and the natural or biological sciences. The emphasis is cultural and general—a preparation for life rather than a preparation for a profession or a career.

But for the faculty member, research is particular and special, and the man really living at the edge of knowledge will frequently find that participation in survey or introductory courses requires an abrupt change of gears. Small wonder that instruction for the first two years finds relatively few of the greatest scholars either willing or able to make the necessary adjustments. Introductory courses for future majors will sometimes attract them from their research lairs, but a room full of freshmen ready to fulfill a distribution requirement can be a forbidding prospect. Pressure to perform will only encourage acceptance of the next offer from a more sympathetic institution.

There have been two main answers to this problem. The first has been to separate the graduate and the undergraduate faculties. This resolves, in part, the problem of intellectual schizophrenia; no professor is expected to perform at two different levels at the same time. But the price is separation within the university—an undergraduate college whose faculty members suffer from the suspicion that they are second-class or, at best, that they are involved in a university activity at the second level of importance.

The other answer has been to maintain the single faculty, but to divide it by age—the novices for teaching and the established professors for research. Of course, the final solution must involve some compromise of these extreme positions, because there are many famous full professors who bend their backs to contribute to the improvement of undergraduate instruction. In many cases the problem is resolved by a discreet distribution of teaching loads within departments, based upon tacit assumptions of the teaching and research capabilities of individual faculty members. Sometimes there is an equally subtle distribution of teaching responsibilities among departments. History and government faculty, for example, have traditionally carried a heavier load of teaching hours than anthropology and sociology professors, because the behavioral wing of the social sciences is more scientifically oriented and less digestible by students in pursuit of a general education.

The problem at best is a very difficult one, but we have enormously complicated its solution by acting as if undergraduate education in a university can be the same thing as undergraduate education in a four-year liberal arts college. We suffer, I suggest, from the fallacy buried in the assumption that the first two years of higher education should be the same in all institutions, be they independent colleges or universities. We also suffer from the even more profound fallacy that all students who enter the liberal arts college or the university have the same educational needs and motivations.

These two broadly held and fallacious assumptions are at the heart of the strain between the instruction and research at our universities. Those who hold them insist on a generality of studies that serves only to drive out of the lecture halls many faculty who are committed to research. We have often assumed that where teaching and research do not mesh, the research faculty should be punished and the teaching faculty rewarded. Special inducements for teaching may well be necessary, and they may help reduce the problem. But the means are artificial.

The fact is that undergraduate instruction and admissions policies need modification in order to assure the internal coherence and integrity of the university through a closer coordination of the teaching and research functions. I shall not lay out a blueprint here, but some general observations are in order.

First, I think we must break the lock step that would keep all institutions and students working in the same patterns and at the same pace. We must be prepared to recognize that undergraduate instruction can and must be different in a university than it is in a college, for example, and that it can and must appeal to a special category of student. The trend to design different programs to fit different institutions and different students has already begun; we must accelerate it.

Second, we shall have to hold tight to the ideals of a liberal education but recognize that, in the face of rapidly improving secondary education and the multi-concerns of the modern university, the style of liberal education will have to be adapted to its environment.

We might all agree that the threefold purpose of liberal education is to learn to know nature, society, and ourselves; to acquire certain skills, such as clear expression and a grasp of the scientific method and discipline; and finally, to embrace certain values, such as intellectual honesty, tolerance, and the capacity for wise judgment.

But the curriculum and the system for assuring a liberal as well as a professional education must surely take into consideration the missions of the university. This will mean, among other things, a reexamination of the idea that general education is something that is sandwiched between secondary-school and upper-class work. Rather than occupy

two or more years of pre-professionsal study, liberal education may have to run on a track parallel with professional work. For the student who wants to specialize, therefore, liberal education will have to be provided either by the secondary school or by a special program that includes liberal along with professional studies—or a combination of both. After all, a liberal education is the objective of a lifetime. Why assume it should be crowded into the first two post-secondary years?

The improvement of liberal education in the university will also require attention to the way subject matter is presented. There can be a liberal and a professional way of treating any subject. In a university it becomes particularly important that the research-oriented professors have as broad a view of their subject as possible. Just as instruction will have to be adapted to interest the professor, so will the professor have to teach his subject in a liberal style to interest the student.

Third, the flexibility and independence of graduate-level work will have to characterize a larger proportion of undergraduate education, too. This is already beginning to happen in the upper-class years; it may have to be extended down into the first two years for those students who are ready for it—and there are many more than we think. Honors work and educational experimentation can also help lighten the heavy dough of our undergraduate course programs. Whatever solutions we provide, we will have to give our fullest attention to improving our programs for our best students if they are not to be lost in the crowd.

Finally, we must know a great deal more about the kind of preparation, maturity, and motivation that should determine the selection of students for university-level work. Those who need the sense of security that comes from being a member of a smaller, tighter community should not come to the university. For when they do, they keep looking for a kind of faculty-student relationship that can best be found in an independent liberal arts college, a fruitless search that adds to the problem of internal cohesion in the university.

The application of these criteria might drastically modify the number of undergraduates who would come to the university as opposed to the college. Such criteria would surely affect the whole tone and purpose of the university, and they would make possible the reintroduction of the undergraduate to the research professor. But most of all, they would tend to bring teaching and research together and so help make our university communities coherent again.

Let us examine next the relations between the transmission and application of knowledge—between instruction and public service. Too frequently, I am afraid, we view the intellectual development of the student, to paraphrase Alfred North Whitehead, as if he had neither a body nor a soul. But even when we don't, we consign his physical and spiritual requirements to the area of extracurricular activities—a term frequently conjured up to secure the intellectual purity of the classroom.

Still, the student needs some connection between his studies and his concerns, between what he reads and what he sees, between what he thinks and what he does. This is complicated, because university-level study should require long periods of solitary study and reflection.

But the underclassman is not yet a library or laboratory scholar and must not be treated as one. Otherwise he will seek outlets for his concerns without the benefit of the moderating influence of his studies upon his actions. The head of the student government can discover to his lasting benefit that his experiences in campus affairs and his studies of public administration have some relation to each other. The same is true of the sociology student just returned from the South.

We have not been very inventive about how to relate studies and experience or thought and action, and the result can be frustration, or apathy, or even revulsion on the part of good students. There is an excitement and an important feedback that comes from actually seeing and experiencing the relevance of intellectual exercises.

Unquestionably, the notion that knowledge can and should be pursued for its own sake is at the heart of our lack of interest in connecting studies and concerns. We pay the price in student disinterest and in the proliferation of activities which do not have the discipline of intellectual content. A closer coordination of the student's two lives would bring the university into better focus, and it would serve to aid the development of appropriate extracurricular activities, as well as add an important stimulus to intellectual growth. If there be doubters, I suggest they talk with a professor who has just seen his first book on publication day, or an anthropologist who has just returned from working with the Andean Indians, or an astrophysicist who has just seen his theories confirmed by recent descriptions of the moon's surface. The excitement of these men will be a reminder that the connection between thought and action, or between

theory and results, which is so important to adults on the faculty, is even more important to students in the university.

In a larger sense, the ultimate use or application of knowledge must be brought under the restraints of research and instruction or the university is likely, in my view, to become unhinged. The pressing requirements of government and industry are, for the faculty member, full of the heady aroma of larger public purpose or prospective private gain. Both sensations are pleasant to an academic fraternity which for decades has been caricatured as impractical and which believes, with good reason, that it has been financially starved. In these circumstances, it is not surprising that faculty have taken to consulting with zest.

Again, we need criteria that will be useful in determining the directions and the merits of extra-university activity, and these criteria are to be found in our model of the three interconnected missions of the university. We must refer to the other two missions if we are to make valid decisions about the university's outside involvements. How can these strengthen the research and teaching functions?

Let me promptly remove from the discussion those matters which occupy the faculty in their capacities as private citizens. Everyone owes a part of his life to his society for public service, whether or not this service is directly connected with his profession. For those with a trained intelligence, such calls will not be lacking: they will increase as expert and disinterested service for the general welfare is in greater and greater demand.

But the outside activity which has a professional connection should, in general, have some feedback or use to the research interests of the professor and to the students who are dependent on him. Otherwise, the professor is just in business, or moonlighting, and his students are being shortchanged. Activities that are simply training projects, or are merely involved in implementing established knowledge and are not answering questions, should fall outside the boundaries of acceptable public activities for the university faculty.

The integrity of the university involves, then, a resistance to overexpansion of any of its three institutional functions, and the accompanying requirement that each institution will select its field of specialization. Integrity involves, perhaps even more importantly, an insistence that all of the university's activities advance its capabilities to pursue each of its missions—that, as Whitehead has said, "all its various parts are coordinated and play into each other's hands."

This is a fine prescription, but it is idle to lay it down without talking about how it is to be a-chieved. Who is going to "manage" integrity? Who will select and control the complex and tightly interrelated tasks to be undertaken by the university? Who is to make the critical decisions that will prevent each phase of activity from growing out of balance and stifling the others? Who is to make the university and its missions a coherent whole?

It is clear, at the outset, that the answers will not be precise or unequivocal. The university is not an orderly structure that yields to authoritarian management as does the military division or the corporation. The university's function is to serve the private processes of faculty and students, on the one hand, and the large public interests of society on the other. In this sense, it has no balance sheet of its own, no single product that can be annually measured, no performance tables for judging success. Even when seniors do well on admission to graduate school, there is always the haunting suspicion that success may be due more to the skill of the admissions committee than to the performance of the students.

Three groups participate in university management—the students, the faculty, and the administration. Let us talk about the student first. The undergraduate is generally on the campus no more than four years, a fact that tends to put the leadership of student movements in other countries more often than not in the hands of graduate students, and sometimes in the hands of those who make careers of student activities. The most vigorous student activities in the developing nations are led by students who have been enrolled for ten years and work full time at the business. But in this country, it is difficult to be a student and not attend classes sometimes. Furthermore, the prospects of a career are so bright that most students don't wish to delay their departures. Hence, management of the university is generally only on the edge of student interest.

In any case, management is not just a matter of deciding what would be good to do. Most importantly, it involves what is timely and what is possible. It involves what is wise. And wisdom requires, among other things, an understanding of the spirit of a particular institution, the interests

of its campus leaders, its financial prospects, and the priorities it gives to various academic ventures. There is no substitute for careful observation of people and events over time. This kind of experience is denied the young, and it is an almost fatal disability for constructive participation in most university decisions.

Finally, the student is a student. He is at the university to learn, not to manage; to reflect, not to decide; to observe, not to coerce. The process of learning, like the process of research, is in the end a most private affair, requiring for the most part detachment and not engagement. If we learn to involve the student more highly in the formal learning process, we may even further reduce his desire for management.

But there are two comments that must be made on the other side of the argument. Some students will become strongly interested in university affairs. The student body will always include some with talents as administrators or leaders. These young people gravitate naturally into student government or the campus newspaper, seeking outlets for their interests. Their participation in university institutional activities is important for them because the university machinery is an immediate outlet for their organizational proclivities. It is also good for the university, which, at least as much as any other organization, is most likely to be improved by the ideas and the enthusiasms of imaginative, energetic young people.

There are, in connection with all of this, powerful forces at work that are raising the political temperature of the student and increasing his interest in university affairs. He is the product of an age of earlier freedom and later responsibility. Left on his own as a teenager, he is coming to the university and finding that the faculty is as peripatetic as his parents. He encounters a vacuum at the point of his greatest need—wisdom and advice on how to become an adult. He also finds a community which frequently seems not much interested in his education. He may well be mistaken in many cases, but he does feel an impersonality about the campus and a concentration on matters that involve him only tangentially. For many the answer is the access to the machinery of the university—they want to reorder its priorities in their favor.

It would be foolish to deny the elements of justice in this line of reasoning. It would be equally foolish to refuse to listen to those who wish to be heard. We welcome them as freshmen with speeches that tell them they are now adults, and so we must expect to treat them as adults.

There is another point to be made. Students do not like to be excluded, in principle, from the machinery of the university. Nor, indeed, does anyone else. A careful selection of places where student participation can be accepted because of known interest or known talent will most frequently be a stabilizing and integrating act rather than the contrary.

The disabilities of the students' short stay, inexperience, and scholarly preoccupations remain. But as long as students feel they have entered a place where there are no priorities, or where the priorities work against their real interests as students, the pressure for involvement will be strong and perhaps irresistible. Uncontrolled, this will ruin good scholars and good universities. Dealt with sympathetically it will help bring about successful campus integration.

The faculty, as managers of the modern university, also offer certain limitations, arising from quite different circumstances. The community of masters was a noble and even feasible idea when there were only the four faculties of medicine, theology, law, and philosophy, and when the professor lectured several times a week and rarely saw students—as individuals—except in the corridors. The universities were in the big cities and the faculties were given appointments in the university but continued to participate in the main stream of city life. Outside the lectures there was precious little to administer in the university, so faculty decision-making was largely limited to appointments to the faculty itself. The nearest analogy would be to a modern departmental meeting, although the departmental meeting deals with academic affairs and logistical considerations in far more detail than did the whole university faculty of even a century ago.

But apart from size and complexity, the faculty as faculty has faced the additonal difficulties we have noted in the enormous fractionalizing of the fields of knowledge, combined with an equally great increase in outside activities. The faculty has now become dispersed in several faculties, colleges, and departments; it has been divided into C. P. Snow's two worlds; and it has turned increasingly outward, away from the institution of the university, to the "guilds" that the scholars' special interests have led them to set up for themselves.

Partial views which are based upon increasingly specialized interests make it difficult for the faculty as faculty to have a point of view on broad institutional matters. Consequently, the faculty's administrative stance contains elements of senatorial courtesy—maximum permissiveness with respect to individual faculty desires, combined with maximum protection if anyone would interfere with this permissiveness. Such a posture is exactly right for the protection of the classroom, but it is quite inadequate for educational or institutional management.

So the university can never again run on the assumption that it commands or can command the full-time interest and attention of all its faculty. The nature of knowledge today is such that it requires minds and talents of quite a different order from those needed to make administrative deci-1 sions. And the faculty should be left as free as possible of administrative duties in order to do its work. As the interests of the disciplines and professions cut increasingly across institutional lines, faculty members must have access to the stimulation and fresh ideas that will certainly come from the interchange of outside meetings and conferences among specialists. The role of the university is to provide a framework and an environment where these ideas can be put to use—laboratories, libraries, classrooms, and studios—where creative work can be conceived, tested, explained, reformulated and tested again, and then sent out into the world.

But if faculty as a corporate body cannot be expected to manage the university, individual faculty members are indispensable to the management process. Indeed, I would put high on any university priority list the identification and support of those members of the faculty whose viewpoint is broad, who have that rare quality of seeing problems in operational terms, and whose faculty standing is solidly based on a specialized competence. They do not have to be drawn into full-time or even part-time administration. But they are the mainsprings of the university works, the heartbeat of its body, and the real initiators of reform and progress. Any university with a dozen such men as Mike Oates of Princeton and Mac Black of Cornell can expect to grow and prosper; without them it will surely be bound in shallows and in miseries. Presidential leadership consists, in large part, of discovering these faculty leaders and then staying at their elbows, supporting their ideas, finding them money, guiding them when necessary, and encouraging them when the going seems rough.

Finally, there is the administrator, who is, in the end, charged with managing the integration of these many different and at times conflicting elements. The leadership of individual faculty members has brought new vigor to the university and will always be indispensable in accomplishing the particular tasks that interest them. And the faculty must always largely determine the shape and content of educational standards and educational policy.

But someone must be concerned with the institution as a whole, the activities it supports, the public face it presents, and the private concerns with which it is occupied. This job cannot be divided among disparate elements of the university. So it is the administrator—the president and others with managerial responsibility, cooperating with faculty and student leaders—who must be concerned both with the apparatus of the university and with the idea it represents. He must be able to involve himself directly in the central academic business of the university, to exert educational leadership, to be an agent for both stability and change. He must be capable of institutional justice and personal compassion. He must not fear power or be afraid to exercise it, because he must know that power cannot be the direct concern of either student or teacher. He must always be sensitive to the difference between the process of management and the process of education, and he must understand that the former must always serve the latter. Few large faculties have been able to provide this leadership for themselves. But without their general support, leadership cannot be effective.

It is this combination of institutional management and educational leadership that makes academic administration a unique and vital business. And it is this combination that is so necessary if any of the internal developments we have outlined are to have a chance to succeed.

The internal coherence of the university involves, then, attention to the missions of the university, their interdependence, and the optimum roles of student, teacher, and administrator in the management of this complicated task. It involves internal restraints in the pursuit of each mission, and the restraints that come from the necessity of considering the university missions as a coordinated whole. It involves clarity with respect to an educational philosophy that is appropriate to a university. It involves understanding of the respective roles and contributions of administration, faculty, and students to the internal management of the university.

In the center of this complicated community there are a group of students with strong administrative and educational instincts, a much larger group of faculty with strong institutional instincts,

and a group of administrators sensitive to student values and aspirations and to faculty interests and attitudes. No university can function properly unless it has a balance of these groups who are preoccupied with its health and vitality. No university can develop in sensible ways unless a general consensus has been achieved at the heart of its institutional life among those concerned with its future. But it will be, I suggest, those who spend full time at the business of direction and management who must assure this consensus—who must see to it that educational purpose and institutional interests develop in harmony.

Even when the community has mastered the difficult task of internal self-government, the task of university direction, stability, and growth has not been stated in its full complexity. We have already said that the university is no longer a self-sufficient world: it has a central role in the drama of higher education in the world at large. The university must achieve not only an internal harmony, but a harmony that is in a state of constant adaptation to the outside world. It is to this matter of the evolving role of the university in the total structure of higher education that we must turn next.

THE AMERICAN UNIVERSITY: PART I

Henry David Aiken

It has become a sociological commonplace that we have been moving into a post-capitalist, even a post-industrialist era in which, along with much prestige and money, residual power now passes to the university men. From this one might infer that we also are witnessing at last the decline of the nation-state. But the nation-state remains a powerful institution, and those who serve it or receive its aid, even on a per diem basis, generally wind up as state's men. This is as true of academicians as of lawyers, corporation presidents, or poets. It is arguable indeed that the academicians have given the nation-state a new lease on life. For they make possible, for the first time, the conversion of a mode of government into a politico-social organism, a true Republic as it were, whose educator-guardians supply the rationale, the indispensable training, and the continuing fund of personnel for its maintenance and protection. All this and the open society too. For all his worries about alloys, Plato, the ur-academician, would have been enchanted.

Such, in effect, is the premise of Professor Daniel Bell's new book, The Reforming of General Education, a work that offers by far the most articulate presentation by a university state's man of the problems and possibilities of liberal education in the university age. Bell regards self-consciousness as a proper benefit of liberal education; he himself is also more conscious of his premises and of the terms of his own guardian's role than are most other members of his class. What they casually see, his sociological eye automatically places in a selective historical context; what they take for granted, his ever-available pen explicitly affirms. Because of this, certain chapters of his book, which is formally preoccupied with problems of undergraduate education in one great national university (Columbia) provide a useful preface to the whole spate of writings by still more highly placed leaders of the university set who are concerned with the unprecedented situation of the American university as the central institution for higher learning and the indispensable service agency for the American "national society."

The concept of the "national society" deserves the italics which Bell gives it in the following quotation, for it provides the implicit frame for a great deal of establishmentarian thinking about feasible reforms in the great American universities:

> . . . within recent decades . . . the United States [has] passed from being a nation to becoming a national society in which there is not only a coherent national authority, but where the different sectors of the society, economy, polity, and culture are bound together in a cohesive way and where crucial political and economic decisions are now made at a "center."

Remembering the day, some may feel that, construed as sociology, this statement is overdrawn. But there can be no question as to its usefulness as a thesis of centrist educational ideology. And anyone who hopes to save something from the wreck of general and liberal education in our universities must confront it as a pervasive over-belief of our university leaders.

Professor Bell describes a palpable fact when he points out that more centralized power has lately accrued to the state than has ever before existed in this country, and that as this power increases so do ties to the nation's scientific technology become ever stronger and tighter. And as the national government becomes the mainstay of our ever more technical and expensive scientific research, so reciprocally the university, where so much advanced research and teaching occurs, is a new force to reckon within our national polity. For it forms the base of a whole new intellectual class whose "leaders," as Bell carefully phrases it, are accorded "both national importance and moral authority."

Here an interesting parallel comes to mind. What Oxford and Cambridge were to England in the time of its greatness, so Harvard, California, Columbia, and other national universities are now to the world-powerful United States. The all-important difference is that the forms of education in

*From H. D. Aiken, "The University, Part I," New York Review of Books, October 20, 1966. Reprinted with permission from The New York Review of Books. Copyright (c) 1966, The New York Review.

which the English universities excelled—the individual tutorial, classical studies, humanistically oriented history and politics, and philosophy—are precisely the areas which seem least useful and relevant to the going concerns of our present national society. Where the English university tended to produce cultivated non-specialists whose gifts were those of developed critical common sense and judgment, and acute if informal logical sense, the contemporary American university characteristically, though by no means always, turns out highly trained scientific technicians, sometimes capable of contributing to the advancement of learning, but only within a restricted sphere of inquiry. Where the Englishman received, so to say, a common law education which led him from case to case and from precedent to precedent, developing along the way his sense of analogy and relevance, the American, within the range of his specialty, is trained to be methodical, exact, and systematic. Outside his professional range, he remains rather clumsy and impressionable, likely to be opinionated in a speculative way, but where something is to be done, curiously indecisive, ready to place the burden of obligation on someone else who can supply a more "informed" judgment.

From many converging sources, the impression emerges that, whatever may be their importance, our academic leaders are unprepared for the moral roles that have been thrust upon them. Yet it is precisely these same leaders whose limiting attitudes and aptitudes at once set the tone and determine the aims and functions of the contemporary university itself. Everywhere within the university, including the humanities, their influence and their example are as pervasive as their sufferance is indispensable. There seem to be exceptions: for example, President Pusey of Harvard is distinguished as an educator for his rehabilitation of the Harvard Divinity School and for his support of the study of religion within Harvard College. But this emphasis has not seriously modified the drift of things at Harvard, as the recent review of Harvard's general education program by the so-called Doty Committee illustrates.[1] And at California,

at Cornell (as we shall shortly see), even at Columbia, where the idea of general education originated and where the emphasis on liberal studies in the College has always been vocal, the pull is overwhelmingly in the direction of the forms of specialized research and instruction which are useful to the national society and which therefore receive the largesse of its government.

To a non-leader or anti-leader (in Bell's sense) it may be dispiriting, though it should not be surprising, to find that of the many prominent university spokesmen who have written about the "crisis" of the university, few (Jacques Barzun is one erratic and strangely self-defeating exception) have any fundamental objection to make to the way things are going there. Nowhere among our leaders can one find a president or dean with the radical independence and crusading zeal of Hutchins, the imaginative cross-fertilizing passions for language, poetry, and science of I. A. Richards (at the top of his form), or the leonine philosophical imagination of Dewey,

---

[1] It is no accidnet that the chairman (Professor Paul M. Doty) of the Doty Committee (the full title of its report is "Report of the Special Committee to Review the Present Status and Problems of the General Education Program") and most of its leading members were scientists and that its report accurately reflected attitudes prevalent at Harvard's scientific center. Only very eloquent opposition, in part by certain humanistically oriented scientists, prevented a radical revision of the general education program which would have broken down the uneasy three-fold distinction between the natural sciences, the social sciences, and the humanities into a new two-fold distinction between "the sciences" and "the humanities," with the "true social sciences," now properly oriented in the direction of exact "behavioral science," grouped with the natural sciences, and the humanities themselves ranged with history and with those historically oriented parts of social science that cannot quite cut the "behavioral" mustard. The defeat of the Doty Committee's proposal, I may add, astonished us all. It also showed, implicitly, how anxious are many professors about the take-over of university policy and the idea of liberal educacation by exponents of a culture whose mind belongs wholly to the purposes and uses of positive science. Nor is it wholly an accident that it should be a leading social scientist who was invited by the Dean of the College to make a corresponding report to the faculty concerning the general education of Columbia. Professor Bell is more of a traditionalist regarding the formal groupings of academic disciplines than his Harvard counterparts. But this does not, I think, reflect fundamental differences of orientation between the points of view that prevail, respectively, at the "centers" of Harvard and Columbia.

with its interlocking educational concerns for logic and history, for nature and experience, for settlement houses and Cezanne, for methods of resolving problematic situations and the consummatory activities that can make a life worthwhile or a civilization significant. Nowhere, if it comes to that, can one find someone bold or strong enough to assert, however outrageously and ambiguously, what I once heard Paul Tillich say at an elegant dinner for Harvard general educators: that without a relation to the ultimate concerns of genuine religion the modern university cannot possibly be the educational center of an acceptable human culture. How serviceable, and how undistinguished, are the words of our present-day university leaders. How barely distinguishable from one another are these foxes, these well-meaning inside men, whose only thought as educators is to advise the prince, to be of use to the national society.

This does not mean that what they say is of no consequence. Just the opposite. Because they instinctively know what is "possible" within the context of the national society, it is to them we must turn in order to learn what may become of the university, and hence of us all, in the years ahead. And when they describe—as, for example, President Clark Kerr of California did a couple of years ago—the "uses" of the "multiversity," as he called it, we are forewarned that, if there are none to oppose them, such indeed will be the uses of the university in our time.

It is in this spirit that we must take The University in Transition, by James A. Perkins, currently President of Cornell and a Bellean national society leader if ever there was one. Perkin's pedigree is impeccable: it includes everything from a Ph.D. and assistant professorship in political science to the assistant directorship of a "School" of Public and International Affairs, and from government service to the vice-presidencies of a distinguished liberal arts college and of a great foundation. The names of the national governmental and educational advisory bodies on which he serves read like a catalogue of great problems for a course in Contemporary Civilization. When he informs us, therefore, that the distinctive feature of the American university is its commitment, not only to the accumulation and transmission of knowledge, but also to its application as a public service, we do not have to reach for his idea of "public service." By public service he means, essentially, service to the national society and its government. Nor are we in

doubt that the service rendered may include the person of the applicator himself.

President Perkin's account of that knowledge worthy to be impressed upon the minds of university students holds no surprises. Homogeneous with the prose that invests it, it reads like the precis of an entry on "Knowledge" from the University Administrator's own Book of Knowledge. President Perkins may be called a rationalist and a gnostic; for him, that is, all knowledge is a product of "reason," and human good is an emanation from knowledge. He dutifully reaffirms "the Greek affirmation" of man as the rational animal, declares knowledge to be the result of "reason's application to the results of observation," and confidently states that knowledge, so viewed, is applicable to "the whole range of human experience." He does not spend himself in definitions of "reason"; so often, however, is "knowledge equated with the products of "research," that one feels that, even without research, one knows what he has in mind. Nor does he plague us with uncertainties about the ranges or limits of the life of reason, much less with the possibility that reason and the standards to which "reasonable men" hold themselves liable may be subject to critique. President Perkins, so to say, takes a positive view of reason just as he takes a positive view of science. And he takes the American university, at least on the side of its research, as a going cognitive concern, as of course within limits it unquestionably is. My quarrel is not at all that he raises no doubts about the validity of scientific research or the importance of its transmission and use. Rather it is that he seems not to see that there may be precious forms of knowledge, possibilities of human study and learning, worthy of a great university's concern, which simply are not products of "research" and which do not fall reasonably within the purview of most American (or Greek) academicians' notions of reason.

To be fair, President Perkins, himself trained as a political scientist, would probably not wish to be held to strict interpretations of such concepts as science and reason. Undoubtedly he would repudiate the notion that all knowledge, or science, must be formulable in mathematically exact terms. Yet what he says about "the humanities," and it isn't much, suggests that he conceives them, at least for university purposes, primarily as those products of historical and philological inquiry which would be publishable in the Proceedings of the Modern Language Association. It does not include the sort of informal critical and philosophical

reflections upon literature and the arts that one encounters, say, in the prose writings of Coleridge,
or Arnold, or Nietzsche and, in our time, in the
essays of Eliot, Camus, or, particularly in his
earlier period, Trilling. In its current usage, the
cant word "research" is a perfectly apt term for
the work of the experimental psychologist or comparative linguist, and hence for the preliminary
investigations that are often invaluable to the man
of letters, the humanist, and the philosopher. It
is not, I believe, a word that is appropriate to what
the latter are doing when they finally close with the
"objects" of their concern, nor is it the word for
what they are doing in performing their own characteristic jobs of work.

President Perkins fancies the three primary
activities of the American university as "missions."
If his account of the first mission is an academic
stereotype, one part of what he says about the second mission—which he habitually calls the "transmission" of knowledge—is not. Indeed, his is the
first published expression I have encountered of a
powerful trend among those members of the academic establishment who would streamline the whole
university curriculum so that it can more readily
serve the interests of research and public service.
For nearly a decade not only general education but
also, in its older senses, liberal education have
been under quiet but increasingly severe attack in
the universities. And the rash of reexaminations
of general education—which scarcely two decades
ago was regarded as the educational reform of our
age—is in fact less a function of an understandable
desire to improve, let alone expand, existing general education programs than to curtail their role
in the undergraduate curriculum and to make it
easier for "bright" students to avoid their requirements.

Now it must be acknowledged that many "G.E."
course are uninspired (so, by the way, are many
departmental courses), boringly taught to phleg-
matic students who want to get on with their careers and lives. Further, the better secondary
schools, and particularly the private schools, are
currently giving students great lashings of general
and liberal studies. The average freshman from
Choate or Loomis sometimes reminds one of T. S.
Eliot's Prufrock, who has "known them all already,
known them all," from Plato's dialogues to the
plays of Genet, and from set theory to the dark
night of the soul. What really remains for such
a creature but to move on as rapidly as possible

to graduate school? The new device in many universities of admitting precocious freshmen to something called "advanced standing" has many justifications, among them the avoidance of an expensive
fifth year of high school at Harvard or Cornell, another prolonged course, that is, of general and liberal studies. Moreover, as President Perkins and
Professor Bell both ask, in effect, "Who, nowadays,
wants to teach General Education?" (Young Ph.D.s
with their careers and of them go where the prestige,
the security, and the hard money are, and at most
universities this is not the office of the Committee
on General Education.)

Not, certainly President Perkins. His argument
has force. Like Kerr, Perkins is a pluralist about
higher education, but he would achieve the ends of
the university by different means. Kerr, an imper-
ialist and a federalist, would let the university di-
versify its activities more or less as it will within
one great academic union. Perkins, however, belongs to the Ivy League. He wants to maintain a
greater internal coherence within the university so
that none of the missions he ascribes to it will be
overwhelmed by the rest. This means, in practice,
that the job of transmitting knowledge must be constantly geared to the demands of advancing research
and service. Perkin's ploy is thus to "break the
lock step that would keep all institutions and students
working in the same patterns and at the same pace."
In a university, undergraduate instruction "can and
must be different . . . than in a college, and that
it can and must appeal to a special category of student." This difference, as Perkins describes it,
is a direct consequence of his thesis that the university is the place, among institutions of higher
learning, where the advancement and application
of learning in the interests of society are primary
missions. Such an institution may "hold fast to the
ideals of a liberal education." But it must "recognize that, in the face of rapidly improving secondary
education and the multi-concerns of the modern
university, the style of liberal education will have
to be adapted to its environment." Hence, for the
student "who wants to specialize"—clearly the university, as distinct from the ordinary college, student—liberal education will have to be provided
either by the secondary school or by " a special
program that includes liberal along with professional
studies—or a combination of both." "After all," as
Perkins blandly says, "a liberal education is the
objective of a life time. Why assume it should be
crowded into the first two post-secondary years?"

Why indeed? The only trouble is that, like so many others, President Perkins himself obviously would shed no tear if liberal studies were conducted mainly in the secondary schools or else in four-year liberal arts colleges, which would thereby become glorified finishing schools run by professor-masters for whom research and service are not true missions. Plainly, the university is here being unveiled by Perkins as America's great center for advanced studies, which admits into its precincts only clever young apprentices whose interest in learning is, from the beginning, entirely professional. President Perkins only slightly blurs his tracks. "There can be," he reminds us, "a liberal and professional way of treating any subject." Yes. In a university where the missionary pressures on student and teacher alike are wholly on the professional side, "it becomes particularly important that the research-oriented professors have as broad a view of their subject as possible." Yes. But how is this to happen in a context where there is only a "special program" of liberal studies, and when even this perfunctory hat-tipping in the direction of liberality is at once forgotten? We are warned that "the flexibility and independence of graduate-level work will have to characterize a larger proportion of undergraduate education too." Already this is happening in the junior and senior years; for those "who are ready for it—and there are many more than we think," it doubtless will have to be extended into the first two years. Obviously the next step must be to get rid, not of the Ph. D. degree (as some have argued), but of the B.A., at least as a university degree. This done, the incoming freshmen can proceed, without ado, to the work that will enable them shortly to swell the ranks of the professor-missionaries of the American university.

President Perkin's formula for preserving coherence and balance within the university in the face of its "multi-concerns" has a certain plausibility; formally, it preserves the identity of the university as an educational institution of sorts, as Kerr's multiversity does not. The formula is this: ideally each of the missions should positively strengthen the other two; that is, no training for public service that doesn't reinforce research, no research (presumably) that fails to strengthen the curriculum; but also, note will, no curriculum and no teaching that fail to strengthen research and service. In practice this implies that no additions should be made to the university staff which do not strengthen the research and service corps, no courses added that fail to prepare students for their work as proto-

researchers and servicemen, no "extra-curricular" artistic, literary, or intellectual activities which can't be justified by the power they add to the missions. Not a word is said about those dimensions of teaching whose only justification is the enlargement of the human imagination, the quickening, in part by subtle processes of emulation and identifications, of the student's impulse to become a more fully human being. President Perkins talks of the mission of service, but he quite ignores that service which a university ought to render its own members, students, faculty, and administrators alike: the provision of an example of a community of mutually developing persons, at once learned and cultivated, dedicated to their own work but responsive to achievements of orders different from their own. Why is it that virtually a whole generation of the choicest students and junior faculty are so revolted by the grubbiness, pretentiousness, and vulgarity of the multiversity, by its remoteness and impersonality, by its deadly "functions," including, among others, its incredible "commencement" days with their honorary degrees for retired generals, and the ghost-written speeches in justification of some manifest destiny or other? Having read several books about the Berkeley student revolt and having witnessed something of the sort in my own university, I am convinced that what animates these uprisings is not so much a demand for greater political or social freedom, or a desire to participate in the day-to-day running of the university, as a desperate, angry reaction to the meagerness and meanness of so much ordinary university life.[2] President Perkins remarks that young people who "keep looking for a

_____
[2] This sense of drabness, drift, confusion, and above all of pervasive hypocrisy is reinforced and deepened by a book published this summer by Nicholas van Hoffman entitled The Multiversity, A Personal Report on What Happens to Today's Students in American Universities, Holt, Rinehart and Winston, 1966. The book, which is cast mainly in (presumably factual) dialogue form, necessarily misses a good deal of those sides of university life in which students cannot directly observe and which—one sometimes thinks—they would misconstrue if they did; particularly is this true of the serious, independent intellectual life of the faculty. There is an inwardness, an intellectual passion, and a sweetness which can pervade the study of a dedicated professor or student which Mr. van Hoffman does not fully appreciate. But his indictment, impressionistic though it is, remains overwhelming.

kind of faculty-student relationship that can best be found in an independent liberal arts college" are involved in a fruitless search which merely adds to the problem of internal cohesion (never forget the missions!) in the university. And he tells them that if they need a sense of security that comes from being a member of a smaller, tighter community, "they should not come to the university." But, then, who should come? Youthful computers, already programmed for research and service? What he does not, will not, see it that everyone, whether student or professor or administrator, suffers from the anonymous life of anxiety-ridden specialized and professionalized missionary work to which the university anti-community commits its members. The brutal fact remains that for all too many of its inhabitants, including its students, the central institution of higher learning in our time is not remotely a "mission" (to update slightly Cardinal Newman's image of the university as an "active cloister") but a factory town whose industry (to employ some figure of the university leaders themselves) is a kind of knowledge.

Such reflections are further darkened as one follows President Perkin's later ruminations on the universities' struggles for internal coherence and self-control in the face of mounting external interference, particularly by the national government. But I have no space, even if I had the heart, to do more than mention his suave defense of the burgeoning, immensely costly administrative bureaucracy, with its lunatic hierarchy of trustees, presidents and vice presidents, chancellors and provosts, and department "heads," its subtly influential administrative and secretarial assistants for whom frequently not only the student but the ordinary faculty members are figures in a committee report. Nowhere is there a touch of irony, a casual note of self-deprecation, an awareness of the appaling menace of full-time university executives and their appendages, who indeed make a mission of administration and whose relations to what goes on in the classroom or the laboratory, not to mention the dormitory or the common room, are not sufficiently developed to be called ceremonial. Not even vaguely does President Perkins intimate that a distinction might be drawn between something called "institutional management" and "educational leadership"; that in fact the kind of institutional life American university managers must lead usually insulates them from the educational life of the university. It is no accident I think that, as Time magazine

cheerfully pointed out in a recent issue, leaders of business and heads of universities have become interchangeable parts. In fact, as our universities move, in Perkin's phrase, "from autonomy to systems" (as the University of California has already done) the president of a multiversity is nothing but the executive officer of a "knowledge industry."[3]

---

[3] In this connection it is amusing to recall a revealing tiff last year between President Clark Kerr and two Berkeley professors, Sheldon S. Wolin and John H. Shaar, in the pages of this Review (March 11, 1965). In the course of a devastating but not intemperate review of the student revolt at Berkeley entitled "The Abuses of the Multiversity," Wolin and Shaar had something to say about Kerr's deep, if largely unconscious, acquiescence in the idea of the university as a business. Along with a number of genuine quotations from Kerr's writings which illustrated the point, the phrase "knowledge factory" was ascribed to him. In a heavily ironical reply, which here and there does score off Wolin and Shaar, Kerr points out that "knowledge factory" is not his phrase but Mario Savio's and that the phrase he had used in his book—"knowledge industry"—was itself quoted from Professor Fritz Machlup—a "concept" (save us) which, as Kerr says, "he used in quite a different sense than 'factory'." But, so far as education is concerned, what a difference! In the passage at issue, Kerr, following Machlup, talks with a face even straighter than Perkins's about "the production, distribution, and consumption" of knowledge which now accounts for "29 per cent of gross national product" (sic) and which "is growing at about twice the rate of the rest of the economy." And the "center" of the industry which has accomplished this prodigious feat, says Kerr, is the university. Of course, Machlup's concept of the "knowledge industry" is not the same as Savio's bitter "knowledge factory." But what Kerr sees more than Perkins is that if one treats the production of knowledge as an industry and the university as its center, one has defined the university's institutional function in industrial terms. And if, as Kerr also says, the university is, in what are plainly metaphorical terms, "the city of the intellect," then that city, like, say, Dearborn, is an industrial city. Nor is that overwhelming fact mitigated by the presence within the "university" of an art gallery, a campanile, a daily newspaper, a resident string quartet, and some other "departments" which supply remedial reading to hoi polloi. And if the president of the university likes to think

If one cares to learn something about the actual ways of university administrators, more is to be learned from Herbert Stroup's sardonic Bureaucracy in Higher Education than from a dozen books of apology by national university leaders such as Perkins and Kerr. Stroup, a sociologist as well as Dean of Students at Brooklyn College, reminds one at times of Veblen. Unfortunately his book is uneven and offers no real alternative to existing trends. Indeed, Stroup defends academic bureaucracy as "a stabilizing and regularizing influence on the social body, " whose very existence "tends to stave off haphazard, quixotic and even irrational efforts on the part of powerful minorities. " He also argues, following the political scientist, C. J. Friedrich, that bureaucracy may be a positive help to the maintenance of a democratic society.

Nonetheless in the case of the university, Stroup himself contends that "the college worker" is not less but "more amenable to the dictates of interest groups than are others in society. " He reminds us of the melancholy fact that of all groups composing the Nazi party, teachers were the best represented, and he quotes (Dean Stroup has a gift for quotation which he overworks) approvingly a statement of Hans Gerth and C. Wright Mills to the effect that scientists and technicians just because of their narrow training and limited knowledge are the most easily manipulated of all groups in modern society. For my part I do not know this to be true. But on general grounds I find it believable. The very organization of the American university, with its absentee owners (trustees) and quasi-military chain of command, at once relieves the ordinary professor and student of responsibilities for what happens to the institution itself and systematically unfits him for sustained political action in spheres outside his immediate field of professional interest. For most of us academicians, in fact, major decisions and policies adopted by "the university" are like fate, and we uncheerfully accept them as such.

_____

of himself as a mayor, or rather, since he is not elected but appointed by a board of regents, as a kind of town manager, it must be understood that his job is not vaguely that of leader and coordination of a company of his peers, whose scholar-teacher vocation remains his own and to which, hopefully, he will soon return. His town is, in quite a different sense, a company town, and he, its manager, is a company man. When a strike or riot occurs, his role is to protect the company's interests. Never, never is it to join his fellow citizens in their strike against the established order.

If it is true, as M. C. Dimock remarks in a statement quoted by Stroup at the end of his book, that "an institution tends to take on the character of its leadership, " those concerned with the quality of academic life in our universities have reason to be alarmed. For our top university leaders, as Stroup demonstrates, are largely and effectively insulated from that life. They may know something about it by description, but they do not share it, any more than the captains of other industries share the ordinary life of workers. Invariably this face is reflected in their public utterances. Indeed, the fatal limitation of the books, and minds, of university hierarchs like James Perkins, who so gladly preach to the rest of us about missions in which they themselves participate—perhaps can any longer participate—only ritually, is their utter remoteness from the educational process. What their discourses really amount to are managers' briefs for those parts or aspects of the national industry over which they preside but which, even as presiding officers, they understand only imperfectly. The rest—and it is a very great deal—is not their "business. "

President Perkins, no more than President Kerr, offers a remotely acceptable account of the idea of the university. But if I have to choose between them, I will take Kerr's account, both because it is more accurate as a statement of fact, and because, construed as prescription and prophecy, it leaves open the possibility that the university may remain something more than an advanced technological institute. A multiversity may be an educational department store with attached service stations of various sorts, but, like Sears, it sells everything, including, conceivably, a half-liberal education.

Admittedly the sort of undergraduate education which a university makes possible differs in important ways from that afforded by even a first-rate liberal arts college like Oberlin or Swarthmore. For undergraduates as well as graduate students, a range of educational possibilities, informal as well as formal, exists within the environment of a university, even of the second rank, which even the most richly endowed four-year college cannot match. Correspondingly, the university college has liabilities which not all undergraduates are able to offset. But "getting lost" is not, as President Perkins contends, by any means the whole problem. An undergraduate can get lost at Oberlin as well as at Cornell, and many students at smaller universities such as Brandeis have readier access to what is left of their teachers' minds than they do at large city colleges. The point is rather that the university college itself is subject to both intellectual and (shall I say) moral strains, and has peculiar problems of identity and integrity that are owing to the fact that it is incysted within a university whose academic departments and institutes have educational and professional commitments that frequently (although by no means always) lead away from the concerns of liberal education. Quite apart from the existence of the professional schools, which can greatly enrich the undergraduate curriculum, there are the graduate school and the graduate students whose presence is felt, often for the better, throughout the college. Further, in a university college, the opportunity, as well as the pressure, to specialize and to do it quickly is commonly greater than in most other colleges. For these reasons, the issue of liberal education—what it is and what it is worth, especially to the exceptional student—may be more keenly felt in the university than in the four-year college. And partly because of this the general education movement itself and most of the current proposals for its reform have originated within the universities.

But the significance of liberal education, and hence of the problems of general education in the impending era of the multiversity and the university system, is unlikely to be intensely felt by anyone not directly involved in the primary educational experience of the university college. This is true enough, God knows, of many research professors, anxious to "get on with their work." How much more so must it be of professional administrators, such as President Perkins, bemused by the incessant demands of all the far-flung missions over which they preside. This is a question, not of good will or personal endowment, but of experience and of the focus which experience alone makes possible. To write significantly and imaginatively about what is at stake in the contemporary crisis of the university college—and this, I have come to think, lies at the very heart of the wider crisis of the university and of the whole higher learning in our time—one must be constantly involved as a teacher, writer, and person in the fundamental life of the mind. Only so can one realize what an incomparable endowment a truly liberal education can be for young people just now coming into full possession of their powers. But only so, also, can one appreciate the sense of divided loyalties and aspirations, and the feeling of attenuation and loss which pervade the contemporary university college. Plainly, the task is, in the full etymological sense of the term, a philosophical one, well beyond the range of interest or experience, I should add at once, of most academic philosophers, themselves tied to the routines of an increasingly specialized profession. It requires someone who, like Daniel Bell, is himself (if he will not mind my saying so) caught in the cross-fire between the scholar and the intellectual, and who, one suspects, finds it impossible to satisfy all the aspirations of his own commodious mind within the limits set by even so sprawling an academic discipline as sociology. In the second part of this essay, we shall consider with what success Professor Bell, a philosopher now almost in spite of himself, has coped with the monumental job of work to which he has been called as historian, critic, and (conceivably) reformer of general education in one great university college, Columbia.

Part 6

A MASS SOCIETY

THE MASS SOCIETY*

C. Wright Mills

In the standard image of power and decision, no force is held to be as important as The Great American Public. More than merely another check and balance, this public is thought to be seat of all legitimate power. In official life as in popular folklore, it is held to be the very balance wheel of democratic power. In the end, all liberal theorists rest their notions of the power system upon the political role of this public; all official decisions, as well as private decisions of consequence, are justified as in the public's welfare; all formal proclamations are in its name.

I

Let us therefore consider the classic public of democratic theory in the generous spirit in which Rousseau once cried, 'Opinion, Queen of the World, is not subject to the power of kings; they are themselves its first slaves.'

The most important feature of the public of opinion, which the rise of the democratic middle class initiates, is the free ebb and flow of discussion. The possibilities of answering back, of organizing autonomous organs of public opinion, of realizing opinion in action, are held to be established by democratic institutions. The opinion that results from public discussion is understood to be a resolution that is then carried out by public action; it is, in one version, the 'general will' of the people, which the legislative organ enacts into law, thus lending to it legal force. Congress, or Parliament, as an institution, crowns all the scattered publics; it is the archetype for each of the little circles of face-to-face citizens discussing their public business.

This eighteenth-century idea of the public opinion parallels the economic idea of the market of the free economy. Here is the market composed of freely competing entrepreneurs; there is the public composed of discussion circles of opinion peers. As price is the result of anonymous, equally weighted, bargaining individuals, so public opinion is the result of each man's having thought things out

for himself and contributing his voice to the great chorus. To be sure, some might have more influence on the state of opinion than others, but no one group monopolizes the discussion, or by itself determines the opinions that prevail.

Innumerable discussion circle are knit together by mobile people who carry opinions from one another, and struggle for the power of larger command. The public is thus organized into associations and parties, each representing a set of viewpoints, each trying to acquire a place in the Congress, where the discussion continues. Out of the little circles of people talking with one another, the larger forces of social movements and political parties develop; and the discussion of opinion is the important phase in a total act by which public affairs are conducted.

The autonomy of these discussions is an important element in the idea of public opinion as a democratic legitimation. The opinions formed are actively realized within the prevailing institutions of power; all authoritative agents are made or broken by the prevailing opinions of these publics. And, in so far as the public is frustrated in realizing its demands, its members may go beyond criticism of specific policies; they may question the very legitimations of legal authority. That is one meaning of Jefferson's comment on the need for an occasional 'revolution.'

The public, so conceived, is the loom of classic, eighteenth-century democracy; discussion is at once the threads and the shuttle tying the discussion circles together. It lies at the root of the conception of authority by discussion, and it is based upon the hope that truth and justice will somehow come out of society as a great apparatus of free discussion. The people are presented with problems. They discuss them. They decide on them. They formulate viewpoints. These viewpoints are organized and they compete. One viewpoint 'wins out.' Then the people act out this view, or their representatives are instructed to act it out, and this they promptly do.

Such are the images of the public of classic democracy which are still used as the working justifications of power in American society. But now we must recognize this description as a set of images out of a fairy tale: they are not adequate even as an approximate model of how the American system of power works. The issues that now shape man's fate are neither raised nor decided by the public at large. The idea of the community of publics is not a description of fact, but an assertion of an ideal, an assertion of a legitimation masquerading —as legitimations are now apt to do—as fact. For now the public of public opinion is recognized by all those who have considered it carefully as something less than it once was.

These doubts are asserted positively in the statement that the classic community of publics is being transformed into a society of masses. This transformation, in fact, is one of the keys to the social and psychological meaning of modern life in America.

I. In the democratic society of publics it was assumed, with John Locke, that the individual conscience was the ultimate seat of judgment and hence the final court of appeal. But this principle was challenged—as E. H. Carr has put it—when Rousseau 'for the first time thought in terms of the sovereignty of the whole people and faced the issue of mass democracy.'[1]

II. In the democratic society of publics it was assumed that among the individuals who composed it there was a natural and peaceful harmony of interests. But this essentially conservative doctrine gave way to the Utilitarian doctrine that such a harmony of interests had first to be created by reform before it could work, and later to the Marxian doctrine of class struggle, which surely was then, and certainly is now, closer to reality than any assumed harmony of interests.

III. In the democratic society of publics it was assumed that before public action would be taken, there would be rational discussion between individuals which would determine the action, and that, accordingly, the public opinion that resulted would be the infallible voice of reason. But this has been challenged not only (1) by the assumed need for experts to decide delicate and intricate issues, but (2) by the discovery—as by Freud—of the irrationality of the man in the street, and (3) by the discovery—as by Marx—of the socially conditioned nature of what was once assumed to be autonomous reason.

IV. In the democratic society of publics it was assumed that after determining what is true and right and just, the public would act accordingly or see that its representatives did so. In the long run, public opinion will not only be right, but public opinion will prevail. This assumption has been upset by the great gap now existing between the underlying population and those who make decisions in its name, decisions of enormous consequence which the public often does not even know are being made until well after the fact.

Given these assumptions, it is not difficult to understand the articulate optimism of many nineteenth-century thinkers, for the theory of the public is, in many ways, a projection upon the community at large of the intellectual's ideal of the supremacy of intellect. The 'evolution of the intellect,' Comte asserted, 'determines the main course of social evolution.' If looking about them, nineteenth-century thinkers still saw irrationality and ignorance and apathy, all that was merely an intellectual lag, to which the spread of education would soon put an end.

How much the cogency of the classic view of the public rested upon a restriction of this public to the carefully educated is revealed by the fact that by 1859 even John Stuart Mill was writing of 'the tyranny of the majority,' and both Tocqueville and Burckhardt anticipated the view popularized in the recent past by such political moralists as Ortega y Gasset. In a word, the transformation of public into mass—and all that this implies—has been at once one of the major trends of modern societies and one of the major factors in the collapse of that liberal optimism which determined so much of the intellectual mood of the nineteenth century.

By the middle of that century: individualism had begun to be replaced by collective forms of economic and political life; harmony of interests by inharmonious struggle of classes and organized pressures; rational discussions undermined by expert decisions on complicated issues, by recognition of the interested bias of argument by vested position; and by the discovery of the effectiveness of irrational appeal to the citizen. Moreover, certain structural changes of modern society, which we shall presently consider, had begun to cut off the public from the power of active decision.

II

The transformation of public into mass is of particular concern to us, for it provides an important clue to the meaning of the power elite. If that elite is truly responsible to, or even exists in connection with a community of publics, it carries a very different meaning than if such a public is being transformed into a society of masses.

The United States today is not altogether a mass society, and it has never been altogether a community of publics. These phrases are names for extreme types; they point to certain features of reality, but they are themselves constructions; social reality is always some sort of mixture of the two. Yet we cannot readily understand just how much of which is mixed into our situation if we do not first understand, in terms of explicit dimensions, the clear-cut and extreme types:

At least four dimensions must be attended to if we are to grasp the differences between public and mass.

I. There is first, the ratio of the givers of opinion to the receivers, which is the simplest way to state the social meaning of the formal media of mass communication. More than anything else, it is the shift in this ratio which is central to the problems of the public and of public opinion in latter-day phases of democracy. At one extreme on the scale of communication, two people talk personally with each other; at the opposite extreme, one spokesman talks impersonally through a network of communications to millions of listeners and viewers. In between these extremes there are assemblages and political rallies, parliamentary sessions, law-court debates, small discussion circles dominated by one man, open discussion circles with talk moving freely back and forth among fifty people, and so on.

II. The second dimension to which we must pay attention is the possibility of answering back an opinion without internal or external reprisals being taken. Technical conditions of the means of communication, in imposing a lower ratio of speakers to listeners, may obviate the possibility of freely answering back. Informal rules, resting upon conventional sanction and upon the informal structure of opinion leadership, may govern who can speak, when, and for how long. Such rules may or may not be in congruence with formal rules and with institutional sanctions which govern the process of communication. In the extreme case, we may conceive of an absolute monopoly of communication to pacified media groups whose members cannot answer back even 'in private.' At the opposite extreme, the conditions may allow and the rules may uphold the wide and symmetrical formation of opinion.

III. We must also consider the relation of the formation of opinion to its realization in social action, the ease with which opinion is effective in the shaping of decisions of powerful consequence.

This opportunity for people to act out their opinions collectively is of course limited by their position in the structure of power. This structure may be such as to limit decisively this capacity, or it may allow or even invite such action. It may confine social action to local areas or it may enlarge the area of opportunity; it may make action intermittent or more or less continuous.

IV. There is, finally, the degree to which institutional authority, with its sanctions and controls, penetrates the public. Here the problem is the degree to which the public has genuine autonomy from instituted authority. At one extreme, no agent of formal authority moves among the autonomous public. At the opposite extreme, the public is terrorized into uniformity by the infiltration of informers and the universalization of suspicion. One thinks of the late Nazi street-and-block-system, the eighteenth-century Japanese Kumi, the Soviet cell structure. In the extreme, the formal structure of power coincides, as it were, with the informal ebb and flow of influence by discussion, which is thus killed off.

By combining these several points, we can construct little models or diagrams of several types of societies. Since 'the problem of public opinion' as we know it is set by the eclipse of the classic bourgeois public, we are here concerned with only two types: public and mass.

In a public, as we may understand the term, (1) virtually as many people express opinions as receive them. (2) Public communications are so organized that there is a chance immediately and effectively to answer back any opinion expressed in public. Opinion formed by such discussion (3) readily finds an outlet in effective action, even against—if necessary—the prevailing system of authority. And (4) authoritative institutions do not penetrate the public, which is thus more or less autonomous in its operations. When these conditions prevail, we have the working model of a community of publics, and this model fits closely the several assumptions of classic democratic theory.

At the opposite extreme, in a mass, (1) far fewer people express opinions than receive them; for the community of publics becomes an abstract collection of individuals who receive impressions from the mass media. (2) The communications that prevail are so organized that it is difficult or impossible for the individual to answer back immediately or with any effect. (3) The realization of opinion in action is controlled by authorities who organize and control the channels of such action. (4) The mass has no autonomy from institutions; on the contrary, agents of authorized institutions penetrate this mass, reducing any autonomy it may have in the formation of opinion by discussion.

The public and the mass may be most readily distinguished by their dominant modes of communication: in a community of publics, discussion is the ascendant means of communication, and the mass media, if they exist, simply enlarge and animate discussion, linking one primary public with the discussions of another. In a mass society, the dominant type of communication is the formal media, and the publics become mere media markets: all those exposed to the contents of given mass media.

III

From almost any angle of vision that we might assume, when we look upon the public, we realize that we have moved a considerable distance along the road to the mass society. At the end of that road there is totalitarianism, as in Nazi Germany or in Communist Russia. We are not yet at that end. In the United States today, media markets are not entirely ascendant over primary publics. But surely we can see that many aspects of the public life of our times are more the features of a mass society than of a community of publics.

What is happening might again be stated in terms of the historical parallel between the economic market and the public of public opinion. In brief, there is a movement from widely scattered little powers to concentrated powers and the attempt at monopoly control from powerful centers, which, being partially hidden, are centers of manipulation as well as of authority. The small shop serving the neighborhood is replaced by the anonymity of the national corporation: mass advertisement replaces the personal influence of opinion between merchant and customer. The political leader hooks up his speech to a national network and speaks, with appropriate personal touches, to a million people he never saw and never will see. Entire brackets of professions and industries are in the "opinion business,' impersonally manipulating the public for hire.

In the primary public the competition of opinions goes on between people holding views in the service of their interests and their reasoning. But in the mass society of media markets, competition, if any, goes on between the manipulators with their

mass media on the one hand, and the people receiving their propaganda on the other.

Under such conditions, it is not surprising that there should arise a conception of public opinion as a mere reaction—we cannot say 'response'—to the content of the mass media. In this view, the public is merely the collectivity of individuals each rather passively exposed to the mass media and rather helplessly opened up to the suggestions and manipulations that flow from these media. The fact of manipulation from centralized points of control constitutes, as it were, an expropriation of the old multitude of little opinion producers and consumers operating in a free and balanced market.

In official circles, the very term itself, 'the public'—as Walter Lippmann noted thirty years ago—has come to have a phantom meaning, which dramatically reveals its eclipse. From the standpoint of the deciding elite, some of those who clamor publicly can be identified as 'Labor,' others as "Business,' still others as 'Farmer.' Those who can not readily be so identified make up 'The Public.' In this usage, the public is composed of the unidentified and the non-partisan in a world of defined and partisan interests. It is socially composed of well-educated salaried professionals, especially college professors; of non-unionized employees, especially white-collar people, along with self-employed professionals and small businessmen.

In this faint echo of the classic notion, the public consists of those remants of the middle classes, old and new, whose interests are not explicitly defined, organized, or clamorous. In a curious adaption, 'the public' often becomes, in fact, 'the unattached expert,' who, although well informed, has never taken a clear-cut, public stand on controversial issues which are brought to a focus by organized interests. These are the 'public' members of the board, the commission, the committee. What the public stands for, accordingly, is often a vagueness of policy (called open-mindedness), a lack of involvement in public affairs (known as reasonableness), and a professional disinterest (known as tolerance).

Some such official members of the public, as in the field of labor-management mediation, start out very young and make a career out of being careful to be informed but never taking a strong position; and there are many others, quite unofficial, who take such professionals as a sort of model. The only trouble is that they are acting as if they were disinterested judges but they do not have the power of judges; hence their reasonableness, their tolerance, and their open-mindedness do not often count for much in the shaping of human affairs.

IV

All those trends that make for the decline of the politician and of his balancing society bear decisively upon the transformation of public into mass. * One of the most important of the structural transformations involved is the decline of the voluntary association as a genuine instrument of the public. As we have already seen, the executive ascendancy in economic, military, and political institutions has lowered the effective use of all those voluntary associations which operate between the state and the economy on the one hand, and the family and the individual in the primary group on the other. It is not only that institutions of power have become large-scale and inacessibly centralized; they have at the same time become less political and more administrative, and it is within this great change of framework that the organized public has waned.

In terms of scale, the transformation of public into mass has been underpinned by the shift from a political public decisively restricted in size (by property and education, as well as by sex and age) to a greatly enlarged mass having only the qualifications of citizenship and age.

In terms of organization, the transformation has been underpinned by the shift from the individual and his primary community to the voluntary association and the mass party as the major units of organized power.

Voluntary associations have become larger to the extent that they have become effective; and to just that extent they have become inaccessible to the individual who would shape by discussion the policies of the organization to which he belongs. Accordingly, along with older institutions, these voluntary associations have lost their grip on the individual. As more people are drawn into the political arena, these associations become mass in scale; and as the power of the individual becomes more dependent upon such mass associations, they are less accessible to the individual's influence. *

_____

*See, especially, the analysis of the decline of the independent middle classes, ELEVEN: The Theory of Balance.

*At the same time—and also because of the metropolitan segregation and distraction, which I shall discuss in a moment—the individual becomes more dependent upon the means of mass communication for his view of the structure as a whole.

Mass democracy means the struggle of powerful and large-scale interest groups and associations, which stand between the big decisions that are made by state, corporation, army, and the will of the individual citizen as a member of the public. Since these middle-level associations are the citizen's major link with decision, his relation to them is of decisive importance. For it is only through them that he exercises such power as he may have.

The gap between the members and the leaders of the mass association is becoming increasingly wider. As soon as a man gets to be a leader of an association large enough to count he readily becomes lost as an instrument of that association. He does so (1) in the interests of maintaining his leading position in, or rather over, his mass association, and he does so (2) because he comes to see himself not as a mere delegate, instructed or not, of the mass association he represents, but as a member of 'an elite' composed of such men as himself. These facts, in turn, lead to (3) the big gap between the terms in which issues are debated and resolved among members of this elite, and the terms in which they are presented to the members of the various mass associations. For the decisions that are made must take into account those who are important— other elites—but they must be sold to the mass memberships.

The gap between speaker and listener, between power and public, leads less to any iron law of oligarchy than to the law of spokesmanship: as the pressure group expands, its leaders come to organize the opinions they 'represent.' So elections, as we have seen, become contests between two giant and unwieldly parties, neither of which the individual can truly feel that he influences, and neither of which is capable of winning psychologically impressive or politically decisive majorities. And, in all this, the parties are of the same general form as other mass associations.[2]

When we say that man in the mass is without any sense of political belonging, we have in mind, a political fact rather than merely a style of feeling. We have in mind (I.) a certain way of belonging (II.) to a certain kind of organization.

I. The way of belonging here implied rests upon a belief in the purposes and in the leaders of an organization, and thus enables men and women freely to be at home within it. To belong in this way is to make the human association a psychological center of one's self, to take into our conscience, deliberately and freely, its rules of conduct and its purposes, which we thus shape and which in turn shape us. We do not have this kind of belonging to any political organization.

II. The kind of organization we have in mind is a voluntary association which has three decisive characteristics: first, it is a context in which reasonable opinions may be formulated; second, it is an agency by which reasonable activities may be undertaken; and third, it is a powerful enough unit, in comparison with other organizations of power, to make a difference.

It is because they do not find available associations at once psychologically meaningful and historically effective that men often feel uneasy in their political and economic loyalties. The effective units of power are now the huge corporation, the inacessible government, the grim military establishment. Between these, on the one hand, and the family and the small community on the other, we find no intermediate associations in which men feel secure and with which they feel powerful. There is little live political struggle. Instead, there is administration from above, and the political vacuum below. The primary publics are now either so small as to be swamped, and hence give up; or so large as to be merely another feature of the generally distant structure of power, and hence inacessible.

Public opinion exists when people who are not in the government of a country claim the right to express political opinions freely and publicly, and the right that these opinions should influence or determine the policies, personnel, and actions of their government.[3] In this formal sense there has been and there is a definite public opinion in the United States. And yet, with modern developments this formal right—when it does still exist as a right— does not mean what it once did. The older world of voluntary organization was as different from the world of the mass organization, as was Tom Paine's world of pamphleteering from the world of the mass media.

Since the French Revolution, conservative thinkers have Viewed With Alarm the rise of the public, which they called the masses, or something to that effect. "The populace is sovereign, and the tide of barbarism mounts,' wrote Gustave Le Bon. 'The divine right of the masses is about to replace the divine right of kings,' and already ' the destinies of nations are elaborated at present in the heart of the masses, and no longer in the councils of princes.'[4] During the twentieth century, liberal and even socialist thinkers have followed suit, with

more explicit reference to what we have called the society of masses. From Le Bon to Emil Lederer and Ortega y Gasset, they have held that the influence of the mass is unfortunately increasing.

But surely those who have supposed the masses to be all powerful, or at least well on their way to triumph, are wrong. In our time, as Chakhotin knew, the influence of autonomous collectivities within political life is in fact diminishing.[5] Furthermore, such influence as they do have is guided; they must now be seen not as publics acting autonomously, but as masses manipulated at focal points into crowds of demonstrators. For as publics become masses, masses sometimes become crowds; and, in crowds, the psychical rape by the mass media is supplemented up-close by the harsh and sudden harangue. Then the people in the crowd disperse again—as atomized and submissive masses.

In all modern societies, the autonomous associations standing between the various classes and the state tend to lose their effectiveness as vehicles of reasoned opinion and instruments for the rational exertion of political will. Such associations can be deliberately broken up and thus turned into passive instruments of rule, or they can more slowly wither away from lack of use in the face of centralized means of power. But whether they are destroyed in a week, or wither in a generation, such associations are replaced in virtually every sphere of life by centralized organizations, and it is such organizations with all their new means of power that take charge of the terrorized or—as the case may be—merely intimidated, society of masses.

V

The institutional trends that make for a society of masses are to a considerable extent a matter of impersonal drift, but the remnants of the public are also exposed to more 'personal' and intentional forces. With the broadening of the base of politics within the context of a folk-lore of democratic decision-making, and with the increased means of mass persuasion that are available, the public of public opinion has become the object of intensive efforts to control, manage, manipulate, and increasingly intimidate.

In political, military, economic realms, power becomes, in varying degrees, uneasy before the suspected opinions of masses, and, accordingly, opinion-making becomes an accepted technique of power-holding and power-getting. The minority electorate of the propertied and the educated is replaced by the total suffrage—and intensive campaigns for the vote. The small eighteenth-century professional army is replaced by the mass army of conscripts—and by the problems of nationalist morale. The small shop is replaced by the mass-production industry—and the national advertisement.

As the scale of institutions has become larger and more centralized, so has the range and intensity of the opinion-makers' efforts. The means of opinion-making, in fact, have paralleled in range and efficiency the other institutions of greater scale that cradle the modern society of masses. Accordingly, in addition to their enlarged and centralized means of administration, exploitation, and violence, the modern elite have had placed within their grasp historically unique instruments of psychic management and manipulation, which include universal compulsory education as well as the media of mass communication.

Early observers believed that the increase in the range and volume of the formal means of communication would enlarge and animate the primary public. In such optimistic views—written before radio and television and movies—the formal media are understood as simply multiplying the scope and pace of personal discussion. Modern conditions, Charles Cooley wrote, 'enlarge indefinitely the competition of idea, and whatever has owed its persistence merely to lack of comparison is likely to go, for that which is really congenial to the choosing mind will be all the more cherished and increased.[6] Still excited by the break-up of the conventional consensus of the local community, he saw the new means of communication as furthering the conversational dynamic of classic democracy, and with it the growth of rational and free individuality.

No one really knows all the functions of the mass media, for in their entirety these functions are probably so pervasive and so subtle that they cannot be caught by the means of social research now available. But we do now have reason to believe that these media have helped less to enlarge and animate the discussions of primary publics than to transform them into a set of media markets in mass-like society. I do not refer merely to the higher ratio of deliverers of opinion to receivers and to the decreased chance to answer back; nor do I refer merely to the violent banalization and stereotyping of our very sense organs in terms of which these media now compete for 'attention.' I have in mind a sort of psychological illiteracy that is facilitated by the media, and that is expressed in several ways:

I. Very little of what we think we know of the social realities of the world have we found out first-hand. Most of 'the pictures in our heads' we have gained from these media—even to the point where we often do not really believe what we see before us until we read about it in the paper or hear about it on the radio.[7] The media not only give us information; they guide our very experiences. Our standards of credulity, our standards of reality, tend to be set by these media rather than by our own fragmentary experience.

Accordingly, even if the individual has direct, personal experience of events, it is not really direct and primary: it is organized in stereotypes. It takes long and skillful training to so uproot such stereotypes that an individual sees things freshly, in an unstereotyped manner. One might suppose, for example, that if all the people went through a depression they would all 'experience it,' and in terms of this experience, that they would all debunk or reject or at least refract what the media say about it. But experience of such a <u>structural</u> shift has to be organized and interpreted if it is to count in the making of opinion.

The kind of experience, in short, that might serve as a basis for resistance to mass media is not an experience of raw events, but the experience of meanings. The fleck of interpretation must be there in the experience if we are to use the word experience seriously. And the capacity for such experience is socially implanted. The individual does not trust his own experience, as I have said, until it is confirmed by others or by the media. Usually such direct exposure is not accepted if it disturbs loyalties and beliefs that the individual already holds. To be accepted, it must relieve or justify the feelings that often lie in the back of his mind as key features of his ideological loyalties.

Stereotypes of loyalty underlie beliefs and feelings about given symbols and emblems; they are the very ways in which men see the social world and in terms of which men make up their specific opinions and views of events. They are the results of previous experience, which affect present and future experience. It goes without saying that men are often unaware of these loyalties, that often they could not formulate them explicitly. Yet such general stereotypes make for the acceptance or the rejection of specific opinions not so much by the force of logical consistency as by their emotional affinity and by the way in which they relieve anxieties. To accept opinions in their terms is to gain the good solid feeling of being correct without having to think. When ideological stereotypes and specific opinions are linked in this way, there is a lowering of the kind of anxiety which arises when loyalty and belief are not in accord. Such ideologies lead to a willingness to accept a given line of belief; then there is no need, emotionally or rationally, to overcome resistance to given items in that line; cumulative selections of specific opinions and feelings become the pre-organized attitudes and emotions that shape the opinion-life of the person.

These deeper beliefs and feelings are a sort of lens through which men experience their worlds, they strongly condition acceptance or rejection of specific opinions, and they set men's orientation toward prevailing authorities. Three decades ago, Walter Lippmann saw such prior convictions as biases: they kept men from defining reality in an adequate way. They are still biases. But today they can often be seen as 'good biases'; inadequate and misleading as they often are, they are less so than the crackpot realism of the higher authorities and opinion-maker. They are the lower common sense and as such a factor of resistance. But we must recognize, especially when the pace of change is so deep and fast that common sense is more often common than sense. And, above all, we must recognize that 'the common sense' of our children is going to be less the result of any firm social tradition than of the stereotypes carried by the mass media to which they are now so fully exposed. They are the first generation to be so exposed.

II. So long as the media are not entirely monopolized, the individual can play one medium off against another; he can compare them, and hence resist what any one of them puts out. The more genuine competition there is among the media, the more resistance the individual might be able to command. But how much is this now the case? Do people compare reports on public events or policies, playing one medium's content off against another?

The answer is: generally no, very few do: (1) We know that people tend strongly to select those media which carry contents with which they already agree. There is a kind of selection of new opinions on the basis of prior opinions. No one seems to search out such counter-statements as may be found in alternative media offerings. Given radio

programs and magazines and newspapers often get a rather consistent public, and thus reinforce their messages in the minds of that public. (2) This idea of playing one medium off against another assumes that the media really have varying contents. It assumes genuine competition, which is not widely true. The media display an apparent variety and competition, but on closer view they seem to compete more in terms of variations on a few standardized themes than of clashing issues. The freedom to raise issues effectively seems more to be confined to those few interests that have ready and continual access to these media.

III. The media have not only filtered into our very experience of our own selves. They have provided us with new identities and new aspirations of what we should like to be, and what we should like to appear to be. They have provided in the models of conduct they hold out to us a new and larger and more flexible set of appraisals of our very selves. In terms of the modern theory of the self,[8] we may say that the media bring the reader, listener, viewer into the sight of larger, higher reference groups—groups, real or imagined, up-close or vicarious, personally known or distractedly glimpsed—which are looking glasses for his self-image. They have multiplied the groups to which we look for confirmation of our self-image.

More than that: (1) the media tell the man in the mass who he is—they give him identity; (2) they tell him what he wants to be—they give him aspirations; (3) they tell him how to get that way—they give him technique; and (4) they tell him how to feel that he is that way even when he is not—they give him escape. The gaps between the identity and aspiration lead to technique and/or to escape. That is probably the basic psychological formula of the mass media today. But, as a formula, it is not attuned to the development of the human being. It is the formula of a pseudo-world which the media invent and sustain.

IV. As they now generally prevail, the mass media, especially television, often encroach upon the small-scale discussion, and destroy the chance for the reasonable and leisurely and human interchange of opinion. They are an important cause of the destruction of privacy in its full human meaning. That is an important reason why they not only fail as an educational force, but are a malign force: they do not articulate for the viewer or listener the broader sources of his private tensions and anxieties, his inarticulate resentments and half-formed hopes. They neither enable the individual to transcend his narrow milieu nor clarify its private meaning

The media provide much information and news about what is happening in the world, but they do not often enable the listener or the viewer truly to connect his daily life with these larger realities. They do not connect the information they provide on public issues with the troubles felt by the individual. They do not increase rational insight into tensions, either those in the individual or those of the society which are reflected in the individual. On the contrary, they distract him and obscure his chance to understand himself or his world, by fastening his attention upon artificial frenzies that are resolved within the program framework, usually by violent action or by what is called humor. In short, for the viewer they are not really resolved at all. The chief distracting tension of the media is between the wanting and the not having of commodities or of women held to be good looking. There is almost always the general tone of animated distraction, of suspended agitation, but it is going nowhere and it has nowhere to go.

But the media, as now organized and operated, are even more than a major cause of the transformation of America into a mass society. They are also among the most important of those increased means of power now at the disposal of elites of wealth and power; moreover, some of the higher agents of these media are themselves either among the elites or very important among their servants.

Alongside or just below the elite, there is the propagandist, the publicity expert, the public-relations man, who would control the very formation of public opinion in order to be able to include it as one more pacified item in calculations of effective power, increased prestige, more secure wealth. Over the last quarter of a century, the attitudes of these manipulators toward their task have gone through a sort of dialectic:

In the beginning, there is great faith in what the mass media can do. Words win wars or sell soap; they move people, they restrain people. 'Only cost,' the advertising man of the 'twenties proclaims, 'limits the delivery of public opinion in any direction on any topic.'⁹ The opinion-maker's belief in the media as mass persuaders almost amounts to magic—but he can believe mass communications omnipotent only so long as the public is trustful. It does not remain trustful. The mass media say so very many and such competitively exaggerated things; they banalize their message and they cancel one another out. The 'propaganda

phobia,' in reaction to wartime lies and postwar disenchantment, does not help matters, even though memory is both short and subject to official distortion. This distrust of the magic of media is translated into a slogan among the opinion managers. Across their banners they write: 'Mass Persuasion Is Not Enough.'

Frustrated, they reason; and reasoning, they come to accept the principle of social context. To change opinion and activity, they say to one another, we must pay close attention to the full context and lives of the people to be managed. Along with mass persuasion, we must somehow use personal influence; we must reach people in their life context and through other people, their daily associates, those whom they trust: we must get at them by some kind of 'personal' perusasion. We must not show our hand directly; rather than merely advise or command, we must manipulate.

Now this live and immediate social context in which people live and which exerts a steady expectation upon them is of course what we have called the primary public. Anyone who has seen the inside of an advertising agency or public-relations office knows that the primary public is still the great unsolved problem of the opinion-makers. Negatively, their recognition of the influence of social context upon opinion and public activity implies that the articulate public resists and refracts the communications of the mass media. Positively, this recognition implies that the public is not composed of isolated individuals, but rather of persons who not only have prior opinions that must be reckoned with, but who continually influence each other in complex and intimate, in direct and continual ways.

In their attempts to neutralize or to turn to their own use the articulate public, the opinion-makers try to make it a relay network for their views. If the opinion-makers have so much power that they can act directly and openly upon the primary publics, they may become authoritative; but, if they do not have such power and hence have to operate indirectly and without visibility, they will assume the stance of manipulators.

Authority is power that is explicit and more or less 'voluntarily' obeyed; manipulation is the 'secret' exercise of power, unknown to those who are influenced. In the model of the classic democratic society, manipulation is not a problem, because formal authority resides in the public itself and in its representatives who are made or broken by the public. In the completely authoritarian society, manipulation is not a problem, because authority is openly identified with the ruling institutions and their agents, who may use authority explicitly and nakedly. They do not, in the extreme case, have to gain or retain power by hiding its exercise.

Manipulation becomes a problem wherever men have power that is concentrated and willful but do not have authority, or when, for any reason, they do not wish to use their power openly. Then the powerful seek to rule without showing their power-fulness. They want to rule, as it were, secretly, without publicized legitimation. It is in this mixed —case as in the intermediate reality of the American today—that manipulation is a prime way of ex-ercising power. Small circles of men are making decisions which they need to have at least autho-rized by indifferent or recalcitrant people over whom they do not exercise explicit authority. So the small circles tries to manipulate these people into willing acceptance or cheerful support of their decisions or opinions—or at least to the rejection of possible counter-opinions.

Authority formally resides 'in the people,' but the power of initiation is in fact held by small cir-cles of men. That is why the standard strategy of manipulation is to make it appear that the people, or at least a large group of them, 'really made the decision.' That is why even when the authority is available, men with access to it may still prefer the secret, quieter ways of manipulation.

But are not the people now more educated? Why not emphasize the spread of education rather than the increased effects of the mass media? The answer, in brief, is that mass education, in many respects, has become—another mass medium.

The prime task of public education, as it came widely to be understood in this country, was poli-tical: to make the citizen more knowledgeable and thus better able to think and to judge of public affairs. In time, the function of education shifted from the political to the economic: to train people for better-paying jobs and thus to get ahead. This is especially true of the high-school movement which has met the business demands for white-collar skills at the public's expense. In large part education has become merely vocational; in so far as its political task is concerned, in many schools, that has been reduced to a routine training of na-tionalist loyalties.

The training of skills that are of more or less direct use in the vocational life is an important task to perform, but ought not to be mistaken for liberal education: job advancement, no matter on what levels, is not the same as self-development, although the two are now systematically confused.[10] Among 'skills,' some are more and some are less relevant to the aims of liberal—that is to say, lib-erating—education. Skills and values cannot be so easily separated as the academic search for suppo-sedly neutral skills causes us to assume. And es-pecially not when we speak seriously of liberal edu-cation. Of course, there is a scale, with skills at one end and values at the other, but it is the middle range of this scale, which one might call sensibili-ties, that are of most relevance to the classic pu-blic.

To train someone to operate a lathe or to read and write is pretty much education of skill; to evoke from people an understanding of what they really want out of their lives or to debate with them stoic, Christian and humanist ways of living, is pretty much a clear-cut education of values. But to assist in the birth among a group of people of those cultural and political and technical sensibilities which would make them genuine members of a genuinely liberal public, this is at once a training in skills and an edu-cation of values. It includes a sort of therapy in the ancient sense of clarifying one's knowledge of one's self; it includes the imparting of all those skills of controversy with one's self, which we call thinking; and with others, which we call debate. And the end product of such liberal education of sensibilities is simply the self-educating, self-cultivating man or woman.

The knowledgeable man in the genuine public is able to turn his personal troubles into social issues, to see their relevance for his community and his community's relevance for them. He understands that what he thinks and feels as personal troubles are very often not only that but problems shared by others and indeed not subject to solution by any one individual but only by modifications of the structure of the groups in which he lives and sometimes the structure of the entire society.

Men in masses are gripped by personal troubles, but they are not aware of their true meaning and source. Men in public confront issues, and they are aware of their terms. It is the task of the liberal institution, as of the liberally educated man, continually to translate troubles into issues and issues into the terms of their human meaning for the indi-vidual. In the absence of deep and wide political debate, schools for adults and adolescents could perhaps become hospitable frameworks for just such debate. In a community of publics the task of liberal education would be: to keep the public from being overwhelmed; to help produce the disciplined and informed mind that cannot be overwhelmed; to help develop the bold and sensible individual that cannot be sunk by the burdens of mass life. But educational practice has not made knowledge directly relevant to the human need of the troubled person of the twentieth century or to the social practices of the citizen. This citizen cannot now see the roots of his own biases and frustrations, nor think clearly about himself, nor for that matter about anything else. He does not see the frustration of idea, of intellect, by the present organization of society, and he is not able to meet the tasks now confronting 'the intelligent citizen.'

Educational institutions have not done these things and, except in rare instances, they are not doing them. They have become mere elevators of occupational and social ascent, and, on all levels, they have become politically timid. Moreover, in the hands of 'professional educators,' many schools have come to operate on an ideology of 'life adjustment' that encourages happy acceptance of mass ways of life rather than the struggle for individual and public transcendence. *

There is not much doubt that modern regressive educators have adapted their notions of educational content and practice to the idea of the mass. They do not effectively proclaim standards of cultural level and intellectual rigor; rather they often deal in the trivia of vocational tricks and 'adjustment to life'—meaning the slack life of masses. 'Democratic schools' often mean the furtherance of intellectual mediocrity, vocational training, nationalistic loyalties, and little else.

VI

The structural trends of modern society and the manipulative character of its communication tech-

---

*If the schools are doing their job, 'A. E. Bestor has written, 'we should expect educators to point to the significant and indisputable achievement in raising the intellectual level of the nation—measured perhaps by larger per capita circulation of books and serious magazines, by definitely improved taste in movies and radio programs, by higher standards of political debate, by increased respect for freedom of speech and of thought, by marked decline in such evidences of mental retardation as the incessant reading of comic books by adults.'[11]

nique come to a point of coincidence in the mass society, which is largely a metropolitan society. The growth of the metropolis, segregating men and women into narrowed routines and environments, causes them to lose any firm sense of their integrity as a public. The members of publics in smaller communities know each other more or less fully, because they meet in the several aspects of the total life routine. The members of masses in a metropolitan society know one another only as fractions in specialized milieux: the man who fixes the car, the girl who serves your lunch, the saleslady, the women who take care of your child at school during the day. Prejudgment and stereotype flourish when people meet in wuch ways. The human reality of others does not, cannot, come through.

People, we know, tend to select those formal media which confirm what they already believe and enjoy. In a parallel way, they tend in the metropolitan segregation to come into live touch with those whose opinions are similar to theirs. Others they tend to treat unseriously. In the metropolitan society they develop, in their defense, a blase manner that reaches deeper than a manner. They do not, accordingly, experience genuine clashes of viewpoint, genuine issues. And when they do, they tend to consider it mere rudeness.

Sunk in their routines, they do not transcend, even by discussion, much less by action, their more or less narrow lives. They do not gain a view of the structure of their society and of their role as a public within it. The city is a structure composed of such little environments, and the people in them tend to be detached from one another. The 'stimulating variety' of the city does not stimulate the men and women of 'the bedroom belt,' the one-class suburbs, who can go through life knowing only their own kind. If they do reach for one another, they do so only through stereotypes and prejudiced images of the creatures of other milieux. Each is trapped by his confining circle; each is cut off from easily identifiable groups. It is for people in such narrow milieux that the mass media can create a pseudo-world beyond, and a pseudo-world within themselves as well.

Publics live in milieux but they can transcend them —individually by intellectual effort; socially by public action. By reflection and debate and by organized action, a community of publics comes to feel itself and comes in fact to be active at points of structural relevance.

But members of a mass exist in milieux and cannot get out of them either by mind or by activity, except—in the extreme case—under 'the organized spontaneity' of the bureaucrat on a motorcycle. We have not yet reached the extreme case, but observing metropolitan man in the American mass we can surely see the psychological preparations for it.

We may think of it in this way: When a handful of men do not have jobs and do not seek work, we look for the causes in their immediate situation and character. But when twelve million men are unemployed, then we cannot believe that all of them suddenly 'got lazy' and turned out to be 'no good.' Economists call this 'structural unemployment'—meaning, for one thing, that the men involved cannot themselves control their job chances. Structural unemployment does not originate in one factory or in one town, nor is it due to anything that one factory or one town does or fails to do. Moreover, there is little or nothing that one ordinary man in one factory in one town can do about it when it sweeps over his personal milieu.

Now, this distinction, between social structure and personal milieu, is one of the most important available in the sociological studies. It offers us a ready understanding of the position of 'the public' in America today. In every major area of life, the loss of a sense of structure and the submergence into powerless milieux is the cardinal fact. In the military it is most obvious, for here the roles men play are strictly confining; only the command posts at the top afford a view of the structure of the whole, and moreover, this view is a closely guarded official secret. In the division of labor too, the jobs men enact in the economic hierarchies are also more or less narrow milieux and the positions from which a view of the production process as a whole can be had are centralized, as men are alienated not only from the product and the tools of their labor, but from any understanding of the structure and the processes of production. In the political order, in the fragmentation of the lower and in the distracting proliferation of the middle-level organization, men cannot see the top, and cannot state the issues that will in fact determine the whole structure in which they live and their place within it.

This loss of any structural view or position is the decisive meaning of the lament over the loss of community. In the great city, the division of milieux and of segregating routines reaches the point of closest contact with the individual and the family, for, although the city is not the unit of prime decision, even the city cannot be seen as a total structure by most of its citizens.

On the one hand, there is the increased scale and centralization of the structure of decision; and, on the other, the increasingly narrow sorting out of men into milieux. From both sides, there is the increased dependence upon the formal media of communication, including those of education itself. But the man in the mass does not gain a transcending view from these media; instead he gets his experience stereotyped, and then he gets sunk further by that experience. He cannot detach himself in order to observe, much less to evaluate, what he is experiencing, much less what he is not experiencing. Rather than that internal discussion we call reflection, he is accompanied through is life-experience with a sort of unconscious, echoing monologue. He has no projects of his own: he fulfills the routines that exist. He does not transcend whatever he is at any moment, because he does not, he cannot, transcend his daily milieux. He is not truly aware of his own daily experience and of its actual standards: he drifts, he fulfills habits, his behavior a result of a planless mixture of the confused standards and the uncriticized expectations that he has taken over from others whom he no longer really knows or trusts, if indeed he ever really did.

He takes things for granted, he makes the best of them, he tries to look ahead—a year or two perhaps, or even longer if he has children or a mortgage—but he does not seriously ask, What do I want? How can I get it? A vague optimism suffuses and sustains him, broken occasionally by little miseries and disappointments that are soon buried. He is smug, from the standpoint of those who think something might be the matter with the mass style of life in the metropolitan frenzy where self-making is an externally busy branch of industry. By what standards does he judge himself and his efforts? What is really important to him? Where are the models of excellence for this man?

He loses his independence, and more importantly, he loses the desire to be independent: in fact, he does not have hold of the idea of being an independent individual with his own mind and his own worked-out way of life. It is not that he likes or does not like this life; it is that the question does not come up sharp and clear so he is not bitter and he is not sweet about conditions and events. He thinks he wants merely to get his share of what is around with as little trouble as he can and with as much fun as possible.

Such order and movement as his life possesses is in conformity with external routines; otherwise his day-to-day experience is a vague chaos—although he often does not know it because, strictly speaking, he does not truly possess or observe his own experience. He does not formulate his desires; they are insinuated into him. And, in the mass, he loses the self-confidence of the human being—if indeed he has ever had it. For life in a society of masses implants insecurity and furthers impotence; it makes men uneasy and vaguely anxious; it isolates the individual from the solid group; it destroys firm group standards. Acting without goals, the man in the mass just feels pointless.

The idea of a mass society suggests the idea of an elite of power. The idea of the public, in contrast, suggests the liberal tradition of a society without any power elite, or at any rate with shifting elites of no sovereign consequence. For, if a genuine public is sovereign, it needs no master; but the masses, in their full development, are sovereign only in some plebiscitarian moment of adulation to an elite as authoritative celebrity. The political structure of a democratic state requires the public; and, the democratic man, in his rhetoric, must assert that this public is the very seat of sovereignty.

But now, given all those forces that have enlarged and centralized the political order and made modern societies less political and more administrative; given the transformation of the old middle classes into something which perhaps should not even be called middle class; given all the mass communications that do not truly communicate; given all the metropolitan segregation that is not community; given the absence of voluntary assosiations that really connect the public at large with the centers of power—what is happening is the decline of a set of publics that is sovereign only in the most formal and rhetorical sense. Moreover, in many countries the remnants of such publics as remain are now being frighened out of existence. They lose their will for rationally considered decision and action because they do not possess the instruments for such decision and action; they lose their sense of political belonging because they do not belong; they lose their political will because they see no way to realize it.

The top of modern American society is increasingly unified, and often seems willfully coordinated: at the top there has emerged an elite of power. The middle levels are a drifting set of stalemated, balancing forces: the middle does not link the bottom with the top. The bottom of this society is politically fragmented, and even as a passive fact, increasingly powerless: at the bottom there is emerging a mass society.

Notes

1. See E. H. Carr, The New Society (london: Macmillan, 1951), pp. 63-6, on whom I lean heavily in this and the following paragraphs.

2. On elections in modern formal democracies, E. H. Carr has concluded: 'To speak today of the defence of democracy as if we were defending something which we knew and had possessed for many decades or many centuries is self-deception and sham—mass democracy is a new phenomenon—a creation of the last half-century—which it is inappropriate and misleading to consider in terms of the philosophy of Locke or of the liberal democracy of the nineteenth century. We should be nearer the mark, and should have a far more convincing slogan, if we spoke of the need, not to defend democracy, but to create it.' (ibid. pp. 75-6).

3. Cf. Hans Speier, Social Order and The Risks of War (New York: George Stewart, 1952), pp. 323-39.

4. Gustave Le Bon, The Crowd (London: Ernest Benn Ltd., 1952—first English edition, 1896), pp. 207. Cf. also pp. 6, 23, 30, 187.

5. Sergei Chakhotin, The Rape of the Masses (New York: Alliance, 1940), pp. 289—91.

6. Charles Horton Cooley, Social Organization (New York: Scribner's, 1909), p. 93. Cf. also Chapter IX.

7. See Walter Lippmann, Public Opinion (New York: Macmillan, 1922), which is still the best account of this aspect of the media. Cf. especially pp. 1—25 and 59—121.

8. Cf. Gerth and Mills, Character and Social Structure (New York: Harcourt, Brace, 1953), pp. 84 ff.

9. J. Truslow Adams, The Epic of America (Boston: Little, Brown, 1931) p. 360.

10. Cf. Mills, 'Work Milieu and Social Structure,' a speech to 'The Asilomar Conference' of the Mental Health Society of Northern California, March 1954, reprinted in their bulletin, People At Work: A Symposium, pp. 20 ff.

11. A. E. Bestor, Educational Wastelands (Urbana, Ill.: University of Illinois, 1953), p. 7. Cf. also p. 80.

AMERICA AS A MASS SOCIETY: A Critique

Daniel Bell

. . . a sombre melancholy weighed on people's souls. . . . It would sometimes seem as
if this period had been particularly unhappy,
as if it had left behind only the memory of
violence, of covetousness and moral hatred.
. . . The feeling of genereral insecurity [was
heightened] by the chronic form wars were
apt to take, by the constant menace of the
dangerous classes, by the mistrut of justice
. . . . It was, so to say, bad form to praise
the world and life openly. It was fashion-
able to see only its suffering and misery, to
discover everywhere the signs of decadence
and the near end—in short to condemn the
times or to despise them.

—J. H. Huizinga, The Waning of the Middle Ages

The sense of a radical dehumanization of life
which has accompanied events of the past few decades has given rise to the theory of "mass society." One can say that, Marxism apart, it is
probably the most influential social theory in the
Western world today. While no single individual
has stamped his name on it—to the extent that
Marx is associated with the transformation of personal relations under capitalism into commodity
values, or Freud with the role of the irrational
and unconscious in behavior—the theory is central
to the thinking of the principal aristocratic, Catholic, or Existentialist critics of modern society.
These critics—Ortega y Gasset, Paul Tillich,
Karl Jaspers, Gabriel Marcel, Emil Lederer,
Hannah Arendt, and others—have been concerned
less with the general conditions of freedom in society than with the freedom of the person and with
the possibility, for some few persons, of achieving
a sense of individual self in our mechanized society. And this is the source of their appeal.

The conception of the "mass society" can be
summarized as follows: The revolutions in trans-
port and communications have brought men into
closer contact with each other and bound them in
new ways; the division of labor has made them
more interdependent; tremors in one part of society
affect all others. Despite this greater interdependence, however, individuals have grown more es-
tranged from one another. The old primary group
ties of family and local community have been shattered; ancient parochial faiths are questioned; few
unifying values have taken their place. Most important, the critical standards of an educated elite
no longer shape opinion or taste. As a result,
mores and morals are in constant flux, relations
between individuals are tangential or compartmentalized, rather than organic. At the same time, greater mobility, spatial and social, intensifies concern
over status. Instead of a fixed or known status, sym-
bolized by dress or title, each person assumes a
multiplicity of roles and constantly has to prove himself in a succession of new situations. Because of
all this, the individual loses a coherent sense of self.
His anxieties increase. There ensues a search for
new faiths. The stage is thus set for the charis-
matic leader, the secular messiah, who, by bes-
towing upon each person the semblance of necessary grace and of fullness of personality, supplies
a substitute for the older unifying belief that the
mass society has destroyed.

In a world of lonely crowds seeking individual
distinction, where values are constantly translated
into economic calculabilities, where in extreme
situations shame and conscience can no longer restrain the most dreadful excesses of terror, the
theory of the mass society seems a forceful, realistic description of contemporary society, an accurate reflection of the quality and feeling of modern life. But when one seeks to apply the theory
of mass society, analytically, it becomes very
slippery. Ideal types, like the shadows in Plato's
cave, generally never give us more than a silhouette.
So, too, with the theory of "mass society." Each
of the statements making up the theory, as set forth
in the second paragraph above, might be true, but they
do not follow necessarily from one another. Nor can
we say that all the conditions described are present
at any one time or place. More than that, there
is no organizing principle—other than the general
concept of a "breakdown of values"—that puts the
individual elements of theory together in a logical,
meaningful—let alone historical—manner. And when
we examine the way the "theory" is used by those

who employ it, we find ourselves even more at a loss.

In trying to sort out the ambiguities in the use of the phrase, we can distinguish perhaps five different, and sometimes contradictory, usages:

1. <u>Mass as undifferentiated number.</u> As commonly used in the term "mass media," "mass" implies that standardized material is transmitted to "all groups of the population uniformly." As understood generally by sociologists, a <u>mass</u> is a heterogeneous and undifferentiated audience, as opposed to a <u>class,</u> or any parochial and relatively homogeneous segment. Some sociologists have been tempted to go further and make "mass" a rather pejorative term. Because the mass media subject a diverse audience to a common set of cultural materials, it is argued that these experiences must necessarily lie outside the personal—and therefore meaningful—experiences to which the individual responds directly. A movie audience, for example, is a "mass" because the individuals looking at the screen are, in the words of the American sociologist Herbert Blumer, "separate, detached, and anonymous." The mass "has no social organization, no body of custom and tradition, no established set of rules or rituals, no organized group of sentiments, no structure of status roles and no established leadership."

To become part of the mass is to be divorced— or "alienated"—from oneself. And the instruments which project the dominant social values that men (and women and children) choose as their <u>imago,</u> or ideal image and desire—television, radio, and the movies—impose a mass response on their audience.

2. <u>Mass as the judgment by the incompetent.</u> As first introduced by the late Ortega y Gasset in 1931, in his famous <u>Revolt of the Masses,</u> the terms "masses" and "mass" had a far different meaning than the usage implied by the term "mass media" and its invidious connotations. For Ortega, the word "mass" did not designate a group of persons—the masses were not the workers, even though the revolutionary movements of the time had equated the two—but the low <u>quality</u> of modern civilization, resulting from the loss of a commanding position by the "gentlemen" who once made up the educated elite. Modern taste, for Ortega, represents the judgment of the unqualified. Modern life "makes a <u>tabula rasa</u> of all classicism." Nothing that is in the past can be "any possible model or standard." Even "the famous Renaissance reveals itself as a period of narrow provincialism—

why not use the word?—ordinary." Modern culture, since it disowns the past, seeks a "free expression of what its vital desires"; it becomes, therefore, an unrestrained "spoiled child" with no controlling standards, "no limit to its caprice." In Ortega, one finds the most sweeping attack against all "modernity." His is the disdain of the humanist for the vulgar.

3. <u>Mass as the mechanized society.</u> In German romanticism, in its idealization of nature and the pastoral, one finds the source of much of the protest against modern life. For these writers— and the poets and critics Ernst and Friedrich George Juenger can be taken as typical—the dehumanizing element is technology. The mass society is a mechanical society. Society has become an "apparatus." The machine impresses its style on man, makes life mathematical and precise; existence takes on a masslike character: the steel helmet and the welder's face-guard symbolize the individual's disappearance into his technical function. The regulated, functional man emerges as a new type, hard and ruthless, a cog in the technological press.

4. <u>The mass as the bureaucratized society.</u> Less romantic, but equally critical, are those theorists who see extreme rationalization and extreme bureaucratization—the <u>over-organization</u> of life— as the salient features of the mass society. The idea of "rationalization" goes back to Hegel and Marx, and along with it the notions of "estrangement" or "alienation," "reification," and the "fetishism of commodities"—all of which express the thought that in modern society man has become a "thing," an object manipulated by society, rather than a subject who can remake life in accordance with his own desires. In our time, Georg Simmel, Max Weber, and Karl Mannheim have developed and elaborated these concepts. In Mannheim's work— notably in his <u>Man and Society in an Age of Reconstruction</u>—the diverse strands are all brought together.

Mannheim's argument, put schematically, runs as follows: modern large-scale organization, oriented exclusively to efficiency, creates hierarchies that concentrate all decisions at the top. Even technical decisions are removed from the shop floor and centered in specialized bodies that have no direct contact with work. Since the concern is solely with efficiency, rather than human satisfactions, all solutions to problems are defined in relation to this single value. Mannheim calls this "functional rationality," or direct means-ends relationships, in contrast to "substantial rationality," which is the application of Reason to human affairs.

This concentration of decision-making not only creates conformity but stunts the initiative of subordinates and leaves them unsatisfied in their personal needs for gratification and esteem. (In effect, the demand for submission to extreme rationality deprives the individual of the power to act rationally; i.e., in accordance with reason. This frustration seeks release in irrational ways.) Normally, the routinization of one's job dulls the edge of frustration and provides some security. But when unemployment looms, the helplessness becomes sharpened, and self-esteem is threatened. Since individuals cannot rationally locate the source of their frustration (i.e., the impersonal bureaucratic system itself), they will, under these circumstances, seek scapegoats and turn to fascism.

5. The mass as mob. While for Mannheim, and the neo-Marxists, mass society is equated with monolithic bureaucratization, for Emil Lederer and Hannah Arendt it is defined by the elimination of difference, by uniformity, aimlessness, alienation, and the failure of integration.

In Lederer's view, society is made up of many social groups united by function or self-interest, some rational in purpose, some irrational. So long as society is stratified, these groups can impose only partial control, and irrational emotions are restricted. But when the lines dividing social groups break down, the people become volatile and febrile "masses," ready to be manipulated by a leader.

Hannah Arendt, perhaps because she writes a decade later, sees the masses as already overspilling the bounds. The masses are those who, because of indifference or simply sheer number, do not belong to "political parties or municipal governments or professional organizations or trade unions"—in short, organizations that exist to satisfy a common interest—and they "form the majority of those large numbers of neutral, politically indifferent people who never join a party or hardly ever go to the polls."

Such people already stand "outside" of society. The revolt of the masses is a revolt against the "loss of social status along with which is lost the whole sector of communal relationships in whose framework common sense makes sense. . . The masses become obsessed by a desire to escape from reality because in their essential homelessness they can no longer bear its accidental incomprehensible aspects.

And so, because modern life sunders all social bonds, and because the techniques of modern communication have perfected the means whereby propaganda can manipulate the masses, the "age of the masses" is now upon us.

What strikes one first about these varied uses of the concept of mass society is how little they reflect or relate to the complex, richly striated social relations of the real world. Take Blumer's example of the movie audience as "separate, detached, and anonymous." Presumably, a large number of individuals, because they have been subjected to similar experiences, now share some common psychological reality in which the differences between individual and individual become blurred; accordingly we get the sociological assumption that each person is now of "equal weight," and therefore a sampling of what such disparate individuals say they think constitutes "mass opinion." But is this so? Individuals are not tabulae rasae. They bring varying social conceptions to the same experience and go away with dissimilar responses. They may be silent, separate, detached, and anonymous while watching the movie, but afterward they talk about it with friends and exchange opinions and judgments. They are once again members of particular social groups. Would one say that several hundred or a thousand individuals home alone at night, but all reading the same book, constitute a "mass"?

Because romantic feeling colors critical judgment, the attacks on modern life often have an unduly strong emotional charge. The image of "facelessness," for example, is given a metaphysical twist by Gabriel Marcel:

"The individual, in order to belong to the mass . . . has to. . . divest himself of that substantial reality which was linked to his initial individuality . . . . The incredibly sinister role of the press, the cinema, the radio has consisted in passing that original reality through a pair of flattening rollers to substitute for it a superimposed pattern of ideas, an image with no real roots in the deep being of the subject of this experiment." Perhaps terms like "original reality" and "real roots in the deep being" have a meaning that escapes an empiricist temper, but without the press, the radio, etc., etc.—and they are not monolithic—in what way, short of being everywhere at once, can one learn of events that take place elsewhere? Or should one go back to the happy ignorance of earlier days?

Some of the images of life in the mass society, as presented by its critics, border on caricature.

According to Ernst Juenger, traffic demands traffic regulations, and so the public becomes conditioned to automatism. Karl Jaspers has written that in the "technical mass order" the home is transformed "into a lair or sleeping place." Even more puzzling is the complaint against modern medicine. "In medical practice . . . patients are now dealt with in the mass according to the principle of rationalization, being sent to institutes for technical treatment, the sick being classified in groups and referred to this or that specialized department. . . . The supposition is that, like everything else, medical treatment has become a sort of manufactured article.

The attack on the mass society widens into an attack on science itself. For Ortega, "the scientific man is the prototype of the massman," because science, by encouraging specialization, has made the scientist "hermetic and self-satisfied within his limitations." Ortega draws from this the sweeping conclusion that "the most immediate result of this unbalanced specialization has been that today, when there are more 'scientists' than ever, there are much less 'cultured' men than, for example, about 1750." But how is one to verify such a comparison between 1750 and the present? Even if we could establish comparable categories, surely Ortega would have been the first to shy away from statistical comparisons. Moreover, can we assume that because a man specializes in his work, he is unable, in his leisure and in reflection, to appreciate culture? And what is "culture"? Would not Ortega admit that we have more knowledge of the world than in 1750—knowledge not only of nature but of the inner life of man? Is knowledge to be divorced from culture, or is "true culture" a narrow area of classical learning in which eternal truths reside?

One could argue, of course, that reading a book, to cite my previous example, is a qualitatively different experience from going to a movie. But this leads precisely to the first damaging ambiguity in the theory of the mass society. Two things are mixed up in that theory: a judgment regarding the quality of modern experience—with much of which any sensitive individual might agree—and a presumed scientific statement concerning the disorganization of society created by industrialization and by the demand of the masses for equality. It is the second of these statements with which this essay quarrels.

Behind the theory of social disorganization lies a romantic—and somewhat false—notion of the past, which sees society as having once been made up of small, "organic," close-knit communities (called Gemeinschaften in the terminology of the sociologists) that were shattered by industrialism and modern life, and replaced by a large, impersonal, "atomistic" society (called Gesellschaft) that is unable to provide the basic gratifications, and call forth the loyalties, that the older communities knew. These distinctions are, however, completely riddled by value judgments. Everyone is against atomism and for "organic living." But if we substitute, with good logic, the term "total" for "organic," and "individualistic" for "atomistic," the whole argument looks quite different. In any case, a great weakness in the theory is its lack of history-mindedness. The transition to a mass society, if it be such, was not effected suddenly, explosively, within a single lifetime, but took generations to mature. In its sociological determinism, the hypothesis overlooks the human capacity for adaptiveness and creativeness, for ingenuity in shaping new social forms. Such new forms may be trade unions whose leaders rise from the ranks—there are 50,000 trade unions locals in this country that form little worlds of their own—or the persistence under new conditions of ethnic groups and solidarities.

But more than mere contradictions in usage, ambiguities in terminology, and a lack of historical sense are involved in the theory of the mass society. It is at heart a defense of an aristocratic cultural tradition—a tradition that does carry with it an important but neglected conception of liberty—and a doubt that the large mass of mankind can ever become truly educated or acquire an appreciation of culture. Thus, the theory often becomes a conservative defense of privilege. This defense is at times so extreme as to pose a conflict between "culture" and "social justice." The argument (reminiscent of the title of Matthew Arnold's book Culture and Anarchy) is made that any attempts at social betterment must harm culture. And, while mainly directed against "bourgeois" society, the theory also strikes at radicalism and its egalitarian notions.

The fear of the "mass" has its roots in the dominant conservative tradition of Western political thought, which in large measure still shapes many of the political and sociological categories of social theory—i.e., in authoritarian definitions of leadership and in the image of the "mindless masses." The picture of the "mass" as capable only of violence and excess originates with Aristotle's Politics. In his threefold typology, democracy is equated with the rule of hoi polloi—who are easily swayed by

demagogues—and which must degenerate into tyranny. This notion of the masses, developed in
Hellenistic times, was deepened by the struggles
between plebes and aristocracy in the Roman republic, and by the efforts of the Caesars to exploit
mob support; and the image of the insensate mob
fed by "bread and circuses" became deeply im-
printed on history. (From Plutarch, for example,
came the description of the fickle masses and the
wily tribunes that was drawn upon so directly by
Shakespeare in his tragedy Coriolanus.) Early
Christian theory justified its fear of the masses
with a theory about human nature. In the religious
terms of Augustine—as, later, in the secularized
version of Hobbes—the Earthly City bore an in-
eradicable stain of blood: in Paradise there was
neither private property nor government; property
and police were the consequence of the Fall of Man;
property and police were signs, therefore, not of
man's civilization but of his corruption; they were
necessary means of keeping man in check.

But it was the French Revolution that trans-
planted the image of the "mindless masses" into
modern consciousness. The destruction of the
ancien regime and the rallying cry of "equality"
sharpened the fear of conservative, and especially
Catholic, critics that traditional values (meaning
political, social, and religious dogma) would be
destroyed. For a Tocqueville and an Acton,
there was an irreducible conflict between liberty
and equality; liberty guaranteed each man the right
to be different, whereas equality meant a "leveling"
of tastes to the lowest common denominator. For a
Max Scheler, as well as an Ortega, the mass society
meant a "democracy of the emotions," which could
unleash only irrational forces. For the Catholic de
Maistre, as for the Anglican T. S. Eliot, the equality of men meant the destruction of the harmony
and authority so necessary to a healthy, integrated
society. From this traditionalist point of view,
Nazism has been characterized not as a reaction
against, but the inevitable end-product of, democracy. Hitler is seen as a replica of the classical
demagogue swaying the mindless masses and leading them in nihilistic revolt against the traditional
culture of Europe.

Important as these conceptions are, as remind-
ers of the meaning of liberty, and of excellence,
they reflect a narrow conception of human potentialities. The question of social change has to be seen
against the large political canvas. The starting
point of modern politics, as Karl Mannheim has
pointed out, came after the Reformation, when
chiliasm, or religiously inspired millennial striving
to bring about heaven on earth, became an expression
of the demands for social and economic betterment
of the lower strata of society. Blind resentment
of things as they were was thereby given principle,
reason, and eschatological force, and directed to
definite political goals. The equality of all souls
became the equality of all individuals and the right
of everyone, as enlightened by progressive reve-
lation, to make a judgment on society.

Comte, the father of modern sociology, expressed
great horror at the idea of this universal right to
one's own opinion. No community could exist, he
wrote, unless its members had a certain degree
of confidence in one another, and this, he said, was
incompatible with the right of everyone to submit
the very foundations of society to discussion whenever he felt like it. In calling attention to the dangers
of free criticism, Comte pointed to the decline in
public morals as evidenced by the increase of divorces, the effacement of traditional class distinctions, and the ensuing impudence of individual
ambitions. It was part of the function of government, he thought to prevent the diffusion of ideas
and the anarchic spread of intellectual freedom.

Modern society, apparently, does not bear Comte
out: though the foundations of privilege go on being
challenged in the name of justice, society does not
collapse. Few moralists would now uphold the
bleak view once expressed by Malthus, that "from
the inevitable laws of human nature some human
beings will be exposed to want. These are the unhappy persons who in the great lottery of life have
drawn a blank." The most salient fact about
modern life—capitalist and communist—is the ideological commitment to social change. And by change
is meant the striving for material, economic betterment, greater opportunity for individuals to exercise
their talents, and an appreciation of culture by
wider masses of people. Can any society deny
these aspirations?

It is curious that in these "aristocratic" critiques
of modern society, refracted as they are through
the glass of an idealized feudal past, democracy is
identified with equality alone. The role of constitu-
tionalism and of the rule of law, which, with universal
suffrage, are constituent elements of the Western
democratic structure, are overlooked. The picture
of modern culture as debauched by concessions to
popular taste—a picture that leaves out the great
rise in the general appreciation of culture—is
equally overdrawn. If it is granted that mass society
is compartmentalized, superficial in personal

relations, anonymous, transitory, specialized, utilitarian, competitive, acquisitive, mobile, and status-hungry, the obverse side of the coin must be shown, too—the right to privacy, to free choice of friends and occupation, status on the basis of achievement rather than of ascription, a plurality of norms and standards, rather than the exclusive and monopolistic social controls of a single dominant group. For it, as Sir Henry Maine once put it, the movement of modern society has been from status to contract, then it has been, in that light, a movement from a fixed place in the world to possible freedom.

The early theorists of the mass society (Ortega, Marcel) focused attention of the "deterioration of excellence," while the later theorists (Mannheim, Lederer, Arendt) called attention to the way in which the over-organization and, at the same time, the disruption of the social fabric facilitated the rise of fascism. Recently, in the light of Communist successes, the argument has been advanced that the mass society, because it cannot provide for the individual's real participation in effective social groups, is particularly vulnerable to Communist penetration, and that the mass organization, because it is so unwiedly, is peculiarly susceptible to Communist penetration and manipulation. Certainly, the Communists have scored enormous successes in infiltration, and their "front organization" may be counted as one of the great political inventions of our century. But without discounting Communist techniques, the real problem here lies less with the "mass society" as such (aside from the excuse it affords disaffected intellectuals for attacks on modern culture) than with the capacity or incapacity of the given social order to satisfy the demands for social mobility and higher standards of living that arise once social change is under way. This is the key to any radical appeal.

It is not poverty per se that leads people to revolt; poverty most often induces fatalism and despair, and a reliance, embodied in ritual and superstitious practices, on supernatural help. Social tensions are an expression of unfulfilled expectations. It is only when expectations are aroused that radicalism can take hold. Radical strength is greatest (and here the appeal of communism must be seen as a variant of the general appeal of radicalism) in societies where awareness of class differences runs deep, expectations of social advancement outstrip possibilities, and the establishments of culture fail to make room for aspiring intellectuals.

It is among industrial workers rather than apathetic peasants (in Milan rather than Calabria), among frustrated intellectuals rather than workers long unionized (e.g., India), that radicalism spreads. Resentment, as Max Scheler once noted, is among the most potent of human motives; it is certainly that in politics. It is in the advanced industrial countries, principally the United States, Britain, and northwestern Europe, where national income has been rising, where mass expectations of an equitable share in that increase are relatively fulfilled, and where social mobility affects ever greater numbers, that extremist politics have the least hold. It may be, as the late Joseph Schumpeter pessimistically believed, that in newly awakened societies, like Asia's, the impatient expectations of key social strata, particularly the intellectuals, may so exceed the actual possibilities of economic expansion that communism will come to look like the only plausible solution to the majority. Whether this will happen in India and Indonesia is one of the crucial political questions of the next decade. But at any rate it is not the mass society, but the inability, pure and simple, of any society to meet impatient popular expectations that makes for a strong response to radical appeals.

From the viewpoint of the mass-society hypothesis, the United States ought to be exceptionally vulnerable to the politics of disaffection. In our country, urbanization, industrialization, and democratization have eroded older primary and community ties on a scale unprecedented in social history. Yet, though large-scale unemployment during the depression was more prolonged and more severe here than in any country in Western Europe, the Communist movement never gained a real foothold in the United States, nor has any fascist movement on a European model arisen. How does one explain this?

It is asserted that the United States is an "atomized" society composed of lonely, isolated individuals. One forgets the truism, expressed sometimes as a jeer, that Americans are a nation of joiners. There are in the United States today at least 200,000 voluntary organizations, associations, clubs, societies, lodges, and fraternities, with an aggregate (but obviously overlapping) membership of close to 80 million men and women. In no other country in the world, probably, is there such a high degree of voluntary communal activity, expressed sometimes in absurd rituals, yet often providing real satisfactions for real needs.

"it is natural for the ordinary American," wrote Gunnar Myrdal, "when he sees something that is wrong to feel not only that there should be a law against it, but also that an organization should be formed to combat it."   Some of these voluntary organizations are pressure groups—business, farm, labor, veterans, trade associations, the aged, etc. —but thousands more are like the National Association for the Advancement of Colored People, the American Civil Liberties Union, the League of Women Voters, the American Jewish Committee, the Parent-Teachers Associations, local community-improvement groups, and so on, each of which affords hundreds of individuals concrete, emotionally shared activities.

Equally astonishing are the number of ethnic group organizations in this country carrying on varied cultural, social, and political activities. The number of Irish, Italian, Jewish, Polish, Czech, Finnish, Bulgarian, Bessarabian, and other national groups, their hundreds of fraternal, communal, and political groups, each playing a role in the life of America, is staggering.

Even in urban neighborhoods, where anonymity is presumed to flourish, the extent of local ties is astounding. Within the city limits of Chicago, for example, there are 82 community newspapers with a total weekly circulation of almost one million; within Chicago's larger metropolitan area, there are 181. According to standard sociological theory, these local papers providing news and gossip about neighbors should slowly decline under the pressure of the national media. Yet the reverse is true. In Chicago, the number of such newspapers has increased 165 per cent since 1910; in those forty years, circulation has jumped 770 per cent. As sociologist Morris Janowitz, who studied these community newspapers, observed: "If society were as impersonal, as self-centered and barren as described by some who are preoccupied with the one-way trend from 'Gemeinschaft' to Gesellschaft' seem to believe, the levels of criminality, social disorganization and psychopathology which social science seeks to account for would have to be viewed as very low rather than (as viewed now) alarmingly high."

It may be argued that the existence of such a large network of voluntary associations says little about the cultural level of the country concerned. It may well be, as Ortega maintains, that cultural standards throughout the world have declined (in

everything?—in architecture, dress, design?), but nonetheless a greater proportion of the population today participates in worthwhile cultural activities. This has been almost an inevitable concomitant of the doubling—literally—of the American standard of living over the last fifty years.

The rising levels of education have meant a rising appreciation of culture. In the United States, more dollars are spent on concerts of classical music than on baseball. Sales of books have doubled in a decade. There are over a thousand symphony orchestras, and several hundred museums, institutes, and colleges are purchasing art in the United States today. Various other indexes can be cited to show the growth of a vast middlebrow society. And in coming years, with steadily increasing productivity and leisure, the United States will become an even more active "consumer" of culture. *

----

*Some further ambiguity in the use of the mass-society concept derives from the confusions in the use of the anthropological and the humanist meanings of the word "culture." Thus some critics point to the "breakdown" of local folk or regional practices—speech differences, cooking, songs, dances, humor—and their replacement by uniform national patterns as an indication of the leveling of the mass society and of the decline of culture. These changes, which are real, are meaningful, however, only in anthropological usage, as a change from parochial to more universal cultural forms. But such changes are not necessarily a judgment about the humanist quality of the culture. (It is curious that in the past the breakdown of rustic forms was seen as a necessary prelude to the growth of a "high culture." Today the breakdown of the rustic forms is seen as part of the destruction of humanist culture.) The distinctions should be made clear. The anthropological concept of culture is relativistic. It implies no judgment of any one culture and cannot be used as a stick to criticize "high culture." The fact that the nature of satisfactions has changed from country dances and folksy humor to Brazilian sambas and Broadway flippancy is analytically a different question than that of the character of the culture. As these criticisms are made, one deals with the presumed disorganization of society the other with the quality of the culture. Again, it is the purpose of this essay to point out that the invocatio of the notion of tradition (Gemeinschaft, etc.) to make a judgment about the disorganization of the society is scientifically spurious and conceals a value. The othe criticism, which is serious, lies outside the scope

It has been argued that the American mass society imposes an excessive conformity upon its members. But it is hard to discern who is conforming to what. The New Republic cries that "hucksters are sugarcoating the culture." The National Review, organ of the "radical right," raises the banner of iconoclasm against the domination of opinion-making in our society by "the liberals." Fortune decries the growth of "organization man." Each of these tendencies exists, yet in historical perspective there is probably less conformity to an over-all mode of conduct today than at any time within the last half century in America. True, there is less bohemianism than in the twenties (though increased sexual tolerance) and less political radicalism than in the thirties (though the New Deal enacted sweeping reforms.) But does the arrival at a political dead center mean the establishment, too, of a dead norm? I do not think so. One would be hard put to find today the "conformity" Main Street exacted of Carol Kennicott thirty years ago. With rising educational levels, more individuals are able to indulge a wider variety of interests. ("Twenty years ago you couldn't sell Beethoven out of New York," reports a record salesman. "Today we sell Palestrina, Monteverdi, Gabrielli, and Renaissance and Baroque music in large quantities.")

The curious fact, perhaps is that no one in the United States defends conformity. Everyone is against it, and probably everyone always was. Thirty-five years ago, you could easily rattle any middle-class American by charging him with being a "Babbitt." Today you can do so by accusing him of conformity. The problem is to know who is accusing whom. In December, 1958, the Reader's Digest (circulation twelve million) reprinted an article from Woman's Day (circulation five million) with the title, "The Danger of Being Too Well—Adjusted." The point of the article is that great men were not adjusted, and the article quotes a psychiatrist who says that "we've made conformity into a religion"; we ought to remember, however, that each child is different "and ought to be."

Such citation is not proof that there is not "conformity" in the middle class; but if there is, there

is also a great deal of anxiety and finger pointing about it. Certainly those who live on the margin of society—the Upper Bohemians, whose manners soon become the style for the culture—seek frantically to find different ways of emphasizing their non-conformity. In Hollywood, where Pickfair society in the twenties counterfeited a European monarchy (and whose homes crossed Louis XIV with Barnum & Bailey), "non-conformity," according to Life magazine (in its jumbo Entertainment issue of December 22, 1958—readership twenty-five million), "is now the key to social importance and that Angry Middle-Aged man, Frank Sinatra, is its prophet and reigning social monarch." The Sinatra set, Life points out, deliberately mocks the old Hollywood taboos and is imitated by a host of other sets that eagerly want to be non-conformist as well. Significantly—a fact Life failed to mention—the reigning social set and its leaders, Sinatra, Dean Martin, Sammy Davis, Jr., are all from minority groups and from the wrong side of the tracks. Sinatra and Martin are Italian, Davis a Negro. In earlier times in American life, a minority group, having bulled its way to the top, would usually ape the style and manners of the established status community. In Hollywood, the old status hierarchies have been fragmented, the new sets celebrate their triumph by jeering at the pompous ways of the old.

At the margins of the literary life, and a different social phenomenon, are the Beatniks, a hopped-up, souped-up, self-proclaimed group of outcasts who are rebelling against the "highly organized academic and literary movement employment agency of the Neoanti-reconstructionist who form a dense crust of custom over American cultural life." But the singular fact is, as Delmore Schwartz recently argued, that these Beatniks are imaginary rebels, "since the substance of their work is a violent advocacy of a nonconformism which they already possess . . . since nonconformism of almost every variety had become acceptable and respectable and available to everyone. Unlike the Bohemianism of the past, which had to attack the dominant Puritanism and Victorianism of respectable society in a variety of forms, including the censorship of books, Prohibition and a prudery enforced by the police, the new nonconformism has no genuine enemy. . . hence the new rebel bears a great deal of resemblance to a prize fighter trying to knock out an antagonist who is not in the ring with him. The additional sardonic fact is that the man in the gray flannel suit, the presumed target of the Beatniks, is, as, Russell Lynes

of this essay. (For a discussion of the issues of "high vs. "middlebrow" culture, see Clement Greenberg, "The Plight of Our Culture," Commentary, June and July, 1953. See also, Mary Mc Carthy, "America the Beautiful," Commentary, September, 1947.)

pointed out, especially if he is in advertising, or the entertainment media, an Upper Bohemian himself. The job is accepted as a means of obtaining an income in order to sport and flaunt his presumed, idiosyncratic tastes in dress, food, travel, and the like.* The problem for all these multiple sets is not conformity but added novelty.

To add one more paradox, the early theorists of mass society (e.g., Simmel) condemned it because in the vast metropolitan honeycombs people were isolated, transient, anonymous to each other. Americans, sensitive as they are to the criticism of others, took the charge to heart and, in building the postwar suburbs, sought to create fraternity, communality, togetherness, only to find themselves accused of conformity. In the new, recent trend of people returning to the city, it is clear that, in recoil, people will once again establish barriers and will thus bring on the charge, in the next inspection by European sociology, of anonymity, isolation and soullessness, and anomie.

One hears the complaint that divorce, crime, and violence demonstrate a widespread social disorganization in the country. But the rising number of divorces may indicate not the disruption of the family but a freer, more individualistic basis of choice and the emergence of the "companionship" marriage. And as regards crime, I have sought to demonstrate (see Chapter 11) that there is actually much less crime and violence (though more vicarious violence through movies and TV, and more "windows" onto crime, through the press)

---

*In the richly appointed Lake Shore Drive apartment of Chicago Financier Albert Newman, the guests chatted animatedly, gazed at the original Picasso on the wall, and the Monet, the Jackson Pollock. On tables and shelves stood Peruvian fertility symbols, jade bracelets, sculptures that looked like the superstructure of a Japanese battleship. . . . (The guests) had come to meet 32-year old Allen Ginsberg of Paterson, N. J., author of a celebrated, chock-full catalogue called Howl ("I saw the best minds of my generation destroyed by madness, starving hysterical naked."). . . . At length Poet Ginsberg arrived wearing blue jeans and a checked black-and-red lumberjacking shirt with black patches. . . . With the crashing madness of a Marx Brothers scene run in reverse, the Beatniks (Ginsberg and two friends) read their poetry, made their pitch for money for a new Beatnik magazine, The Big Table, and then stalked out. . . The trio was an instant hit with the literary upper

than was the case twenty-five and fifty years ago. Certainly Chicago, San Francisco, and New York were much rougher and tougher cities in those years. But violent crime, which is usually a lower-class phenomenon, was then contained within the ecological boundaries of the slum; hence one can recall quiet, tree-lined, crime-free areas and feel that the tenor of life was more even in the past. But a cursory look at the accounts of those days—the descriptions of the gang wars, bordellos, and street-fighting in San Francisco's Barbary Coast, New York's Five Points, or Chicago's First Ward—would show how much more violent the actual life of those cities was in the past.

At this point, it becomes quite apparent that such large-scale abstractions as "the mass society," with the implicit diagnoses of social disorganization and decay that derive from them, are rather meaningless without standards of comparison. Social and cultural change is probably greater and more rapid today in the United States than in any other country, but the assumption that social disorder and anomie inevitably attend such change is not borne out in this case.

This may be due to the singular fact that the United States is probably the first large society in history to have change and innovation "built into" its culture. Almost all human societies, traditionalist and habit-ridden as they have been and still are, tend to resist change. The great efforts to industrialize underdeveloped countries, increase worker mobility in Europe, and broaden markets —so necessary to the raising of productivity and standards of living—are again and again frustrated by ingrained resistance to change. Thus, in the Soviet Union, change has been introduced only by dint of wholesale coercion. In the United States— a culture with no feudal tradition, with a pragmatic ethos, as expressed by Jefferson, that regards God as a "workman"; with a boundless optimism and a restless eagerness for the new that have been bred out of the original conditions of a huge, richly endowed land—change, and the readiness to change, have become the norm. This indeed may be why those consequences of change predicted by theorists basing themselves on European precedent find small confirmation.

The mass society is the product of change—and is itself change. It is the bringing of the "masses"

---

crust. . . . (the next evening) at the Sherman Hotel, the Beatniks read more poetry for a curious crowd of 700 (who paid $1 and up). . ." (Time, February 9, 1959).

into a society, from which they were once excluded. But the _theory_ of the mass society affords us no view of the relations of the parts of the society to each other that would enable us to locate the sources of change. We may not have enough data on which to sketch an alternative theory but I would argue that certain key factors, in this country at least, deserve to be much more closely examined than they have been: the change from a society once geared to frugal saving and now impelled to spend dizzily; the breakup of family capitalism, with the consequent impact on corporate structure and political power; the centralization of decision-making, politically, in the state and, economically, in a group of large corporate bodies; the rise of status and symbol groups replacing specific interest groups—these indicate that new social forms are in the making and, with them, still greater changes in the complexion of life under mass society. With these may well come new status anxieties—aggravated by the threats of war—changed character structures, and new moral tempers.

The moralist may have his reservations or give approval—as some see in the breakup of the family the loss of a source of essential values, while others see in the new, freer marriages a healthier form of companionship—but the singular fact is that these changes emerge in a society that is now providing one answer to the great challenge posed to Western—and now world—society over the last two hundred years: how, within the framework of freedom, to increase the living standards of the majority of people and at the same time maintain or raise cultural levels. For these reasons, the theory of the mass society no longer serves as a description of Western society but as an ideology of romantic protest against contemporary life.

McCutchan Publishing Corporation